THE LEGEND *of the* FOUNDING FATHERS

THE LEGEND *of the* FOUNDING FATHERS

Wesley Frank Craven

Cornell Paperbacks

CORNELL UNIVERSITY PRESS

ITHACA, NEW YORK

Foreword

THE following lectures, sponsored by the Stokes Foundation, were given at New York University in the spring of 1955. Except for occasional revision and the addition of footnotes, the lectures are printed as they were originally delivered. The footnotes will indicate the type of source upon which I have depended, but I have not attempted to document the text fully.

As is stated in the first lecture, I have assumed that the lecture platform is an appropriate place for exploration of a subject. The subject, in this instance, was suggested by the common inclination of the American people to look back to the origins of their country for an explanation of its essential character. I have elected to treat the subject historically, with attention in successive periods of time to the development of popular interest in the question of our national origins. This approach necessarily threw the emphasis first on the place of the colonial fathers in our national legend, and I have allowed the focus to remain on them except in the last two lectures, which deal with the period since the Civil War. I cannot claim to have explored the historiography of our interest in the Revolutionary fathers as closely as perhaps I should have. The reader will discover that I have leaned heavily, possibly too heavily, upon the record of ceremonial observances for the purpose of suggesting the relative importance to us at different times of the colonial and Revolutionary fathers. By way of excuse, I can cite only the claim of other duties on my time and the fact that the Phelps Lectureship provides for no more than six lectures. I hope very much that any distortion of which I have been guilty will serve at least as a warning against the distortion that can result from an assumption that earlier generations of Americans viewed their history exactly as we do.

I am indebted to Thomas J. Pressly of the University of Washington for his willingness to listen to some of my thoughts at a stage when they badly needed clarification. Richard S. Dunn of the University of Michigan rendered a similar service, and in addition assisted me greatly with the research, as did also Theodore Jacobs. The lectures could not have been completed on time without a term's relief from teaching duties that was made possible by the officers of Princeton University, and without a grant from its research fund that made the assistance of Mr. Dunn available to me during the summer of 1954. I am grateful to Chancellor Heald of New York University for an invitation to join the distinguished company of Phelps lecturers. Most of all, I appreciate the willingness of my former colleagues at New York University, and especially Dean Joseph H. Park, to have me as a lecturer in the University once more.

WESLEY FRANK CRAVEN

April 1956

Contents

THE LEGEND *of the* FOUNDING FATHERS

CHAPTER I

Why Came We Here?

As a caption for this first lecture I have used a question repeatedly put to the people of early New England by their Puritan clergymen: "Why came we here?" In the seventeenth century that question usually foretold an effort to rally the congregation to Puritan standards of orthodoxy by reminding its members of the high purposes for which they or their fathers had undertaken a settlement in the new world. The device strikes the modern American as a familiar one, for he is no less subject to the demand that he remember the purposes for which the nation was originally founded. Of the many different ways of calling the common tradition to witness as to the right and the wrong of a current issue, none has been so favored among Americans as the simple and direct appeal to a standard presumably raised by the founding fathers. Indeed, it might almost be said that we have cut ourselves off from the benefit of a historical tradition, properly speaking, by the veneration we show for the achievement of men who are increasingly removed from the age in which we live.

Comment on this national trait for the most part has tended toward disapproval, because of a belief that the conservative forces in our society have gained thereby a distinct advantage. That the tactic has been frequently and effectively employed by the conservative is, of course, beyond dispute. But have not all of us, whatever may be our political persuasion, done the same? Certainly, Lincoln at Gettysburg—the classic example of appeal to the fathers—spoke for something more than the spirit of reaction. Certainly, too, it would not be difficult to offer other examples in evidence of our common inclination to assume that the principles that guided the fathers should in some measure guide us. For better or for worse, the American community has consistently looked to its origins for an explanation of its distinctive qualities and thus for an indication of what its future should hold.

In these lectures I propose to explore the history of this habit of ours and, more particularly, to comment on some of the important influences that have shaped popular interest, at successive stages of our history, in the question of our national origins. The discussions that follow can be best described perhaps as basically historiographical, but I have gone beyond formal histories to sample the evidence presented by the political leader, the patriotic orator, and the clergyman. I have taken some notice of ceremonial observances, and I have spent a good deal of time with the records of a varied group of organizations that have undertaken to interpret and so to mold the common tradition. My use of the term "legend" is intended to convey nothing more than a hope that I may find in each period the broad base of popular attitude and feeling. Since I could add little to what others have done to show that tradition and historical fact often fail to square, I shall make few attempts to correct the popular view.

At the present time the Revolution and the federal Constitution so dominate our concept of the nation's origins that any reference to the founding fathers immediately calls to mind the leaders of the Revolution and, perhaps first of all, the members of the Constitutional Convention of 1787.[1] But this has not always been the case, and few of us even today would under-

---

[1] Such is the evidence offered by Mathews' standard *Dictionary of Americanisms,* which in 1951 gave this definition of the founding fathers: "The statesmen of the Revolutionary period, especially the members of the

take to explain the American ideal without reference, let us say, to the Pilgrim Fathers or Roger Williams. It may be help-ful to recall the history on which the nation at first depended. Unlike what we teach our students today, it did not begin in 1776 or even in 1765, but had its beginning with the settlement of the colonies in the seventeenth century and reached a grand and logical climax with the story of the Revolution. In that context, the colonial fathers—those we are now likely to de-scribe, for convenience of distinction, as our forefathers—be-came in a very real sense the true fathers of the country, for to them was given the credit of having first planted on these shores the standards their descendants had so recently and so magnificently defended.

For that interpretation of its history the young republic was heavily indebted to Puritan New England, where even before the enactment of the Stamp Act a traditional view of the causes for the settlement of that region had come to emphasize, as I hope to demonstrate in this initial lecture, the very ideals to which the nation would soon be dedicated. Other colonists had been slower than were the New Englanders to develop an interest in their history, but the political controversy touched off by the Stamp Act lent such utility to arguments based on the history of American settlement as to encourage a general acceptance of propositions identifying the purposes of the orig-inal settlers with the cause for which the Revolution was fought. And after independence had been won, there were other influences to stimulate a fuller development of that view, by no means the least being the need felt by a new nation for some historical sanction.

I do not mean to discount the fundamental importance of

Convention of 1787." The common use of the term "founding fathers" seems to be a relatively recent development. The fact that the examples given by Mathews for this usage bear no earlier date than 1941 counts per-haps for little, but I believe an investigation might show that the term is a surprisingly modern one. Lincoln's "our fathers" and such other descriptions as "the fathers of the Republic" are certainly more represent-ative of the common usage through most of our history.

the Revolution to the shaping of our national tradition, if only because it was the Revolution that in large measure now governed the interpretation given the years of our first settlement. My purpose, instead, is to suggest the influences that have placed a dual concept of the country's origins at the very heart of that tradition. It was a concept, of course, well fitted to the main outlines of our history. However much we might owe our independence to the Revolution, we owed our very presence in North America to the migration of our forebears, and it was only natural that we should seek in the purposes that had inspired them a helpful clue to the national character. Further encouragement to find the roots of our national life in the story of our colonial beginnings came from the fact that the Revolution had marked a less drastic break with the past than might have been the case. Similarly, our federal type of union, which imposed no explicit limitation on older loyalties, helped to channel much of the growing interest in questions of national origins into fields of state and local history reaching back to the first years of settlement. Intensive investigation of these earlier years has also been stimulated by the modern interest in genealogy and this, in turn, through the aid it gave to the establishment of social distinctions based upon priority of immigration, has challenged more recent immigrant groups to find satisfying evidence of their own identification with the great American adventure at its beginning. Whatever may be the tendency in our own day, the Revolutionary fathers have enjoyed no monopoly of the special honors reserved in this country for its founders.

As this brief summary has no doubt suggested, our colonial fathers will figure more prominently in the following discussions than any others. Perhaps I should confess that this emphasis, which I take to be not inappropriate to the purposes of the Phelps Lectureship, may reflect too much of my personal bias in favor of the earliest chapters of American history. But I have assumed that the lecture platform is an appropriate place to explore such a subject as this, and that this emphasis may provide a helpful corrective to current assumptions regarding a significant feature of our national life. I shall try to give enough attention to the place of the Revolutionary fathers in a developing legend to avoid distortion, but I make no claim to complete coverage of the subject even within the limits indicated. Though I have tried to sample enough of the literature to provide a safe guide to the main trends of popular interest, my choice has often been arbitrary and fortuitous. Through much of the investigation I have relied upon the familiar time-saving device of using Massachusetts and Virginia for the special significance of their examples. The results are necessarily somewhat impressionistic, but I hope they may prove of interest to others and helpfully suggestive as to some of the problems of our common history.

In any study of the American historical tradition, one of the first questions to be faced is that of why Puritan New England has so largely shaped the development of that tradition. It is a question you will perhaps allow me to approach by asking another question: Why is it that the colony of Virginia has not exerted a comparable influence? We have been a nation ever inclined to concede the importance of priority, as is only natural in a new country. Our histories are full of claims to first honors, and our social conventions have consistently recognized the advantage of membership in the first families of the state, county, or town. We still find it convenient to speak of the first citizens of the community when we mean its leading citizens. There are even those among us who find satisfaction in the fact that on the Sabbath they worship God in the first rather than the second Presbyterian church. And who can dispute that Virginia came ahead of New England?

But the story of early Virginia, for all its undisputed priority and for all its significance, has its difficulties. Its prologue at Roanoke Island, ending in the mystery of the lost colony, has invited us to celebrate in song and verse the sacrifice of those who first settled in the new world,[2] and has given us a prized identification of the American adventure with Queen Elizabeth

---

[2] As in Paul Green's *The Lost Colony, an Outdoor Play in Two Acts* (Chapel Hill, 1937).

and Sir Walter Raleigh. But neither Elizabeth nor Raleigh can be converted into an American, and the same point must be made when one turns to the leading figures in the settlement of Jamestown. Whether one favors Sir Thomas Smith or Sir Edwin Sandys, the Earl of Southampton or the Earl of Warwick, the leaders of the project remained Englishmen who never set foot on American soil. As for the Englishmen who came to Virginia in the early years, their lot was so marked by tragedy and disillusionment that the founders themselves in this instance seem to have done all they possibly could to destroy one another's reputation. It is difficult to find a single leader of the early colony whose record is not debatable by the testimony of his own associates. Whether the charges are always true is another question, and one often made difficult by the incompleteness of the record. Out of the bickering and strife only Captain John Smith, who as historian of the settlement got the last word, managed to emerge with anything approaching heroic stature, and there has been many a debate, even in our own day, on the issue of his character.

Similarly, we have had trouble on the question of the motives which guided the first settlers of Virginia, and not only because that was a subject on which they themselves at times had a few not too well chosen words to speak. The motivation inspiring the Virginia project is as complex a problem as that of explaining the entire English interest in America. It has not been easy to bring this question to a sharp focus on some single motive that is readily identified with the accepted ideals of later generations, as it has been, for instance, in the case of the Pilgrim Fathers.

Hardly less influential has been the attitude of later generations of Virginians. When the Virginians in the nineteenth century elected descent from the Cavalier migrants of the mid-seventeenth century they were by no means the first inhabitants of the Old Dominion to dismiss, as it were, the earliest years of its history. If we may judge by the first history of the province written by a native Virginian, that of Robert Beverley in 1705,[3] the colonists at the opening of the eighteenth century tended to find the true beginning of their community in the new life that had gradually infused the colony after the dissolution of the Virginia Company in 1624. Beverley dutifully records, with a heavy dependence on Smith's history, the narrative of Virginia's origins that still does service in our schoolbooks today—a story featuring chiefly Queen Elizabeth, Sir Walter Raleigh, Captain John Smith, and, for romance, Princess Pocahontas. But in lieu of a tribute to the early adventurers he recorded a judgment that "the chief Design of all Parties concern'd was to fetch away the Treasure from thence, aiming more at sudden Gain, than to form any regular Colony, or to establish a settlement in such a manner, as to make it a lasting Happiness to the Country." [4] In marked contrast to the reverent regard for the original settlers which inspired the early histories of New England stands the following irreverent comment of William Byrd in the 1730's on the beginnings of American settlement. Said he: "As it happen'd some Ages before to be the fashion to Santer to the Holy Land, and go upon other Quixot adventures, so it was now grown the Humour to make a trip to America." [5]

In 1747 the Rev. William Stith, in his *History of the First Discovery and Settlement of Virginia,*[6] began to work out a significant identification of the colony's early history with the constitutional conflict between the English Parliament and the

[3] *The History and Present State of Virginia,* first printed in London in 1705. Citations here are to an edition edited by Louis B. Wright for the Institute of Early American History and published in 1947 by the University of North Carolina Press.

[4] *Ibid.,* 55.

[5] *William Byrd's Histories of the Dividing Line betwixt Virginia and North Carolina,* with introduction and notes by William K. Boyd (Raleigh, 1929), 2.

[6] William Stith, *The History of the First Discovery and Settlement of Virginia: Being An Essay towards a General History of this Colony* (Williamsburg, 1747). As the full title suggests, the author intended to go beyond this first volume, but the response discouraged him from any further effort.

Stuart kings. Having an opportunity through the courtesy of William Byrd to use the minutes of the Virginia Company during the critical last years of its existence, Stith directed his reader's attention chiefly to the period between 1619 and 1624, when Sir Edwin Sandys controlled the company and when significant reforms in its policy had been initiated. Sandys was by no means wholly responsible for these reforms—which included renewed assurances as to the protection of the common law and provision for the first representative assembly in the colonies—but no such disclaimer appeared in the minutes of the company and Sir Edwin was a leading figure in the growing opposition of Parliament to the policies of James I.

In an appendix, Stith published the three Virginia charters and the instructions of 1621 to Sir Francis Wyatt that remain even today the earliest extant provision for the Virginia Assembly. In his text, he used the instructions given by the royal council for the government of the very first colonists to indict the king with the exercise of despotic authority because the legislative power had been placed in the president and council "without any Representation of the People, contrary to a noted Maxim of the English Constitution; That all Freemen are to be governed by Laws, made with their own Consent." [7] He hailed the establishment of the Assembly in 1619 as "the Introduction of the British Form of Government," and the renewed guarantee of common-law rights as a restoration of the colonists' birthright. There is much here that will help to explain the readiness of the Virginia planters to fight for their rights as Englishmen. One finds here also significant parallels with the views of American history that were currently popular in New England, but one finds also a significant difference. It is evident that the tradition in Virginia continued to emphasize the closest identification with the English tradition, whereas the New Englanders, however much they might draw upon the history of seventeenth-century England, attributed to their own

[7] *Ibid.,* 41.

founders the establishment of a new order of human liberty.

At only one point did Stith find occasion to argue that Virginians had been ahead of other Englishmen in the assertion of their rights. In reviewing the laws enacted by the Assembly of 1624, the earliest he had been able to find, he described statutes prohibiting the imposition of any tax or public service upon the colonists except by act of Assembly as "a Petition of Right passed, above four Years, before that Matter was indubitably settled and explained in England." That action, said Stith, showed how early the colonists, "out of the memory of their past Miseries and oppressions," had become "studious and careful to establish our Liberties." [8] But the liberties remained the liberties of any Englishman.

The people of New England were no less conscious of their rights as Englishmen than were the inhabitants of Virginia. As a people who had filled their maps with English place names and who had been inclined to boast over the years that no part of America so faithfully reflected the best of England,[9] they were as alert as any Virginian to the value of the rights they had inherited from their English forebears. At the same time, however, New England enjoyed the additional advantage of a highly developed historical tradition of its own.

It is difficult to pick the first history of New England without resort to an arbitrary decision. One thinks immediately of Bradford's classic history of Plymouth and Governor Winthrop's invaluable journal, which he planned to revise for publication as a history, but neither of these documents got publication before the Revolution and thus both may be omitted here. Edward Johnson's *Wonder-working Providence of Sion's Saviour in New England,* a work published in London in

[8] *Ibid.,* 320.

[9] As in Cotton Mather's statement at the beginning of his *Magnalia Christi Americana* (Bk. I, 3): "It will be enough if I entertain [the reader] with the History of that English Settlement, which may, upon a Thousand accounts, pretend unto more of True English than all the rest, and which alone therefore has been called New-England."

1653,[10] might be selected as the first published history to present the story of New England on an ambitious scale, but Johnson belonged to the first generation of settlers and his history, like that of Smith for Virginia and of Bradford for Plymouth, can be regarded as basically a chronicle written by an active participant in the events described. By this process of elimination the honor goes to Nathaniel Morton's *New-Englands Memoriall,* which was first published in 1669.[11] It is an appropriate choice, for Morton wrote chiefly of Plymouth and drew heavily on the manuscript of Governor Bradford's history. If he accomplished nothing else, he provided assurance that the Plymouth settlers, who were destined to become the most honored of our earliest founders, would have a secure place in New England's developing tradition. But Plymouth, for all its importance as the first settlement in New England and for all the readiness of New England's historians to give it due recognition, had remained a relatively unimportant member of that community. The dominant influence of the Puritan settlement of Massachusetts Bay gave much greater importance to histories having their chief focus on the Bay Colony. Of these first mention belongs to Cotton Mather's monumental *Magnalia Christi Americana: or, The Ecclesiastical History of New-England from Its First Planting in the Year 1620, unto the Year of Our Lord, 1698,* which was published in 1702,[12] well before the centennial of settlement in that region. Thomas Prince's *Annals of New England,* an ambitiously conceived chronicle of bare factual data, remained incomplete at his

[10] Published in London as *A History of New-England. From the English planting in the Yeere 1628, untill the Yeere 1652,* and reprinted by J. Franklin Jameson, with introduction and notes, in the *Original Narratives of Early American History* (New York, 1910).

[11] *New-Englands Memoriall: or, A brief Relation of the most Memorable and Remarkable Passages of the Providence of God, manifested to the Planters of New-England in America; with special Reference to the first Colony thereof, called New-Plymouth* (Cambridge, Mass., 1669).

[12] At London. The title as given above is full.

death midway in the eighteenth century,[13] but New England was soon enjoying the initial volume of Thomas Hutchinson's justly celebrated *History of Massachusetts,* published in 1764. A second volume, carrying the narrative from the late seventeenth century to 1750, followed in 1767.[14]

Merely to list these histories is to go far toward answering the question of New England's special influence on the development of our national historical tradition. When the long controversy with Parliament after 1763 lent political utility to arguments based on the original character of English colonization in America, the only part of that story that had been at all well documented was the story of the Puritan settlements. In 1776 only Virginia, New York, and New Jersey, outside New England, had a published history of any consequence, and none of these could even be compared with the single work of Hutchinson. The gap for other states would in several instances not be filled until well after the Revolution had ended. Meanwhile, New England's initial advantage was further strengthened through its continuing leadership in the study of American history. But it is not enough to emphasize this leadership or to point out, as we have been fond of doing, that most of our school texts were for so long written by New Englanders. We must not lose sight of the obvious fact that the New England view of our origins could not have been so influential as it has been without its being, for most Americans and in its broader outlines, a very acceptable view.

[13] The first volume, published in 1736, carried the title *Chronological History of New England in the Form of Annals.* In 1754 parts of a second volume began to appear as the *Annals of New England,* the third and last part appearing in 1755. Prince did not get beyond 1633.

[14] See *The History of the Colony and Province of Massachusetts-Bay. By Thomas Hutchinson. Edited from the Author's own copies of Volume I and II and His Manuscript of Volume III, With a Memoir and Additional Notes.* By Lawrence Shaw Mayo (3 vols., Cambridge, Mass., 1936). The third volume, completed in the author's exile, was first published with editing by a grandson in 1828.

I have no time here for full discussion of the special circumstances that have helped to make this view acceptable, but let me comment briefly on the early histories of New England in the hope that I may suggest some of the reasons for the extraordinary influence of the tradition they represent. The more important of these histories may be described perhaps as belonging to a general category we have come to define as regional history, as distinct from the more limited type of provincial history. Indeed, it might almost be said that the first strictly provincial histories in New England were written after the Revolution. If Thomas Hutchinson's *History of Massachusetts* seems to refute this proposition, let me turn the point around and say simply that his work demonstrates that provincial history could be written in colonial New England with a better perspective than has characterized most of the state histories written since that time. I argue for no exact parallel with the modern type of regional history, but Puritanism had so largely shaped the origins of the eastern provinces that the history of Puritan settlement naturally took precedence over less significant subjects. As a result New England's early histories gained a breadth of view that made of them, whatever their other limitations, an especially useful starting point for study of the still broader subject of English colonization in North America.

This same emphasis on Puritanism also made of New England's history the story primarily of a God-fearing community dedicated to the fulfillment of a religious ideal. I do not mean to suggest that the Puritans have been a generally acceptable group of founding fathers, for we must later give attention in these discussions to a not inconsiderable body of historical literature that has been devoted to vigorous attacks upon them. But we have liked to think that the founders of this country were men of God—men of principle and conviction, men who were willing to sacrifice their interest for their faith, men such as you will find in the early New England histories.

No less significant was the close identification of the story re-

corded in these histories with the Protestant tradition. In recent years we seem to have found more occasion to comment
on the significance of our English origins than of our Protestant
origins. I have no desire to discount the important influence
on our national tradition of the fact that the first settlers were
overwhelmingly English by birth, but it should be recalled
once more that they were also overwhelmingly Protestant in
their faith and that many of them came to America in the
strong belief that the promise of the Protestant Reformation
might be better realized here. Even in the settlement of Virginia, where economic and political considerations undoubtedly
outweighed others, all participants were given to understand
that their efforts served to protect the Protestant Church
settlement of Elizabeth, to cut down the pretensions of Catholic
Spain, and ultimately to save the North American Indian from
the errors of the Roman Church. Only in Maryland did one
find a significant body of Catholic colonists, and they soon became a decided minority in their own colony. The whole story
of New England's settlement may be profitably viewed as an
important chapter in the history of the English Reformation,
and later colonizers were no less Protestant, whether one thinks
of the Quakers, the Huguenots, the Irish and Scottish Presbyterians, or the especially large migration of German sectarians
in the eighteenth century. Not only were our colonial forefathers overwhelmingly Protestant, but they were in very large
part representative of the more extreme forms of Protestantism
—a fact well understood by Edmund Burke when in 1775 he
admonished the House of Commons to remember that the
Americans were Protestant "and of that kind which is most
adverse to all implicit submission of mind and opinion." [15]
There is little cause for wonder that so many of us during the
formative stage of our national tradition showed a marked
inclination to trace our beginnings back, as had William Bradford and other New England historians, to the troubles beset-

[15] Taken from Max Beloff, *The Debate on the American Revolution,
1761–1783* (London, 1949), 208.

ting "the Lord's free people" at the time of the Reformation.

It may be helpful to remember, too, that the larger part of the colonists seem to have been Calvinists. Statistics on church identification in colonial America are a very uncertain quantity, but Ralph Barton Perry's estimate that over half the white colonists in 1776 "were in the broad sense adherents of Calvinistic or closely allied sects" cannot be far wrong.[16] Perhaps this will explain in part our common tendency to honor the founders of the country for virtues that have been especially emphasized by the disciples of John Calvin.

In any case, the pattern we have consistently followed in paying tribute to our fathers, of whatever group, was first worked out by men thoroughly identified with a Calvinist tradition and undoubtedly owes its original form to the peculiar needs of New England as a religious community. It was a pattern that emphasized the community's mission in America and gave the place of first honor to those who had taken the lead in its founding, but did not neglect to stipulate that the special honors conferred upon these leaders belonged ultimately to the larger body of men for whom they acted.

The parallel with the modern attitude toward the Revolutionary fathers is easily established. Few of us today would respond to Cotton Mather's statement of the Puritan's mission in America: " 'Tis possible, That our Lord Jesus Christ carried some Thousands of Reformers into the Retirements of an American Desart, on purpose, that, with an opportunity granted unto many of his Faithful Servants, to enjoy the precious Liberty of their Ministry, . . . He might there, To them first, and then By them, give a Specimen of many Good Things, which He would have His Churches elsewhere aspire and arise unto. . . ." [17] But who can question that there are found here the essential points in a proposition to which the later American has repeatedly subscribed: that as Americans we have been

[16] Ralph Barton Perry, *Puritanism and Democracy* (New York, 1944), 80.

[17] *Magnalia,* Introd., para. 3.

engaged in a great experiment testing fundamental truths whose establishment as truth will have great meaning for the betterment of mankind? The modern experiment has been political and social rather than religious, but we have been nonetheless a nation which has considered itself dedicated, to use Lincoln's term, to the accomplishment of a high purpose.

Listen also to Mather's tribute to John Winthrop: "Accordingly when the Noble Design of carrying a Colony of Chosen People into an American Wilderness, was by some Eminent Persons undertaken, This Eminent Person was, by the Consent of all, Chosen for the Moses, who must be the Leader of so great an Undertaking. How Prudently, how Patiently, and with how much Resignation to our Lord Jesus Christ, our brave Winthrop waded through these Difficulties, let Posterity Consider with Admiration. And know, that as the Picture of this their Governour, was, after his Death, hung up with Honour in the State-House of his Country, so the Wisdom, Courage, and Holy Zeal of his Life, were an Example well-worthy to be Copied by all that shall succeed in Government." [18] Is this not the likeness of Washington as he has been depicted in countless public tributes? And before passing on, let us notice again the patriot's portrait as it hangs in the public building to lend its own peculiar authority to the law.

One finds no essential difference between the argument for modern laws requiring that our youth be instructed in American history and the justification Mather gave for his *Magnalia*. "I shall count my Country lost," said Mather, "in the loss of the Primitive Principles, and the Primitive Practices, upon which it was at first Established: But certainly one good way to save that Loss, would be to do something . . . that the Story of the Circumstances attending the Foundation and Formation of this Country, and of its Preservation hitherto, may be impartially handed unto Posterity." [19] One lingers momentarily over the word "impartially," for Mather already had confessed to a difficulty since then experienced by more than one

[18] *Ibid.*, Bk. II, 8–9.   [19] *Ibid.*, Bk. I, 1.

historian writing on the American Revolution. Protesting his purpose to write honest history, Mather then asked: "But how can the Lives of the Commendable be written without Commending them?" [20]

Commendations were by no means reserved for the top commanders. The prototype of the pioneer, who dominates the story of later settlement in the West, will be found in the traditional picture of the early colonist, who had endured the storms of the Atlantic, broken a wilderness to the purposes of civilized man, and won for his children a goodly inheritance in deadly strife with the native savage. The literature is not wanting in passages that could even be fitted into the epic of the Oregon Trail. For example, there is Governor Hutchinson's description of the overland march presumably made from Massachusetts in 1635 by the first settlers of Connecticut: ". . . and then about an hundred persons in the first company, some of them had lived in splendour and delicacy in England, set out on foot to travel an hundred and twenty or thirty miles with their wives and children, near a fortnight's journey, having no pillows but Jacob's, and no canopy but the heavens, a wilderness to go thro' without the least cultivation, in most places no path nor any marks to guide them, depending upon the compass to steer by, many hideous swamps and very high mountains, besides five or six rivers or different parts of the same winding river . . . not every where fordable, which they could not avoid." [21]

Since the first settlers more frequently moved by water, as indeed may have been the case in this instance,[22] opportunities for such passages were rare. Nevertheless, the record offered numerous invitations to strike the familiar theme of the obligation falling upon succeeding generations as a result of the sacrifices made by the founders. In paying tribute to the Plymouth Pilgrims, Mather borrowed the word spoken by Peter Martyr

[20] *Ibid.*, Introd., para. 5.   [21] Hutchinson, I, 42.
[22] See Charles M. Andrews, *The Colonial Period of American History* (New Haven, 1934–38), II, 72n.

in tribute to an earlier group of Spanish adventurers: "With their Miseries this People opened a way to those new Lands, and afterwards other Men came to Inhabit them with ease, in respect of the Calamities which these Men have suffered." [23]

Happily, Perry Miller's penetrating studies of *The New England Mind* make it easy to determine the influences which first gave shape to the legend of New England's founding.[24] It was a legend that rested basically upon the strong sense the Puritan fathers had had of their own special mission in America. Whatever other forces may have helped to stimulate the settlement of Massachusetts, its early history, together with the interpretations placed upon it by later generations, can be understood only in the terms of a purpose to establish the true church of God according to the Puritan interpretation of what that church should be. John Winthrop provides the key to the extraordinary sense of dedication that guided the community through its first years in his "Model of Christian Charity," a lay leader's sermon written aboard the *Arbella* on the way to America. "Thus stands the cause betweene God and vs," he wrote, "wee are entered into Covenant with him for this worke, we haue taken out a Commission, the Lord hath giuen vs leaue to draw our owne Articles wee haue professed to enterprise these Accions vpon these and these ends, wee haue herevpon besought him of favour and blessing: Now if the Lord shall please to hear vs, and bring vs in peace to the place wee desire, then hath hee ratified this Covenant and sealed our Commission." [25] Winthrop was speaking here of the external or national covenant, something distinct from the covenant of grace which bound men as individuals. It was a covenant embracing the entire community of settlers, including the unredeemed as well as the redeemed. It was a way of reminding those he led

[23] *Magnalia*, Bk. I, 10.
[24] Especially his recent *The New England Mind; From Colony to Province* (Cambridge, Mass., 1953).
[25] Quoted in Perry Miller, *The New England Mind; The Seventeenth Century* (Cambridge, Mass., 1954), 477.

that the community in its whole life had been dedicated to the highest purpose man could conceive. As Winthrop explained in this same place, the colony would be like a city set upon a hill. Its mission was to provide an example, to demonstrate the true way of God, and thus to give assurance that the full promise of the Protestant Reformation would in time be realized.

In a community so founded and so dedicated it was natural that the Puritan clergy should have become the chief molders of its tradition, and that the growth of this tradition should have been marked by repeated appeals to the precedents established by the founders. In the second half of the seventeenth century these appeals to "ancestral precedent" took a form that Professor Miller has aptly described as the jeremiad, and he would have us view the some 1,400 pages of Cotton Mather's *Magnalia* as the most "colossal" of all the jeremiads.[26] It was a form, exploiting a plentiful supply of texts in Isaiah or Jeremiah, which balanced the glories of New England's founding with lamentations for a more recent fall from grace. The theme at least will strike you as a familiar one, for surely most of us have caught the orator's suggestion on the Fourth of July that a generation of giants has been succeeded by a lesser breed of men.

It is a theme that you will immediately, and not improperly, identify with the resistance of Puritan orthodoxy to the demands of time and place for change. But it was more than that. The Puritans had migrated to America for a purpose greater than that of achieving merely their own salvation. They hoped to save England, then following the false preaching of William Laud, and they identified their efforts with the broadest objectives of the Protestant Reformation. They remained in close touch with the leaders of the Puritan movement in England, and not a few of the New England Puritans remigrated when the English civil war brought the promise of a Puritan triumph at home. But that promise ended in disappointment, and New

[26] Miller, *From Colony to Province,* 33.

England's Puritanism soon found itself isolated in the American wilderness, not so much by the great distances of the Atlantic as by the course of history. At home, though Archbishop Laud had been defeated, the victors had not taken the course plotted for them by Massachusetts. Instead, they had turned to Presbyterianism and, worse still, to sectarianism, even to a doctrine of religious tolerance, as though God had not decreed one true way to serve Him or anything better in the way of a social order than the babble of voices which disgraced Rhode Island. The end result had been the restoration of Anglicanism and the house of Stuart, whose policies showed an early hostility to Massachusetts and to the Bay charter that had guaranteed the Puritan's right first to serve God. And how had these calamities—to which in a few years was added the dreadful slaughter of King Philip's War—befallen God's people?

There could be but one answer from the pulpit. Winthrop had given a warning aboard the *Arbella* that God would expect "a strickt performance of the Articles" and would make the people "knowe the price" of their breach.[27] And so, on special fast days and in the annual election sermons, the Puritan Jeremiahs, while compiling an impressive record of New England's sins, called to mind again and again *New England's Errand into the Wilderness.*[28]

Thus early was the thought of New England turned inward upon itself and to an examination of its own peculiar experience. It was now that William Stoughton made his oft-quoted statement that God had "sifted a whole Nation that he might send choice Grain over into this wilderness," [29] and now that the meetinghouse echoed the recurrent demand: "Why came

[27] See note 25.

[28] See Perry Miller, "Errand Into the Wilderness," *The William and Mary Quarterly*, 3d ser., X (Jan., 1953), 3–19, an especially helpful discussion which takes its title from Samuel Danforth's election sermon of 1670: *A Brief Recognition of New England's Errand into the Wilderness.* Another helpful discussion is Miller's "Declension in a Bible Commonwealth," American Antiquarian Society *Proceedings*, new ser., LI (April, 1941), 37–94.

[29] Miller, *From Colony to Province*, 135.

we here?" It was now that Increase Mather, among others, expressed the hope that the history of New England's founding might be preserved for posterity,[30] a task that would be completed on a most generous scale by his son. In short, it was now that New England began seriously to build the legend of its founding.

Had that legend served only to recall the religious objectives of the original settlement, or merely as a prop for conservatism, it could not have been so influential as it later became. But the story of this legend is a story of growth and adaptation to the needs of a changing community. Even as it first took form, one can detect a growing emphasis on the political ideals of the founding fathers. They had been, of course, a group of men who never lost sight of the connection between their rights of self-government and their freedom to pursue the religious objectives which had brought them to America. Not only had the charter and the full governing structure of the Massachusetts Bay Company been transferred to the colony at the beginning of the Puritan migration, but the magistrates thereafter had been careful to protect the colony against interference from England, even by a friendly government.[31] When a leading clergyman in 1673 gave thanks that "God hath not given us Rulers that would fleece us, that would pull the bread out of our mouthes, that would grinde our faces and break our bones, that would undermine and rob us of our Liberties, Civil and Religious, to the enslaving of this people and their children," [32] he expressed a sense of the interdependence of political and religious rights that had been strongly fixed in the New England mind from the first. The original basis on which this sense rested was explained well enough by Cotton Mather when he declared: "we came hither because we would have our Posterity

[30] Kenneth B. Murdock, *Increase Mather, the Foremost American Puritan* (Cambridge, Mass., 1925), 37.

[31] A subject ably discussed by Richard S. Dunn in his "John Winthrop, John Winthrop, Jr., and the Problem of Colonial Dependency in New England, 1630–1676," an unpublished Ph.D. dissertation at Princeton University, 1955.

[32] Quoted in Miller, *From Colony to Province*, 132.

settled under the pure and full Dispensations of the Gospel;
defended by Rulers that should be of our selves." [33] The difference at the time Mather wrote was simply that the right of self-
government had become a right increasingly valued for itself,
and not just as a means for the protection of a peculiar church
system.

The circumstances which had brought this subtle shift of
emphasis constitute one of the more complex chapters in New
England's history, but they must be summarized here only in
very brief form. It is a story that centers about a newly forming
imperial policy that found in New England an especially serious challenge to the authority of the home government.
Through the efforts of the Lords of Trade and their agent,
Edward Randolph, Massachusetts lost its charter in 1684, and
soon became the center of a new experiment in imperial administration that looked to the establishment of a single
Dominion of New England embracing all the colonies from
the Delaware eastward. From this disturbing prospect Massachusetts and the other New England colonies were saved by
the Glorious Revolution of 1688–89 in England—a revolution
made doubly glorious by the fact that the New Englanders had
been prompt in turning out the minions of a Catholic king on
the basis of reports from England which fortunately proved to
be well founded. Subsequently, Increase Mather negotiated
with the government of William and Mary a second Massachusetts charter, one that now required the colony to accept a
royal governor but that in other ways restored to the province
valued privileges of self-government.

The new charter naturally became the palladium of the
colony's liberties, and encouraged every attempt to ground the
defense of those liberties in a claim to the full benefits of
the English Revolution. As a result the Revolution acquired an
especially important place in New England's historical tradition, and undoubtedly gave to the inhabitants a new sense of
their rights as Englishmen. But the charter was easily viewed
as nothing more than the confirmation of rights previously

[33] *Magnalia*, Bk. III, 6.

enjoyed, and there were advantages in confronting the new
royal governor with a claim to ancient privileges. However
English in character those privileges might be and however ad-
vantageous it might be to stress their confirmation in the second charter, their enjoyment by New Englanders continued to
be identified with the special care their fathers had shown for
the establishment of the colony's liberties at the time of its
first settlement. A new emphasis on the political considerations
that had guided the first settlers is suggested by Increase
Mather's argument in 1689 that the Puritans would not have
emigrated "if their Reward after all must be to be deprived of
their English Liberties." [34]

When one looks ahead to the observances which marked the
centennial of New England's founding, he finds evidence not
only of a continuing disposition to view the liberties of the
community as an inheritance from its fathers but also a tendency to attribute to the founders the establishment of a new
order of human freedom. Apparently, the centennial celebrations were few and by modern standards they were not too
impressive. But the mere fact that there were any celebrations
at all has more than passing significance, for they mark the
beginning in any country, so far as I know, of the centennial
type of observance that has become all too familiar to the modern American. That such an observance should be an American
invention is not surprising, for we are a country whose origins
can be specifically and rather easily dated, but the centennial in
1707 of Virginia's settlement seems to have passed without
formal notice. The evidence in the case of Plymouth in 1720
is conflicting.[35] My own belief is that the first centennial was

[34] Miller, *From Colony to Province,* 159.

[35] S. E. Morison in the introduction to his recent edition of Bradford's
history (New York, 1952, p. xxxi) declares that the centenary of the *Mayflower's* voyage was celebrated at Plymouth in 1720. But Albert Matthews'
paper on the history of centennial celebrations (*Publications of the Colonial
Society of Massachusetts,* XXVI, 405–6) concludes that there was no observance in 1720 and that the "first centenary was held August 6, 1729" at
Salem.

celebrated at Salem in 1729. In any case, it was a Puritan community that staged the first centennial.

Late in 1728 the Rev. Samuel Fisk, pastor of the First Church of Salem, held the congregation together after services to remind its members of the approaching centennial of "the 1st Congregational Church that was compleatly form'd and organiz'd in the whole American Continent." As a result of this prompting, the congregation held in the next year special services attended by "a considerable confluence of People both from this place and the Towns about." [36] Nothing, of course, could have been more appropriate to the New England tradition than that the first centennial observance should have recalled the establishment of a church, but it is no less significant that the connection between man's right of worship and his right of self-government did not go unnoticed. In 1731, this same Samuel Fisk of Salem preached the annual election sermon before the General Court of Massachusetts—a sermon that began with the observation that "we are now, in the Affairs of this Day, entring on the second Century of choosing our Magistrates," and went on to express the hope that "this may be the happy beginning of a second Century of Elections." [37]

How many other instances could be cited I do not know.[38] It seems reasonable to suppose that not a few of the clergy found occasion through the 1730's for appropriate comment on the founding of church and town, but such detail need not bother us. It will be more helpful to notice that the people of New England during these centennial years found occasion to recognize that they had prospered and to credit the founding fathers with an impressive social achievement. Such is the evidence offered by Thomas Prince in the dedication of his *Annals* in 1736 to the governor and other ranking political leaders of

[36] Matthews as cited in preceding note, 406–7.

[37] *Ibid.*, 410. In 1730 Thomas Prince had taken note, in the annual election sermon, of the approaching "Close of the First Century of our Settlement." *Ibid.*, 408–9.

[38] Matthews lists sermons by Foxcroft at Boston, Dexter at Dedham, Hancock at Braintree, and Callender at Newport, Rhode Island. *Ibid.*, 409–11.

the province. He asked that "the worthy Fathers of these Plantations" be remembered "not only for their eminent self-denial
and piety" and for their concern that "Vital and Pure Chris-
tianity, and Liberty, both civil and ecclesiastical, might be continued to their successors," but also for the establishment of a
society "as happy as any on earth." New England at the time of
the colonists' first coming had been, in Prince's words, a "hideous wilderness," but it was now a place of pleasant houses,
fruitful fields, growing towns and churches, wholesome laws,
precious privileges, grammar schools and colleges, pious and
learned ministers, an informed common people, and magistrates who understood the virtues of sobriety and religion.[39]
Prince did not undertake to dispute the overriding importance
of the religious motivation of the fathers, as would John Adams
a few years later, but it was already clear to New England that
the founders had dedicated their efforts to much more than the
establishment of the true church.

Of comparable significance was a fundamental change in
New England's concept of the religious liberty their fathers
had sought in America. It was a change that turned, as Perry
Miller has indicated,[40] upon New England's experience immediately before and after the English Revolution. With the
loss of the Massachusetts charter in 1684, it had become apparent to the leaders of the church that an unsympathetic government might destroy the very experiment to which the
community had been dedicated by its founders. The fear thus
aroused became greater when a Catholic king succeeded to the
throne in 1685, and was further strengthened by the disturbing
effect of Sir Edmund Andros' efforts to establish the Dominion
of New England. The Protestant Revolution of 1689 saved
New England from this immediate threat, but wisdom advised
that the protection of the new English Act of Toleration might
be needed in an uncertain future. Consequently, the leaders of

[39] Thomas Prince, *A Chronological History of New England* (Edinburgh:
Bibliotheca Curiosa, Vol. 42, 1887–88), I, 9–10.

[40] See especially Miller's discussion of the "Profile of a Provincial Men-
tality" in his *From Colony to Province*, 149 ff.

the colony rushed to embrace the doctrine of toleration as a defensive weapon and with this shift of position on the part of the descendants, the founding fathers were on the way to becoming the apostles of religious liberty—not the liberty they had understood, which was the liberty to do God's will and to require that all others in their midst conform, but the liberty which John Locke suggested was the natural right of all men.

Let me be understood here. I do not mean to suggest that the Puritans suddenly "got religion" on this question of toleration, or that the community immediately experienced a radical departure from previous practices. For many years yet the chief beneficiaries of the new policy would be a small but growing body of Anglicans, whose right of worship must be attributed to the insistence of the English government rather than to the initiative of a people who remained overwhelmingly identified with the faith of their fathers. The Puritans, in a very real sense, had simply made a virtue out of necessity, and in so doing had set up a new defense against the risk that the English government, under the second charter, might demand an even more drastic revision in New England's church policy. Indeed, for better than a century thereafter the New England Puritan would remain so reluctant to concede true equality in his own community to denominations other than his own that the contrast between his professed devotion to religious freedom and his actual practice often invited sharp criticism.

At the same time, it should be said that the Puritan's profession of a new faith was not wholly lacking in sincerity. The New Englander, in common with other Europeans, was moving out of the seventeenth century into the age of enlightenment. He had begun to qualify his own doctrine of strict conformity even before the loss of the first charter, at least to the extent of doubting the justification for the fearful punishment inflicted on the Quakers in the middle of the century.[41] It must be remembered that the last example of harsh persecution in Puritan New England had come no later than the 1670's, when the Anabaptists stirred an old fear, and that the witchcraft

[41] In the case of Increase Mather, see Murdock, 133–34, 142–43.

hysteria of 1692 can be viewed as the final gasp of an old super-
stition. It does seem, however, that the political consideration
played an especially significant part in winning New England's
adherence to the principle of religious freedom. Not only was
the transition somewhat abrupt, but one cannot fail to notice
that it was the Anglican missionary of the Society for the Prop-
agation of the Gospel who so frequently stirred the New England clergy to eloquent affirmations of their new faith.

The Anglican Church had been slow to recognize its responsibilities in America until its own contest with nonconformity
in England had been settled in the Act of Toleration. But in
the eighteenth century the S.P.G. sent to the colonies over 300
missionaries, some of them to (of all places) New England. The
act was in itself offensive to a community so long dedicated to
the service of God, and that boasted of meetinghouses on every
village square. It was difficult to understand, as William Douglass complained in his history of the British settlements in
1755, why the missionaries should direct their attention "to
our most civilized and richest towns where are no Indians, no
want of an orthodox christian ministry, and no Roman catholics." [42] The S.P.G.'s recurrent interest in the establishment of
an American bishopric, moreover, had a way of conjuring up
the specter of Archbishop Laud, with results which helped to
make of the settlement of New England a simple flight from
religious persecution. "Will they never let us rest in peace?"
cried Jonathan Mayhew in 1763. "Is it not enough," he continued, "that they persecuted us out of the old world? . . . What
other new world remains as a sanctuary for us from their oppression, in case of need? Where is the Columbus to explore
one for, and pilot us to it, before we are consumed by the
flames, or deluged in a flood of episcopacy?" [43]

[42] William Douglass, *Summary, Historical and Political, of the First
Planting, Progressive Improvements, and Present State of the British Settlements in North-America* (Boston, 1755), II, 127–28.
[43] Quoted by Clinton Rossiter in *Seedtime of the Republic; the Origin
of the American Tradition of Political Liberty* (New York, 1953), 232.

If the presence of the Anglican missionary helped to re-emphasize the fundamental importance of the religious motive in New England's settlement, the same presence served also to remind men that their forefathers had not been indifferent to their political liberties. The advantages enjoyed by the Anglican Church in eighteenth-century New England had an obvious dependence upon the authority represented by the royal governor, on whom the lower house of representatives kept a jealous watch that frequently encouraged its members to give attention to the long contest between king and Parliament in seventeenth-century England. When some of the Anglicans in Boston at mid-century so far forgot the part Puritanism had played in the opposition to Charles I as to hold services in commemoration of his execution, Mayhew replied in anger with his most famous sermon. It was a sermon vigorously rejecting the doctrine of unlimited submission. He pictured the resistance to Charles I as "a most righteous and glorious stand, made in defense of the natural and legal rights of the people, against the unnatural and illegal encroachments of arbitrary power." [44] Mayhew was no old line Puritan; indeed, in the opinion of some of his fellows, he stood dangerously close to deism. But he knew the history of his people, and thus he knew how to rally their support in the cause of political and religious freedom.

So too did the youthful John Adams, who in the early part of 1765 recorded in his journal "A Dissertation on the Canon and Feudal Law" that is of the first importance to an understanding of the New England tradition on the eve of the Revolution.[45] The essay was published in the Boston *Gazette* during the following August as a contribution to the current fight

[44] Alden Bradford, *Memoirs of the Life and Writings of Rev. Jonathan Mayhew, D.D., Pastor of the West Church and Society in Boston, from June, 1747, to July, 1766* (Boston, 1838), 113.

[45] Charles F. Adams, ed., *The Works of John Adams* (Boston, 1850–56), III, 447–64. With some deletions, it has been included by Adrienne Koch and William Peden in *The Selected Writings of John and John Quincy Adams* (New York, 1946).

against the Stamp Act. Its argument for continued resistance to Britain's new policy depended upon an appeal to history, and more particularly the history of New England.

According to Adams, man had entered the modern age as the victim of a twin tyranny, ecclesiastical and civil. He had begun to break the bonds of his enslavement at the time of the Reformation and then, "under the execrable race of Stuarts, the struggle between the people and the confederacy . . . of temporal and spiritual tyranny" had become "formidable, violent, and bloody." It had been "this great struggle," Adams continued, "that peopled America." Contrary to the common belief, it had not been "religion alone" but "a love of universal liberty, and a hatred, a dread, a horror, of the infernal confederacy before described, that projected, conducted, and accomplished the settlement of America." The Puritans—"a sensible people" persecuted "for no other crime than their knowledge and their freedom of inquiry"—had fled to the wilderness of America in order to establish a plan "of ecclesiastical and civil government, in direct opposition to the canon and feudal systems." Their purpose had been "to establish a government of the church more consistent with the Scriptures, and a government of the state more agreeable to the dignity of human nature, . . . and to transmit such a government down to their posterity, with the means of securing and preserving it forever."

Adams then went on to consider the means given the children for the preservation of their great inheritance. The Puritans, he said, had been content enough "to hold their lands of their king," but they had refused any other homage to "mesne or subordinate lords" and had "transmitted to their posterity a very general contempt and detestation of holdings by quitrents." The fathers had also recognized that the defense of their children's liberties would depend upon "knowledge diffused generally through the whole body of the people." And so they had established their college and their schools, with the result "that all candid foreigners who have passed through this country, and conversed freely with all sorts of people here, will allow, that they have never seen so much knowledge and civility among the common people in any part of the world." Indeed, Adams declared, a "native of America who cannot read and write is as rare an appearance as a Jacobite or a Roman Catholic." The general level of intelligence among the people owed hardly less to their forefathers' care to introduce the art of printing. It had been a cardinal principle of New England, Adams affirmed, "that it should be easy and cheap and safe for any person to communicate his thoughts to the public."

It would be easy to quarrel with some of Adams' assumptions, and especially with his attribution to the Puritan fathers of a love of universal liberty. But it would also be pointless in the context of our present discussion. The time will be better spent in some attempt to comprehend the full meaning for him of this term "universal liberty." As he saw it, New England had come as close perhaps as was humanly possible to the ideal of a society whose members were free, informed, virtuous, and economically independent. Except for his training at Harvard and his reading, Adams was completely provincial in his background, but he understood something of the contrast between the conditions of life in New England and in other parts of the world—a contrast that struck Benjamin Franklin with special force during his long residence in Britain. Writing to Dr. Joshua Babcock in January, 1772, on the subject of a recent tour he had made through Ireland and Scotland, Franklin reported: "I thought often of the Happiness of New England, where every man is a Freeholder, has a vote in publick Affairs, lives in a tidy, warm House, has plenty of good Food and Fewel, with whole cloaths from Head to Foot, the Manufacture perhaps of his own Family. Long may they continue in this Situation! But if they should ever envy the Trade of these Countries, I can put them in a Way to obtain a Share of it. Let them with three fourths of the people of Ireland live the Year round on Potatoes and Buttermilk, without Shirts, then may their Merchants export Beef, Butter, and Linnen. Let them with the

Generality of the Common People of Scotland, go Barefoot, then may they make large Exports in Shoes and Stockings: And if they will be content to wear Rags, like the Spinners and Weavers of England, they may make Cloths and Stuffs for all Parts of the World." [46]

Here, in short, was a social ideal of the first importance to American history—an ideal that a later generation of Americans would associate more particularly with the frontier, where the "meanest farmer's boy" could aspire

> . . . to taste the proud and manly joy
> That springs from holding in his own dear right
> The land he plows, the home he seeks at night.[47]

There was perhaps a certain difference, for in John Adams' New England the meanest farmer's boy had an education to boot.

Adams was advancing no revolutionary doctrine. He had no change in the existing social order to propose, and he sought no more than to stiffen the resistance of his fellow countrymen to an assault upon rights of self-government which, in his mind, carried a guarantee that no New Englander need know the degradation so large a part of the human race did know. In common with many other men of the eighteenth century he attributed that degradation to the oppressive powers belonging to lords spiritual and temporal—that is to say, to the ecclesiastical and feudal confederacy that he considered responsible for an original enslavement of mankind and that in New England had been denied a footing in the very act of first settlement. In identifying him thus with the advanced thought of his age, there is no need to make of John Adams a more enlightened man than he was in 1765. His own deep-rooted Protestant prejudices had much to do with the shaping of his

[46] Albert H. Smyth, *The Writings of Benjamin Franklin* (New York, 1905–7), IV, 362.

[47] Quoted from *The Backwoodsman*, published at Philadelphia in 1818, by Henry Nash Smith in *Virgin Land; The American West as Symbol and Myth* (Cambridge, Mass., 1950), 136.

ideas, as is suggested by his praise for the recently established Dudley lectureship at Harvard "against popery" as an "eternal memento of the wisdom and goodness of the very principles that settled America." In his text he cited Lord Kames and Rousseau, but Adams read the writers of his own age to marvel at how much of their doctrine had been understood by the Puritan fathers.

He admitted "some degree of enthusiasm" in their religious opinions, but argued "that no great enterprise for the honor or happiness of mankind was ever achieved without a large mixture of that noble infirmity." Whatever may have been the imperfections of New England's founders, "their judgment in framing their policy" had been based on "wise, humane, and benevolent principles." They had known, Adams declared, "that government was a plain, simple, intelligible thing, founded in nature and reason, and quite comprehensible by common sense." They had held in contempt "all that dark ribaldry of hereditary, indefeasible right,—the Lord's anointed, —and the divine, miraculous original of government, with which the priesthood had enveloped the feudal monarch in clouds and mysteries, and from whence they had deduced the most mischievous of all doctrines, that of passive obedience and non-resistance." As if commissioned to strike the theme that would dominate the American protest of imperial policy down to 1776, John Adams called upon his fellow countrymen to stand fast in defense of what they already enjoyed by right of inheritance.

It would be difficult to find anything fundamental that has been added to the legend of the founding fathers since Adams wrote his "Dissertation on the Canon and Feudal Law." Here were the fathers who had taken a stand at great cost to themselves for freedom of the body, mind, and spirit. Here were their descendants, a people twice blessed with the privileges of self-government and with the means—knowledge and economic independence—for the defense of a priceless heritage. And here was the question of whether posterity should be denied the right to its inheritance. Here, too, in a single sentence Adams summed up the American mission in words that suggest the authorship of Jefferson or Lincoln: "I always consider the settlement of America with reverence and wonder, as the opening of a grand scene and design in Providence for the illumination of the ignorant, and the emancipation of the slavish part of mankind all over the earth." [48] Thus spoke John Adams in 1765 out of the fullness of New England's provincial tradition.

[48] Interestingly, this statement was omitted in the printed version; whether by oversight of the printer or through the author's choice seems to be unknown.

CHAPTER II

The First and
the Second Founding

IN the first of these lectures I undertook to suggest that popular tradition in New England had come by 1765 to attribute the founding of that community to the very ideals we
associate with the Revolutionary fathers. The parallel immediately invites attention to the years of the great debate with
Britain ending in the American Revolution, and more specifically to two general questions. What influence did traditional
views of American settlement have on the development of that
debate, and thus on the view men came to take of the cause for
which the Revolution was fought? And what influence did the
debate itself have on the development of views regarding the
original settlement of the country? The problem, in short, is
the problem of the influence of established tradition on politics,
and of the influence of political need on tradition.

Let me be the first to suggest that my remarks call for no
major revision in the history of the Revolutionary period. The
idea that tradition had a part in bringing on the Revolution is
familiar enough, and this is especially true in the case of New
England. But have we not, even in that instance, been too much
inclined to consider tradition for little more than the sanction

it gave to certain constitutional arguments, or simply as the resort of clever propagandists? Have we paid too much attention to the role of the lawyer in this debate, admittedly a large one, and too little attention to the role of the historian? Those who sought historical precedent for a redefinition of imperial relationships were as often as not trained in the law, and they might be as much, or even more, concerned with the legal as with the historical precedent. Perhaps no clear distinction between the two kinds of precedent can be established, but there is some difference, however subtle, between the case made by a constitutional lawyer and the type of argument that depends for its effectiveness upon the willingness of the community to admit its validity as a reasonable deduction from the common experience. I have thought, therefore, that there might be some point in considering tradition as a force that in itself may have helped to shape the developing contest with Britain, and of raising the question of the extent to which the colonists' case depended upon an appeal to their own history.

One naturally turns first to New England, where it will not be inappropriate to begin with Plymouth. A few weeks after John Adams had published his "Dissertation on the Canon and Feudal Law," the town meeting at Plymouth adopted formal resolutions of instruction to its representative in the General Court, reading in part as follows: "You Sir Represent a People who are not only Descended From the First Settlers of this Country But Inhabit the very spot the First possesed . . . This place . . . was at First the Asylum of Liberty & we hope will ever be Preserv'd sacred to it . . . to this Place our Fathers . . . Disdaining Slavery Fled to enjoy those Privileges which they had an Undoubted Right to but were Deprived of By the Hands of Violence & Oppression in their native country. We sir their Posterity . . . possessed of the same sentiments & Retaining the same ardour For Liberty think it our indispensible duty on this occasion to express to you these our Sentiments of the Stamp Act." [1] Prompted once more to act in defense

[1] *Records of the Town of Plymouth, Published by Order of the Town* (Plymouth, 1903), III, 166–67.

of ancient liberties, the town in January, 1766, forwarded an
address of congratulation to the citizens of Boston for their
"spirited conduct" through recent months, and soon knew the
gratification of receiving a spirited response drafted by a committee headed by Sam Adams.[2] It was "the fervent wish of the
Metropolis," Boston's greetings concluded, "That the spirit of
our venerable Forefathers, may revive and be diffused through
every Community in this Land: That Liberty Civil and Religious, the grand Object of their View, may still be felt enjoy'd
& vindicated by the present Generation, and the fair Inheritance, transmitted to our latest Posterity." [3]

In 1769, after the Townshend duties had stirred new protests, Plymouth witnessed the first of a long series of celebrations staged on the anniversary of the Pilgrims' landing. The
Old Colony Club, formed in January of that year for the purpose of providing gentlemen of the town an opportunity to
find better company than was afforded by the taverns of the
place, voted in the following December to commemorate the
landing of their "worthy ancestors" at a special dinner.
Through a miscalculation of the difference between the old
and the new calendars, the club scheduled the dinner for December 22d instead of December 21st, the true anniversary, and
thereby unwittingly fixed a custom destined to go uncorrected
until the middle of the nineteenth century.[4] On the 22d, a date
New Englanders came to identify as Forefathers' Day, the members and their guests sat down at a local inn to consume a nine-
course dinner, "dressed in the plainest manner" to avoid an
inappropriate "appearance of luxury and extravagance." After
the meal the diners marched to their hall, where at the entrance
a company of "descendents from the first settlers" paid compli-
ment with a volley of small arms and the young gentlemen of a
school across the street sang a song written for the occasion. The

[2] *Ibid.*, III, 168–71, 175–77.

[3] Harry A. Cushing, ed., *The Writings of Sam Adams* (New York, 1904–
8), I, 71–73.

[4] According to the editor of the *Records of the Town of Plymouth* (III,
457–58), the two hundred and fiftieth anniversary celebration in 1870 was
the first at Plymouth to be held on December 21.

evening was spent in further festivity punctuated by twelve toasts presented by the president of the club from a chair believed to have belonged to no less a saint than Governor Bradford himself. Of the toasts the most noteworthy was this: "May every enemy to civil or religious liberty meet the same or a worse fate than Arch-Bishop Laud." [5]

The anniversary was celebrated in each of the three succeeding years, with the addition of an orator on two of the occasions and with every evidence of a continuing harmony among the sponsors. But political feeling over concessions made to the East India Company ran so high in 1773 that it split the Old Colony Club, which included more than one future loyalist, and brought its existence to an early end. The trouble arose from an effort by the local committee of correspondence to turn that year's celebration to its own purposes. Just what was proposed cannot be said, but, whatever it was, the club vigorously rejected the proposal with a reproachful reminder that some of the committee, as members of the society, had already agreed to plans which featured the Rev. Charles Turner of Duxbury as orator.[6] The scheduled address was delivered by Turner on the 22d, but under whose auspices is somewhat uncertain, for the final entry in the club's records had been made a week before, on December 15, the day preceding the Boston Tea Party. The town itself thereafter assumed the responsibilities of sponsorship, inviting some clergyman each year, through 1780, to deliver an anniversary sermon.[7]

[5] Records of the Old Colony Club in Massachusetts Historical Society *Proceedings*, 2d series, III, 382–444; Albert Matthews, "The Term Pilgrim Fathers and Early Celebrations of Forefathers' Day," Colonial Society of Massachusetts *Publications*, XVII, 293–391; William T. Davis, *History of the Town of Plymouth* (Philadelphia, 1885), 160–62; William S. Russell, *Pilgrim Memorials, and Guide for Visitors to Plymouth Village* (Boston, 1851), 92–95.

[6] For the club's letter to the committee, Records of Old Colony Club, *loc. cit.*, III, 442–43.

[7] *Records of the Town of Plymouth*, especially 45–47, 285–86. Russell's *Guide*, 88, lists the club, the town, and the First Parish as sponsors for 1773.

Nothing could have been more appropriate than to remember the fathers with a good sermon, but the town certainly found more excitement in the attempt by local patriots in 1774 to move Plymouth Rock from the water's edge to the town square as a support for the liberty pole. The very effort carries its own testimony that the rock already was associated in local tradition with the Pilgrims' landing. How long this had been true I do not know. I can only relate to you the story told "with perfect confidence" by a nineteenth-century guide book for tourists. In 1741, according to our guide, the Elder Thomas Faunce of the First Church of Plymouth, then living outside the town at the advanced age of ninety-five, heard of a plan to build a wharf that he feared might cover the rock. Having been born in 1646, eleven years before Governor Bradford died, he remembered that the older settlers had "uniformly declared" the rock "to be the same on which they landed in 1620." And so he went to Plymouth to take "a final leave of this cherished memorial of the fathers" in the presence of many citizens of the town. The Hon. Ephraim Spooner, who served for fifty-two years as town clerk before his death in 1818, had frequently recalled being present (at the age of six) on the occasion of Faunce's last visit to the rock, and Mrs. Jonana White, "who was intimately acquainted" with the family of Elder Faunce and who died in 1810 at the age of 95, had given further confirmation of the elder's testimony. Other "aged persons" had passed on the word to many still living in 1851, when our guide published his book.[8]

It would be perhaps ungracious for us to quarrel with this kind of testimony. Moreover, it is enough for us to know that by 1774 Plymouth Rock had become a symbol worth capturing by the Sons of Liberty. If tradition may be trusted, twenty yoke of oxen were assembled for the job and managed to lift the rock out of its bed, but then—to the dismay of onlookers who saw an omen of coming events—the rock split in two. As one part fell back into its bed, it was decided to proceed

[8] Russell, *Guide*, 9–11.

with the other half to the town square, where it was placed at the foot of the liberty pole and where it remained until 1834, when it was removed to Pilgrim Hall in the featured event of that year's celebration of the Fourth of July. Not until 1880 would the two parts of the rock be reunited, and not even then would the continent's most famous piece of granite find a final resting place.[9] Whatever else may be said of the legend of the founding fathers, it has been very rough on Plymouth Rock.

Among those who noted with interest and approval the early celebration of Forefathers' Day at Plymouth was Sam Adams. He had been the moving spirit behind Boston's proposal to the other towns of Massachusetts in November, 1772, for a system of corresponding committees, and Plymouth had been the first of the towns to respond. He certainly had a part in the hearty congratulations forwarded late in December of that year to the committee in Plymouth "on the return of that great Anniversary, the landing of the first Settlers at Plymouth, & on the religious and respectful Manner" in which it had been recently celebrated. Had it not been for this "handfull of persecuted brave people," the Boston committee concluded, Great Britain might count herself fortunate to hold "such trifling Islands as are now in the possession of the Dane." [10]

It would be easy to dismiss this letter as nothing more than an obvious flattery of local pride, as one more example of Sam Adams' alertness, except for the fact that it carries a major theme in the colonial case against the new imperial policy—that America had been won for England by the settlers themselves at little or no cost to the British nation. This argument served at first perhaps the limited purpose of countering the imperial claim to a right of taxation on the ground of the extraordinary expenses resulting from the recent war with France.[11] But that it had far more important implications is

[9] Davis, *History*, 174; Massachusetts Historical Society *Proceedings*, 2d ser., III, 441n.

[10] *Writings of Sam Adams*, II, 394–95.

[11] See, for example, *ibid.*, I, 8, 42.

indicated by Sam Adams' statement of the proposition in a letter of November, 1765, to George Whitefield. His Majesty, Whitefield was assured, had no more loyal subjects than those of New England, as might be seen from the following review of their history. "As their Ancestors emigrated at their own Expence, & not the Nations; As it was their own & not a National Act; so they came to & settled a Country which the Nation had no sort of Right in: Hence there might have been a Claim of Independency, which no People on Earth, could have any just Authority or Pretence to have molested. But their strong & natural Attachment to their Native Country inclind them to have their political Relation with her continued; They were recognized by her, & they & their Posterity, are expressly declard in their Charter to be entitled, to all the Libertys & Immunitys of free & natural subjects of Great Britain, . . . : So that this Charter is to be lookd upon, to be as sacred to them as Magna Charta is to the People of Britain; as it contains a Declaration of all their Rights founded in natural Justice." [12] By this line of reasoning, Massachusetts' original subordination to England becomes a purely voluntary act, and thus subject to recall at any time the people see fit. The Massachusetts charter is viewed not as the source of rights claimed but a confirmation of their prior existence. The rights themselves are "founded in natural justice." A people who accepted this view of their history, I think it may be said, had taken an important step toward accepting the idea of independence.

Among those who helped the colonists to take such a view of their history was Thomas Hutchinson. Though standing at the opposite pole from Sam Adams on the great issues of the day,[13] Hutchinson, in his *History of Massachusetts,* provided the patriot party with a wealth of material—enough, indeed, to lend

[12] *Ibid.,* I, 28.

[13] This is not to overlook the fact that Hutchinson privately argued against enactment of the Stamp Act. See Edmund S. and Helen M. Morgan, *The Stamp Act Crises; Prologue to Revolution* (Chapel Hill, 1953), 210–14, The text of Hutchinson's argument, written in 1764, has been published by Edmund S. Morgan in the *New England Quarterly,* XXI (1948), 459–92.

credence to Ezra Stiles's observation that the publication of the history in 1764 had "contributed more than anything else to reviving the ancestorial Spirit of Liberty in New England." [14]

Like Sam Adams, Hutchinson marveled at the "addition of wealth and power to Great Britain, in consequence of this first emigration of our ancestors." [15] And like John Adams, whose "Dissertation on the Canon and Feudal Law" was written after the publication of the first volume of the history, Hutchinson attributed to the original settlers a primary desire for "the enjoyment of civil and religious liberty." Merchants and others who sought gain had come later.[16] Hutchinson repeatedly disagreed with the ideas of the founders, but he showed the quality of a true historian in an extraordinarily honest effort to make clear what those ideas were. The statesman (and you will remember that he held high office in the province) intruded upon the work of the historian only to the extent of delivering occasional lectures on the errors which marked the views of the founding fathers. The real tragedy of Thomas Hutchinson perhaps lies not so much in the fact that he died an exile in England as in the fact that his fellow countrymen read his history and turned a deaf ear to his lectures.

In the first volume he found occasion to speculate on what the Puritans would have done had William Laud succeeded in vacating the Massachusetts charter. His conclusion was that they probably would have sought some agreement with the Dutch for removal to New York. Failing that, he declared, they probably "would have sought a *vacuum domicilium* (a favorite expression with them) in some part of the globe where they would, according to their apprehensions, have been free from the controul of any European power." And then he added: "Such a scheme would have consisted very well with their notions of civil subjection, as we shall see in many instances. I

[14] Quoted in John C. Miller, *Sam Adams, Pioneer in Propaganda* (Boston, 1936), 86.

[15] Hutchinson, *History of Massachusetts,* I, xxviii–xxix.

[16] *Ibid.,* I, 81–82.

do not say their notions were just. Allegiance in an English born subject is said to be perpetual, and to accompany him wherever he goes." [17] In commenting upon reported plans by Pym, Hampden, Cromwell, and other leading Puritans to migrate to America in the mid-1630's, he considered their "very strange apprehensions of the relation they should stand in to Great Britain, after their removal to America." Their proposals implied "that they thought themselves at full liberty, without any charter from the crown, to establish such sort of government as they thought proper, and to form a new state as full to all intents and purposes as if they had been in a state of nature, and were making their first entrance into civil society." But the author found comfort in the thought that "this sentiment, in persons of such figure and distinction, will in great measure excuse the same mistake which will appear to have been made by our first settlers, in many instances in the course of our history." [18]

Hutchinson's first volume reached beyond the period of original settlement to include the colony's long defense of its chartered rights in the second half of the seventeenth century. Of particular interest to his contemporaries was the discussion of the colony's attitude toward the English Acts of Trade, which the colony first had ignored and then, being faced in 1677 by a serious threat to its economic life in the form of an embargo of its trade, had accepted by the significant device of enacting a provincial statute that gave force to the parliamentary acts. "The passing of this law," said Hutchinson, "plainly shows the wrong sense they had of the relation they stood in to England." But again he found an excuse for the colonists in William Molyneaux's later effort to assert for Ireland a comparable freedom from the legislative authority of the English parliament. If this friend of John Locke could be so seriously in error, the early settlers of New England could be pardoned their own misunderstanding.[19]

[17] *Ibid.*, I, 78–79.   [18] *Ibid.*, I, 38–39.
[19] *Ibid.*, I, 272–73.

But was it a misunderstanding? This question was thrown back to Hutchinson by Sam Adams in a long communication to the Boston *Gazette* on October 28, 1771.[20] "As I am not disposed to yield an implicit assent to any authority whatever," Adams observed, "I should have been glad if this historian, since he thought proper to pronounce upon so important a matter, had shown us what was the political relation our ancestors stood in to England, and how far, if at all, their posterity are subject to the controul of the parent state." Citing Locke to prove that while every man is born under a perpetual allegiance to his prince he becomes a member of a commonwealth only by his own "express consent," Sam Adams challenged Hutchinson to show that the forefathers had bound themselves by any such "express promise or contract." Adams concluded his essay with a comment on Hutchinson's use of Molyneaux to excuse the colonists' action in 1677. "But we want no excuse for any *supposed* mistakes of our ancestors," he declared. "Let us first see it prov'd that they were mistakes. 'Till then we must hold ourselves obliged to them for sentiments transmitted to us so worthy of their character, and so important to our security." He might have added that he was very much obliged to Thomas Hutchinson for raising the point. Instead, he closed with an ungrateful rejection of "the unsupported opinion of Mr. Hutchinson."

This first volume of Hutchinson's *History* was by no means his last contribution to the Whig cause. The manuscript of the second volume, having been rescued from the street into which it was thrown by the Stamp Act rioters in August, 1765, was published two years later. Covering the period from 1691 to 1730, its text had no such importance for the issues of the day as did its predecessor. But in 1769 he published his *Collection of Original Papers Relative to the History of the Colony of Massachusetts-Bay,* an appendix, as he explained, to the initial volume of the *History* that put in print for the first time the original Massachusetts charter and many other documents

[20] *Writings of Sam Adams,* II, 256–64.

fundamental to an understanding of New England's history from the first settlement through the English Revolution.[21] The use of this collection, at a time when historical precedent for a redefinition of imperial relationships had the broadest interest, was by no means restricted to New Englanders.

Those who actually read Hutchinson, even in New England, constituted no doubt a small percentage of the population. His revealing discussion of New England's first years had its influence on the larger public through such letters to the press as that of Sam Adams in 1771, or through pamphlets such as Josiah Quincy's vigorous protest against the Boston Port Bill in 1774, a paper making liberal use of Hutchinson's work and defining the duty of the hour as a "re-establishment of freedom." [22] More important still, perhaps, were the sermons of the Congregational clergy, who remained in a very special way the custodians of New England's peculiar tradition. The pulpit exerted its influence not only through the spoken word but through printed sermons, some of which presented short and useful histories in a literary form that still enjoyed great popularity in New England. Thus the Rev. Judah Champion of Litchfield, Connecticut, in 1770 published two fast day sermons specifically designed to meet the need for popular history, explaining that "the few histories of the settling of New England now extant, are very scarce among the people in general, and the rising generation in particular are very much unacquainted with the distresses their ancestors encounter'd, whose zeal and virtue should not be forgotten." [23] Though Sam Adams in 1772 felt that some of the clergy were too cautious in recommending

[21] *A Collection of Original Papers Relative to the History of the Colony of Massachusetts-Bay* (Boston, 1769). The work has been reprinted as *The Hutchinson Papers* in two volumes by the Prince Society (Albany, 1865).

[22] *Observations on the . . . Boston Port-Bill; With Thoughts on Civil Society and Standing Armies* (Boston, 1774), in Josiah Quincy's *Memoir of the Life of Josiah Quincy, Junior, of Massachusetts Bay: 1744–1775* (3d ed., Boston, 1875), 293–375.

[23] Quoted in Alice M. Baldwin, *The New England Clergy and the American Revolution* (Durham, 1928), 107.

"the Rights of their Country to the protection of Heaven," [24] the pulpit continued to be one of the more important influences helping to keep fresh the memory of New England's founding and to draw from it lessons appropriate to the day. "But, my friend, have you ever read the history of your own country, wrote by Mather?" asked the Rev. William Gordon in a sermon preached before the General Court of Massachusetts on the first anniversary of American Independence. "If not," he continued, "you have heard of it, let me recommend it to your perusal, you will then find that your difficulties are vastly short of what your forefathers endured." [25]

For evidence that such appeals to the memory of the Puritan fathers continued to have political utility, it is necessary only to notice the prefatory passage of the Suffolk Resolves adopted by the inhabitants of Suffolk County in September, 1774, as a memorial to the Continental Congress. "Whereas the power but not the justice," begins this influential statement of New England's case, "the vengeance but not the wisdom of Great Britain, which of old persecuted, scourged, and exiled our fugitive parents from their native shores, now pursues us, their guiltless children, with unrelenting severity; And whereas, this then savage and uncultivated desart, was purchased by the toil and treasure, or acquired by the blood and valor of those our venerable progenitors; to us they bequeathed the dearbought inheritance, to our care and protection they consigned it, and the most sacred obligations are upon us to transmit the glorious purchase, unfettered by power, unclogged with shackles, to our innocent and beloved offspring. On the fortitude, on the wisdom and on the exertions of this important day, is suspended the fate of this new world, and of unborn millions." [26] Much

[24] *Writings of Sam Adams*, II, 349.

[25] [Frank Moore], *The Patriot Preachers of the American Revolution with Biographical Sketches, 1766–1783* (Printed for Subscribers, n.p., 1860), 185.

[26] Worthington C. Ford, ed., *Journals of the Continental Congress, 1774–1789*, I, 32.

of this, of course, is sheer emotion, reminding us that one function of tradition is to provide a focus for the sentiment that binds men together in hours of trial. But there is more here than mere sentiment. In this text, the American adventure has its beginning in an escape from Europe. The treasure, the toil, and blood expended by the founders support an overriding claim to possession of the new world. The past and the future are linked together in a way that reminds us of our national inclination to make of the past a guarantor of the future.

This discussion of New England is an incomplete one, if only because it depends so heavily upon the record in the leading province of Massachusetts. There were especially interesting developments in Rhode Island during these years, but time requires that we turn our attention southward to the middle provinces.

Important differences had marked the development of the two regions. An extraordinary diversity of population in the one stood in marked contrast to the unusual homogeneity of the other. Without exception the middle provinces reflected the influence of a proprietary pattern of original settlement, while New England proudly boasted the rejection by its founders of all feudal concepts of tenure. That community, moreover, had the maturity that comes with age; in the other, the most important single province, which was Pennsylvania, was kept from being the youngest of the colonies only by the more recent founding of Georgia. On the other hand, settlement in the middle provinces had depended heavily upon the migration of persecuted religious minorities, and most men lived as small farmers with well-developed concepts of the title their own labors had given them to the soil. Here, much more than in the southern provinces, one might expect the development of a tradition comparable to that of New England, with some indebtedness perhaps to the fully developed legend of New England's founding.

An interesting suggestion of borrowing is found in the foreword to Samuel Smith's *History of The Colony of . . . New Jersey,* published in 1765.[27] He found "little reason to doubt, that views of permanent stability to religious and civil freedom" had been the chief inspiration of the original settlers. As a Quaker who also wrote an unpublished history of Pennsylvania, he might have been expected to emphasize the peculiar mission of the Friends in West Jersey; instead, he preferred to draw a parallel with New England's earlier settlement for "motives of like kind." He admitted that some of the settlers had also followed "a distant prospect . . . of improving their estates," but he had the colonist's understanding of the financial risk involved in any colonizing venture and he emphasized the sacrifices made by people of good station at home in crossing 3,000 miles of water "at their own expense" to test an "unprov'd experiment." By their own frugality and industry, with the blessings of Providence, they had laid "the foundation for the present improvement of territory to the mother country." Whether Smith had read the New England historians I cannot say. Whatever the fact, the parallel between his interpretation of New Jersey's history and the familiar view of New England's origins loses none of its significance.

There is little else in the way of formal histories to guide our study of the middle provinces. Samuel Smith's unpublished history of Pennsylvania in its preface described the original settlers as people of "reputation and credit" who had gone "through many hardships to improve the country" without "much charge or difficulty to the parent-state." The text almost comes alive in its account of Penn's dealings with the native Indian, whose place in American history tended now to receive a new emphasis from the colonists' desire to prove that their

[27] *The History of The Colony of Nova-Caesaria, or New-Jersey: Containing an Account of Its First Settlement, Progressive Improvements, The Original and Present Constitution, and Other Events, to the year 1721. With Some Particulars Since; And A Short View of Its Present State.* By Samuel Smith (Burlington, 1765). All citations are to the 2d edition by William S. Sharp, Trenton, 1887.

title to America depended as much upon purchase from the Indian as upon royal grants. But for the most part Smith was content, as in his history of New Jersey, to record by quotation or paraphrase some of the more important documents of Pennsylvania's early political history.[28] Not until the closing years of the eighteenth century would the state have a published history. For New York, William Smith had published in 1757 a useful history covering the period ending in 1739.[29] Cadwallader Colden felt his treatment of the English conquest of the province was calculated to flatter the descendants of the Dutch settlers, but the history actually gave slight notice to the colony's Dutch origins. It may be worth observing that Colden also considered Smith to have been too much under the influence of the New England historians in his judgment of Governor Andros.[30] These three studies by members of the Smith tribe are all we have for the middle provinces.

Tradition, however, does not depend for its existence upon formal histories. The legislator, like the clergyman, by reiterated appeals to a common memory can mold the tradition as effectively as can any other. Many examples could be found, but the one in Pennsylvania focuses our attention upon a major figure in the American legend. William Penn, though jealous of his prerogatives as proprietor of the soil, had shown a generosity of spirit in confirming to the people of his province legal and political rights appropriate to his own convictions as a seventeenth-century Whig. As a result, it had become a commonplace of Pennsylvania politics to use the example of the founder as a check on his sons and successors in the proprietorship. As Benjamin Franklin later explained, it was hoped that

[28] Smith's manuscript was first published as *History of the Province of Pennsylvania* in an edition by William M. Mervine (Philadelphia, 1913).

[29] William Smith, *The History of the Province of New York, from the First Discovery to the year MDCCXXII* . . . (London, 1757). I have used the first volume of The New-York Historical Society reprint of Smith's history and the continuation to 1762 (New York, 1830).

[30] The New-York Historical Society *Collections* (1868), 182, 187–91.

"the Honors done his Character might influence the Conduct of the Sons." [31] And if we may take Franklin's word, the later proprietors became so sickened of repeated admonitions as to the virtues of the original proprietor that they were wont to observe on every announced occasion of some public address to them: "Then I suppose we shall hear more about our Father." [32]

The occasion for this comment by Franklin was a speech of May, 1764, delivered in the Pennsylvania assembly by John Dickinson in opposition to a motion to seek the overthrow of the proprietorship and the appointment of a royal governor. Dickinson spoke of the liberties enjoyed by Pennsylvanians under the Charter of Privileges William Penn had agreed to in 1701 and vigorously opposed the surrender of an inheritance purchased at a "prodigious price" by the original settlers of Pennsylvania. "The inhabitants of remote countries," he declared, "impelled by that love of liberty which allwise Providence has planted in the human heart, deserting their native soils," had "committed themselves with their helpless families to the mercy of the winds and waves, and braved all the terrors of an unknown wilderness in hopes of enjoying in these woods the exercise of those invaluable rights which some unhappy circumstance had denied to mankind in every other part of the earth." He saw danger in surrender of "the liberties secured to us by the wise founders of this Province; peaceably and fully enjoyed by the present age, and to which posterity is so justly entitled." [33]

When published, this speech had a foreword by the Rev. William Smith of the college in Philadelphia which included a verse composed entirely of sentiments extracted from the minutes of the Pennsylvania assembly. I dare not impose the

[31] Smyth, *Writings of Benjamin Franklin,* IV, 346.

[32] *Ibid.*

[33] Paul Leicester Ford, ed., *The Writings of John Dickinson;* Vol. I, *Political Writings, 1764–1774 (Memoirs of the Historical Society of Pennsylvania,* Vol. XIV, Philadelphia, 1895), 21–49, particularly 38, 44.

whole of it upon you, but fortunately the first verse carries
the full import of the others:

William Penn,
A man of principles truely humane,
an advocate for
Religion and Liberty,
Possessing a noble spirit
That exerted itself
For the good of mankind
Was
The great and worthy founder
Of
Pennsylvania [34]

In the foreword to a reply by Joseph Galloway, Franklin conceded the authority of all quotations given, but questioned
that addresses of the sort cited could be taken as "generally the
best repositories of Historical Truth." [35] As these exchanges
suggest, full agreement on the honors that should be awarded
the "great and worthy founder of Pennsylvania" depended
upon a final settlement of the question of the proprietorship,
which awaited the coming of the Revolution.

John Dickinson lost the debate on the proprietorship in
1764, and Franklin sailed for London that fall to press the
assembly's cause with agencies of the crown. But Dickinson
soon found himself with the majority on issues raised by the
Crown's own policy. As a leading member in the Stamp Act
Congress in 1765 he drafted, among other contributions, the
petition to the king which reminded George III that the colonies had been "originally planted" by British subjects who
"by their successful Perseverance in the midst of innumerable
Dangers and Difficulties, with a Profusion of their Blood and
Treasure, have happily added these vast and valuable Dominions to the Empire of Great Britain." [36]

[34] *Ibid.*, 17.
[35] Smyth, *Writings of Benjamin Franklin,* IV, 344–45.
[36] Ford, *Writings of John Dickinson,* I, 193.

Three years later he became in a very real sense the chief spokesman for the colonies in their protest against the Townshend Acts. In addition to his well-known *Letters from a Farmer in Pennsylvania,* he wrote perhaps the most popular patriot song of the pre-Revolutionary years. The verses were forwarded by him to James Otis on July 4, 1768, with an explanation "that indifferent songs are frequently very powerful on certain occasions," and with an attribution of eight unspecified lines to his friend Arthur Lee of Virginia. The song caught on immediately, was widely printed throughout the colonies in newspapers, almanacs, and broadsides, and is the song usually referred to by contemporaries as the Liberty Song.[37] Sung to the tune of "Hearts of Oak," the second and third verses are representative:

> Our worthy Forefathers—let's give them a Cheer—
> To Climates unknown did courageously steer;
> Thro' Oceans to Deserts for Freedom they came,
> And dying bequeath'd us their Freedom and Fame.
>
> Their generous Bosoms all Dangers despis'd,
> So highly, so wisely, their Birth-Rights they priz'd,
> We'll keep what they gave, we will piously keep,
> Nor frustrate their Toils on the Land and the Deep.

In his soberly argued *Letters from a Farmer in Pennsylvania,* which sought this same year to draw some defensible line between a denial of Parliament's right to tax and an admission of its legislative power over certain questions of common imperial concern, Dickinson found little occasion to appeal to ancestral precedent.

The same observation may be made with reference to James Wilson's influential pamphlet of 1774 *On the Legislative Authority of the British Parliament,* which denied the rightful existence of any such authority except by consent of the colo-

---

[37] *Ibid.,* 421–32 for the song and editorial notes. See also Arthur M. Schlesinger, "A Note on Songs as Patriot Propaganda, 1765–1776," *William and Mary Quarterly,* XI (1954), 78–88.

nists and thus helped to move the colonial position toward the principle governing the modern British Commonwealth of Nations. Though Wilson's thesis depended more heavily than had Dickinson's upon assumptions regarding the original character of English colonization, he wrote primarily as a lawyer and, significantly, based his case on the natural rights of man. But like any good lawyer he did not overlook the predilections of the jury. In rejecting all suggestion of a parallel between the settlement of America and the English conquest of Ireland, he had the wit to remind his readers that the first settlers had "never suspected that their descendants would be considered and treated as a conquered people; and therefore they never taught them the submission and abject behaviour suited to that character." [38]

It is a different story with Benjamin Franklin, who was well ahead of Wilson in recording the view that Americans had no choice but to reject all claims of the British Parliament to legislate for the colonies.[39] As Verner Crane has observed, Franklin was no lawyer and his arguments were the least legalistic of those employed by leading champions of American rights. It is also true that he cited Locke infrequently and that his use of the conventional language of natural rights was rare.[40] But he was a student of history, including the history of his own people. His remarks on that subject derive their chief interest from the fact that they were usually addressed to an English audience and thus suggest more strongly the fundamental importance to the American case of what may be described perhaps as the historical argument. He spent most of the critical decade preceding the Revolution in England, first as agent for the antiproprietary party in Pennsylvania and increasingly as the recognized spokesman for the American point

[38] Randolph G. Adams, *Selected Political Essays of James Wilson* (New York. 1930), 73.

[39] See especially Verner W. Crane, *Benjamin Franklin, Englishman and American* (Baltimore, 1936). See also Verner W. Crane, *Benjamin Franklin's Letters to the Press, 1758–1775* (Chapel Hill, 1950), introduction and 46–49.

[40] Crane, *Franklin's Letters to the Press*, xxxviii.

of view. His task was to make that point of view clear to an audience governed by none of the emotional attachments that influenced those addressed by Sam Adams in Boston or Plymouth.[41]

He used the history of American settlement chiefly to refute the popular notion in England that the colonies belonged to Britain. Instead, Franklin argued, as in a letter to Lord Kames in April, 1767, that the colonies had been planted at the expense of private adventurers who came to America by leave of the king, and who then "voluntarily engaged to remain the King's subjects, though in a foreign country; a country which had not been conquered by either King or Parliament, but was possessed by a free people." The first planters had purchased the land they occupied from the natives, and Parliament was so far from having a hand in the work of original settlement that it actually "took no kind of notice of them, till many years after they were established." Georgia and Nova Scotia, both of them eighteenth-century acquisitions, presented examples for which no parallel existed in the period of first settlement. Consequently, the colonies properly were viewed as "so many separate little states, subject to the same Prince," but legislatively independent of Britain.[42]

That Franklin had a New England orientation to his thinking on American history is suggested by more than one passage. His repeated references to New England may reflect, in part, the tendency by Englishmen to single out that section for special criticism as the chief center of trouble in America. It may be that the emphasis belongs to the superior quality of the New England histories, and especially of Hutchinson's work, with which Franklin was acquainted.[43] It may be simply that the story of the Puritan settlements had greater utility, given

[41] See especially Crane's recent collection of Franklin's communications to the press as cited in preceding note.

[42] Smyth, *The Writings of Benjamin Franklin*, V, 19–21.

[43] Crane, *Franklin's Letters to the Press*, 105; Smyth, *Writings of Benjamin Franklin*, V, 297.

the purposes he had in mind. But he spoke the language of
New England's legend as though it were his own, which indeed
it was. For example, there is the following passage from an
anonymous letter to the press in 1768: "Boston man as I am,
Sir, and inimical, as my country is represented to be, I hate
neither England or Englishmen, driven (though my ancestors
were) by mistaken oppression of former times, out of this happy
country, to suffer all the hardships of an American wilderness." [44]

On turning to the South, one finds an interesting contrast.
When Richard Bland, whom Jefferson described as a great
antiquarian and who certainly was a close student of Virginia's
history, wrote in 1766 his *Inquiry into the Rights of the British
Colonies*,[45] he sharply repudiated the idea so popular among
the northern colonists that America had been originally settled
by fugitives from religious and civil oppression in England.
Instead, he argued that the first settlement had been accomplished "by Men who came over voluntarily, at their own Expense," and with appropriate guarantees from the crown for
the establishment of "a civil Government in it as near as
conveniently might be agreeable to the Form of the English
Government and Policy thereof." After "struggling through
immense Difficulties, without receiving the least Assistance from
the English Government," the colony had "attained to such a
Degree of Perfection" that a representative assembly had been
established, an assembly that ever since had exercised the legislative power in that community. Thus far Bland's view was
very close to that of William Stith, whose history in 1747 had
laid the foundation for an interpretation of Virginia's story
that identified the colony with the parliamentary struggle
against the crown, the same struggle that loomed so large in

[44] Crane, *Franklin's Letters to the Press*, 115. See also *ibid.*, 42–43, 54–56;
and Smyth, *Writings of Benjamin Franklin*, V, 206–18, 399–405.
[45] Richard Bland, *An Inquiry into the Rights of the British Colonies*
(Williamsburg, 1766). I have used the reprint edited by Earl G. Swem and
published for the William Parks Club at Richmond in 1922.

John Adams' "Dissertation on the Canon and Feudal Law." A further promise that the discussion might develop along these lines is found in Bland's comment on the dissolution of the Virginia Company in 1624 and on the resultant fear among the colonists that they might then be subjected to "a Prerogative Government." But Bland then veered off to demonstrate that a royalist tradition could be as helpful to the American cause as could any other.

Perhaps it was because he found Stith's work dull, as did Jefferson.[46] Perhaps it was because of the necessity to depend on Beverley's earlier study for the period after 1625, for Beverley was the son of one of Governor Berkeley's supporters at the time of Bacon's Rebellion and had stressed the colony's loyalty to the king during the period of the English civil wars. A more likely supposition is that Bland was guided chiefly by his understanding that the traditional view of Virginia's loyalty to the king offered an effective basis for challenging the right of Parliament to interfere with the legislative independence of the colonies. In any case, his argument focused attention not so much on the first years of settlement as on the period following the company's dissolution. His main exhibits were the royal action of 1634 confirming to the colonists their "full Possession of the Rights and Privileges of Englishmen," the colony's sharp repudiation of an attempt in 1642 through Parliament to reestablish the Virginia Company, a subsequent assurance by Charles I that the colony "should be always immediately dependent upon the Crown, and that the Form of Government should never be changed," and especially the terms of the colony's surrender to the government of Cromwell in 1652. As Bland interpreted the story, the colonists had stoutly resisted the pretensions of Cromwell because of the high value they placed upon the king's assurances as to their rights, and finally had surrendered only on conditions which guaranteed the full privileges of the colony. At the time of the Restoration, the

[46] Paul Leicester Ford, ed., *The Writings of Thomas Jefferson* (10 vols., New York, 1892–99), IV, 102–3.

people of Virginia unanimously had renounced "their Obedience to the Parliament" and had so far anticipated the return
of Charles II "that he was King in Virginia some Time before
he had any certain Assurance of being restored to his Throne
in England."

Thus did Richard Bland undertake to prove that the inhabitants of "the first Colony in North America" were so far
from being "a few unhappy Fugitives" that they actually "were
respected as a distinct State, independent, as to their internal
Government, of the original Kingdom, but united with her,
as to their external Polity, in the closest and most intimate
League and Amity, under the same Allegiance, and enjoying
the Benefits of a reciprocal Intercourse." Here of course is the
substance of a commonwealth concept of empire, which is to
say that Bland's view of colonial rights was as radical as that
advanced by any other man at the time. Like Sam Adams, he
considered the continued association of the colonists with the
empire as a purely voluntary act, arguing that men have a
natural right to emigrate and that in emigrating "they recover
their natural Freedom and Independence." And like John
Adams, he called for stout resistance to an invasion of ancient
and well-established privileges of self-government. But there
was a difference in the tone and the quality of the argument.
One finds here none of the special veneration for the founders
that so marked contemporary discussions in New England, no
suggestion that the colony had been the scene of a new experiment in human liberty, no emotional outburst identifying
America with the hope of mankind.

A contrast with New England is again suggested by Jefferson's *Summary View of the Rights of British America,* a pamphlet published at Williamsburg in 1774 from a draft written
in the vain hope of its adoption as an instruction for the Virginia delegation to the Continental Congress.[47] Jefferson was
more interested in documenting the charge that a long "series

[47] Julian P. Boyd, Lyman H. Butterfield, and Mina R. Bryan, eds., *The
Papers of Thomas Jefferson* (Princeton, 1950–   ), I, 121–35.

of oppressions" proved the existence of "a deliberate, systematical plan of reducing us to slavery" than in elaborating the basis of his claim that these oppressions represented a usurpation of power. On this last point Jefferson's case was essentially the same as that already made by Bland. The first colonists, like their Saxon ancestors, had asserted a natural right to emigrate and to establish in the place of their new abode "such laws and regulations as to them" seemed "most likely to promote public happiness." He admitted no material difference between the Saxon migration to Britain and the British migration to America, and in other ways showed more inclination than had Bland to exploit the Whig view of history that traced English liberties to Saxon origins. He also exploited the ill repute of the house of Stuart, using the grants to Lord Baltimore and other royal "favorites" as examples of an arbitrary parceling out of a country that "had been acquired by the lives, the labors and the fortunes of individual adventurers" who had received not even a shilling from the royal treasury. While condemning the recent penalties imposed on Boston, Jefferson paid tribute to New England's former boldness "against the house of Stuart," but the chief exhibit drawn from the history of his own province remained the articles of surrender in 1652 that Bland before him had used so effectively. In Jefferson's view these articles continued to be of such fundamental importance to the history of Virginia, and of America, that he printed them in full in his later *Notes on Virginia*.[48]

This special dependence on the record of the middle years of the seventeenth century has, I think, more than passing significance in the development of Virginia's historical tradition. Jefferson and Bland found in the articles a most useful means for refuting the claims of Parliament, for these articles had specifically acknowledged that the surrender was "a voluntary act not forced nor constrained by a conquest upon the countrey." The document, moreover, had guaranteed to the Virginians the full rights of "the free borne people of England,"

[48] Ford, *Works of Thomas Jefferson*, IV, 11–15.

had confirmed the established powers of the general assembly, not neglecting to recognize the freedom of the people from all taxes "whatsoever" except those imposed with the consent of the assembly, and had stipulated that the Virginians should "have free trade as the people of England do enjoy to all places and with all nations according to the laws of that commonwealth." [49] All this was very helpful in 1774, but its very helpfulness in the establishment of a larger liberty for Americans undoubtedly served to strengthen the attachment of Virginians to a view of their history that encouraged later claims to a Cavalier descent, for the concessions of 1652 had been won from Cromwell.

It would be easy, however, to overemphasize the differences in 1774 between Virginia and New England. Whether he lived in the North or in the South, the American at that time was at some pains to establish these propositions regarding his origins as a resident of North America: that his forebears had emigrated as free men, that they had paid their own way to America, that in America they had bought the land with their own labor and blood, and that their original devotion to liberty could be demonstrated by instances of stouthearted resistance to encroachment on the rights of self-government. Here certainly was the foundation for a common and very satisfying view of what it was that made of a European, or a Virginian, an American.

While Jefferson labored on the *Summary View,* he had at hand an appeal from Ebenezer Hazard of Pennsylvania for documents from Virginia's records that would illustrate the colony's rise and progress. Hazard ambitiously proposed to publish a collection of the more important documents pertaining to the history of the several provinces, explaining that

[49] I have followed Jefferson's text as cited immediately above. Jefferson himself drew the following conclusion: "The colony supposed, that by this solemn convention, entered into with arms in their hands, they had secured the antient limits of their country, its free trade, its exemption from taxation but by their own assembly, and exclusion of military force from among them." See p. 15.

"when civil States rise into Importance, even their earliest History becomes the object of Speculation." He hoped, therefore, to remove an "Obstruction from the path of Science, and at the same Time to lay the Foundation for a good American History, by preserving from oblivion valuable Materials for that purpose." [50] Jefferson's reply in April, 1775, heartily approved the plan, promised his own co-operation, and recommended that Hazard communicate with Richard Bland.[51] A list of recommendations by Jefferson for inclusion in the collection has survived to bear testimony to his own widening knowledge of colonial history.[52] Hazard's *Historical Collections* would not be published until well after the Revolution. Nevertheless, the initiation of this project on the eve of the first Continental Congress has an obvious significance.

And there are other evidences that the great debate of the preceding decade, with its encouragement for the establishment of a common defense of colonial rights, had given birth to a new concept of an American history. Thus John Adams in his influential "Novanglus" letters, which were serially printed in a Boston newspaper during the interval between the first and second meetings of the Continental Congress, drew from the record of settlement on the Chesapeake evidence to support an argument that the early inhabitants of Virginia and Massachusetts had been in full agreement on their relationship with England, "precisely" as stated by the recent Congress.[53] Differences of tradition seem to have receded into the background as the Second Continental Congress in July, 1775, justified its decision to take up arms against the mother country, for Virginians joined with the representatives of New England in proclaiming that their forefathers had "left their native land, to seek on these shores a residence for civil and religious freedom." At the expense of their own blood, the hazard of their own fortunes, without charge to the mother country, by unceasing labor and through an unconquerable spirit, they had

[50] Boyd, *Papers of Thomas Jefferson*, I, 144–45.
[51] *Ibid.*, I, 164.   [52] *Ibid.*, I, 146–48.
[53] Adams, *Works of John Adams*, IV, 108–12.

accomplished their settlement in the then distant and inhospitable wilds of America.[54] This was a theme drawn chiefly from New England's tradition, and Richard Bland so recently as 1766 had taken exception to some of its implications, but it was too useful a theme in 1775 not to be accepted as good American doctrine. Its acceptance owed much to a certain community of experience binding the colonies together, but it probably owed even more to hard necessity in a common struggle for the freedom of America.

The years of the Revolution afforded little time for the writing of history, except in the case of some of the Tories. It was while an exile in England that Hutchinson completed his great work, and there that Alexander Hewatt wrote his *Historical Account of the Rise and Progress of the Colonies of South Carolina and Georgia,* a two-volume work published in London in 1779 that dealt chiefly with the first of these provinces.[55] Hewatt, who was a Presbyterian clergyman, had no love for the New Englanders, whose fathers he condemned for having fled the intolerance of Europe only to establish it in America, but his discussion of South Carolina's history followed very closely the pattern set by New England's historians. Taking his point of departure from the Revival of Learning and the Reformation in the sixteenth century, he moved by way of the Huguenot settlement in Florida to the colonization of Carolina by "a restless and troublesome party" of dissenters who "were willing to seek liberty of conscience in the deserts of America." [56] Mention might also be given to the history of Pennsylvania written during the Revolution by Robert Proud, a loyalist who remained in America.[57] But the space belongs

[54] Ford, *Journals of the Continental Congress,* I, 142. Cf. 129 for Jefferson's draft.

[55] *An Historical Account of the Rise and Progress of the Colonies of South Carolina and Georgia* (2 vols., London, 1779).

[56] *Ibid.,* I, 54-55.

[57] Robert Proud, *History of Pennsylvania in North America* (2 vols., Philadelphia, 1797-98). See also Charles W. Thompson, "Notices of the Life and Character of Robert Proud," in Historical Society of Pennsylvania *Memoirs,* I (1826), 389-408.

to the work of another Tory, George Chalmers, whose *Political
Annals of the Present United Colonies,* published at London
in 1780,[58] was destined to have a greater influence in this
country than any other historical work dealing with America
that was written between Hutchinson's *History of Massachusetts* and George Bancroft's *History of the United States.*

Chalmers was a Scotsman who had emigrated to Maryland
after the Seven Years' War and had returned to Britain in
1775. His purpose in writing the book was to refute the popular notions regarding the settlement of America which, in his
view, had contributed heavily to bringing on the Revolution,
and in so doing to rebuke those in England who showed sympathy for the American cause. As he explained in his preface,
the American appeal to "ancient privileges" had made it important "to investigate with precision, what immunities the
colonists were originally entitled to possess." For that purpose,
he made good use of the published provincial histories and of
collections like that of Purchas. In the later stages of his study,
which in published form did not reach beyond 1689, he enjoyed
access to state papers that would not be available to American
students for many years to come.[59] It was the authority of the
text and the comprehensiveness of its coverage, rather than the
slight sympathy he showed for the American view, that explain
the extraordinary influence of the book.

Chalmers' treatment of Virginia's early history is representative of the whole. The first settlers, he declared, had enjoyed
no right to emigrate except by permission of the state, and the
Virginia charters demonstrated chiefly the strong sense all
participants in the enterprise had of their dependence upon the
English government. The second charter of 1609, Chalmers

[58] George Chalmers, *Political Annals of the Present United Colonies,
From Their Settlement to the Peace of 1763: Compiled Chiefly from Records, and authorized often by the Insertion of State-Papers,* Book I (London, 1780).

[59] On Chalmers see Grace A. Cockroft, *The Public Life of George Chalmers* (New York, 1939).

observed in passing, had conferred upon the colonists no "one privilege worth contending for." And so far had been the original settlers from enjoying the rights of Englishmen that they actually lived like "soldiers in garrison" under the authority "of a corporation residing in England, in which they were not represented, and over the deliberations of which they had no control." [60] In answer to American proposals for a commonwealth type of imperial relationship, proposals which necessarily gave new emphasis to the prerogatives of the king, Chalmers dated the "happy epoch" of Virginia's history from the establishment of the representative assembly in 1619. He attributed this action by the Virginia Company to its leaders' rejection of the king's assumption that he enjoyed a right to establish colonies as a "mere private estate, descendible to his personal heirs" and subject only to his own prerogative.[61] As for the critical years of the Interregnum, which Bland and Jefferson had used to demonstrate the colonists' devotion to rights of self-government, Chalmers emphasized instead the evidence of a strong devotion to the king rather than to the cause of parliamentary government.[62]

For the New England Puritans, whom he regarded as being so far from John Adams' advocates of "universal liberty" as to be actually a very bigoted and intolerant crew, Chalmers had a special distaste. But he also had a marked respect for them, and especially for their economic achievements. His explanation for New England's early prosperity sounds like a passage lifted from a Fourth of July address: "Freedom then was the enlivening principle of their pursuits; and property, landed and personal, invigorated the nerve of every enterprize." [63] Chalmers also regarded New England as the seedbed of the Revolution. He came to view the Revolution as having had two basic causes. The one was a fundamental weakness in British policy, the other the determination of the colonists, and more

[60] Chalmers, *Political Annals,* 26, 39.
[61] *Ibid.,* 43, 68.   [62] *Ibid.,* 122–25.
[63] *Ibid.,* 99.

particularly the New Englanders, to achieve independence, either within or outside the empire. How far back, in his mind, this determination could be traced is suggested by his discussion of the transfer of the original Massachusetts charter to America. Having condemned the action as highly irregular, as the "first instance of a corporate body that ever sold itself," he went on to observe that the Puritan colonists had "most dexterously" built on this charter not only "the original government of that colony but independence itself." [64] Those of us who have been inclined to attribute the dominant position of New England in our national tradition to the writings of her own historians will do well to read Chalmers' *Political Annals*.

His distaste for the Bay Colony Puritans encouraged him to take a more favorable view of their neighbors. For example, his discussion of the Plymouth settlers stressed qualities of character that have since commended them to the whole of the American people. Roger Williams is presented as a man "fruitful in religious frenzies" (a description not too far off) but as one whose policy of religious tolerance provided a welcome contrast with the rest of New England. [65] Much warmer was his tribute to Lord Baltimore and the colony of Maryland: "What a fine contrast does the christian liberality of the Roman-Catholics of Maryland form to the intolerant temper and practice of the Independents of Massachusetts." [66] In a footnote, Chalmers gave the full text of the Mayflower Compact, [67] and at more than one point he directed attention to other plantation covenants in early New England. While discussing the history of Rhode Island, he argued from Williams' decision to secure a royal charter that the "voluntary" government of the original settlements had failed. Yet Chalmers also credited the founders of Rhode Island with "realising in prac-

[64] *Ibid.*, 136, 151.   [65] *Ibid.*, 156, 270.

[66] *Ibid.*, 218–19.

[67] *Ibid.*, 102n. The document is described as the "Association of New-Plymouth."

tice, because they were few, what has been so often proposed by theorists for mighty nations." [68]

If the Revolutionary fathers had accomplished nothing else by their explorations into colonial history, they had at any rate prodded George Chalmers into giving the new nation a very useful history of its origins. To list the historians of the early national period who leaned heavily upon this work would be to name them all. George Bancroft began serious study for his *History of the United States* with a reading of Chalmers, and even in the later years of the nineteenth century Edward D. Neill still found him helpful.[69] An entire generation of orators drew either directly or indirectly upon Chalmers for the materials out of which they fashioned some of the more favored of their historical themes.

In no way is this more evident than in the monotonous repetition on the Fourth of July, and other occasions, of the proposition with which Chalmers opened his discussion of our colonial origins. "Of these colonies," said he, "it cannot be asserted, as it is of European nations, that their origin is uncertain or unknown; that their ancient history is fabulous and dark; or that their original institutions have come down the current of time, loaded with the disputations of the antiquary. Here, there is as little room for the dreams of conjecture or the obscurities of tradition, as for the regret of the philosopher, that the establishment of nations, which is the most important and instructive part of their annals, is generally the most imperfect." [70] In rough translation, Chalmers was saying that it could be proved by appeal to plain facts of historical record that the American leaders had been talking nonsense. But the plain facts of history are subject to more than one interpreta-

[68] *Ibid.*, 270.

[69] Russel B. Nye, *George Bancroft* (New York, 1945), 94; Cockroft, *Public Life of George Chalmers*, 53n.

[70] Chalmers, *Political Annals*, 1. I do not mean to suggest that Chalmers was the first or the only one to make this point. Hewatt had said substantially the same thing in the preceding year. See his *Historical Account*, I, 57.

tion. In America men read the facts Chalmers so plentifully supplied as suited themselves, and heartily agreed with his opening proposition. "Our origin is within the limits of well-attested history," Chancellor Kent explained to the New-York Historical Society in 1828, and then continued: "This at once dissipates the enchantments of fiction; and we are not permitted, like the nations of ancient Europe, to deduce our lineage from super-human beings, or to clothe the sage and heroic figures who laid the foundations of our empire, with the exaggeration and lustre of poetical invention. Nor do we stand in need of the aid of such machinery. It is a sufficient honour to be able to appeal to the simple and severe records of truth." [71] The student who reviews the varied appeals that have been made to these "records of truth" will detect not a few evidences of poetical invention, but he will also note that in this country, however legendary and misleading may be the popular tradition, it is accepted with the special conviction that proof may be found in the historical record. It would be unfair to charge George Chalmers with fixing this national trait, but certainly he helped to fix it.

Certainly, too, he had a part in determining the interpretation the American people gave to the Revolution they had staged. By his full and well-documented refutation of the historical part of the American case against Britain he made the arguments supporting that case somewhat clearer for a generation of Americans who were beginning to look for a satisfactory interpretation of their Revolution. In so doing, he provided encouragement especially for those who were inclined to assume that the Revolution had been fought not so much for the acquisition of new rights as in the defense of ancient liberties. With Chalmers at hand, it was easy to document the view presented by a speaker before the Phi Beta Kappa Society at Harvard in 1798 who declared: "We contended for preservation, not acquisition, to keep the rights we

[71] *An Anniversary Discourse . . . before The New-York Historical Society, Dec. 6, 1828, By James Kent, President of the Society* (New York, 1829), 6–7.

had, rather than to gain those we never had; and the separation was resorted to chiefly as a necessary means of maintaining the ancient ground." [72]

This, of course, was a conservative view of the Revolution, spoken in Federalist New England midst the fears that had been stirred by the French Revolution. I have no time to discuss the varied influences which encouraged New Englanders to draw a sharp distinction between the two revolutions; nor do I desire to discount any one of them. But in closing I think it worth observing that the Federalist view of the American Revolution was wholly consistent with New England's own and long-established historical tradition.[73] Does it not also reflect the use the Revolutionary fathers had made of tradition?

After the Rev. Samuel Miller of New York City had preached a special sermon on the occasion of George Washington's death, he received an admonition from John Jay for a thoughtless reference to "our glorious emancipation from Britain." If Mr. Miller would take the trouble to read the statements of the Continental Congress in 1774 and 1775, Jay suggested, he would find that the Congress "had regarded the People of this Country as being *Free*" and had resorted to arms only when England "recurred to arms to put a Yoke upon us." And to this Jay added: "I think Truth will justify our indulging the Pride of saying, that we and our ancestors haue kept our Necks free from Yokes, and that the Term *Emancipation* is not applicable to us." [74]

[72] John T. Kirkland, *An Oration, Delivered, At the Request of the Society of PBK, in the Chapel of Harvard College, on the Day of their Anniversary, July 19, 1798* (Boston, 1798), 7.

[73] Notice the use made of Hutchinson's history in Josiah Quincy, *An Oration, Pronounced, July 4, 1798, At the Request of the Inhabitants of the Town of Boston, In Commemoration of the Anniversary of American Independence* (Boston, 1798).

[74] Ltr., Jay to Miller, February 28, 1800, in Princeton University Library.

CHAPTER III

The Shaping of
a National Tradition

IN 1790 James Wilson delivered the first of his famous lectures on law at the University of Pennsylvania. He had emigrated to Pennsylvania from Scotland not long before the Revolution but early enough to play a leading part in the politics of the Revolutionary years. More recently, he had made a contribution to the framing of our federal constitution that has been considered by many scholars second only to that of James Madison, and he had been appointed by Washington to the first Supreme Court. In his inaugural lecture, where he announced a belief that law must be studied as "a historical science," he talked first of American history in general.[1] On the origins of the United States he had this to say: "If the just and genuine principles of society can diffuse a lustre round the establishment of nations, that of the States of America is indeed illustrious. Fierce oppression, rattling, in her left hand, the chains of tyranny; and brandishing, in her right hand, the torch of persecution, drove our predecessors from the coasts of Eu-

[1] James DeWitt Andrews, ed., *The Works of James Wilson* (2 vols., Chicago, 1896), I, 2–6.

rope: liberty, benevolent and serene, pointing to a cornucopia
on one side, and to a branch of olive on the other, invited and
conducted them to the American shores."

If his language seems a bit florid, it must be remembered that
there are occasions which require an orator to come up to the
standards set by convention, and such an occasion was this.
He spoke before a brilliant audience which included the President and Lady Washington, as the first of our first ladies was
often known in Philadelphia, and other dignitaries of the
newly established federal government. After a few such passages, the speaker leveled off to use a prose well suited to the
thoughtful content of his lectures.

As Wilson himself observed, the story of the American states
was at that time imperfectly known even to their own people,
for their histories, with few exceptions, were yet to be written.
But he had no doubt what those histories would show, and
"boldly" ventured, as he put it, to compare the States of America "with the most illustrious commonwealths, which adorn
the records of fame." Said he: "When some future Xenophon
or Thucydides shall arise to do justice to their virtues and their
actions, the glory of America will rival—it will outshine the
glory of Greece."

To support his prediction, the lecturer offered two examples
indicative of the peculiar richness of the American epic. "In
discharging the duties of this office," he declared, "I shall have
the pleasure of presenting to my hearers what, as to the nations
in the Transatlantic world, must be searched for in vain—an
original compact of a society, on its first arrival in this section
of the globe." He referred, of course, to the Mayflower Compact. He had found the Compact in Chalmers' *Political Annals*
and would read it to his audience in a later and especially noteworthy lecture on the Common Law.[2] In this first lecture he
paused only to comment: "How the lawyers, and statesmen,
and antiquarians, and philosophers of Europe would exult, on
discovering a similar monument to the Athenian common-

[2] *Ibid.*, 465–66, where he cites Chalmers, 102.

wealth!" His second example pointed to America's leadership in the development of religious tolerance. Wilson would take nothing from the credit due John Locke for the enunciation of this principle, but he asked, "While immortal honors are bestowed on the name and character of Locke; why should an ungracious silence be observed, with regard to the name and character of Calvert?" It should be made known that "before the doctrine of toleration was published in Europe, the practice of it was established in America."

Wilson brought his introductory remarks to a close by depicting for his audience an American temple of fame—somewhat like our modern Hall of Fame. Already, as one entered its portal there were to be found, on the left hand, the figures of Warren, Montgomery, and Mercer, fallen leaders of Revolutionary battles, and, on the right, Calvert, Penn, and Franklin. Across from the entrance, in a position that dominated the whole, was a special niche reserved for Washington.

Several points in Wilson's remarks invite comment, but they are particularly interesting for the evidence they offer as to the critical importance of the earliest chapters in our history to a newly forming national tradition. Though his choice of heroes indicates a sense of the overriding importance of the Revolution, he is primarily concerned to emphasize the significance of developments associated with the original settlement of the colonies. He assumes, as have most of us since then, that the unifying theme of American history is to be found in the adherence of the American people—a people otherwise marked by great diversity of background and interest—to a common body of principle. But he finds no occasion at all to mention here the Declaration of Independence, which any one of us perhaps would place first in an attempt to support his basic assumption. Instead, he talks of the Mayflower Compact and of Lord Baltimore's statute of religious liberty. In seeking an explanation for this choice of emphasis, it may be helpful to notice that Wilson attributes to the American creed no quality peculiar to America itself. By equating that creed with "the just and genuine principles of society," to which all right thinking men subscribe, he lends to it a quality of universality that has long encouraged us to view the American way of life as a faithful reflection of the goals toward which all men naturally strive. But human nature dictates that a people must have some possessory right in the articles of their own faith, and how better could that need have been met than by laying claim, as does Wilson, to a significant priority among men in the establishment of a social order built on sound principle? It was this need, as much perhaps as anything else, that in the first days of the Republic not only gave special significance to the earliest chapters of American history, but encouraged their interpretation in the light of eighteenth-century standards.

In saying this, I do not mean to suggest that the American people in the early national period found a greater interest in the story of colonization than in the stirring events of more recent years. Indeed, the story of the early settlements, as more than one writer found occasion to comment, often seemed dull by comparison with the momentous developments of the Revolution. It was a story that could not be ignored, if only because of its pertinence to the problem of identifying the several members of the union. But having made the necessary identifications, one could hurry on to the Revolution, as did Noah Webster in the brief history of the United States he compiled in the 1780's for inclusion in his well-known school reader.[3] Webster dutifully identifies each of the thirteen states in terms of their several origins and then, like so many of us since, he jumps over the intervening years to begin, with the Stamp Act, a longer and much more enthusiastic discussion of "the Late War in America."

Modern scholarship has emphasized the poor quality, and

[3] The history is reprinted in Old South Leaflets, 193.

especially the plagiarism from the *Annual Register*, which marred the histories of the Revolution published in the 1780's by William Gordon and David Ramsay,[4] but for our purposes these faults count for little. What matters is that they were written and read, and that they represent the first attempts by Americans to deal comprehensively with an important segment of our common history. Benjamin Trumbull, who was the first to undertake a comprehensive study of the full sweep of our history, did not get beyond 1765 in the initial and only volume published, but his plan had allotted two additional volumes to the Revolutionary period.[5]

It had been the Revolution that had given the American people both their independence and their union. The Revolution, moreover, offered its own claim to priority in pointing the way to a new social and political order. In New England at the time of the Revolution, it had been an easy transition from the long-established view that America had been settled for the sake of political and religious liberty to the view that America had now become the refuge of liberty itself. "From this day will be dated the liberty of the world," cried Jonas Clark in a sermon of 1776 commemorating the Battle of Lexington.[6] A few weeks later, Samuel West, while preaching the annual election sermon in Massachusetts, pictured true religion and liberty "gasping for life" in other parts of the world and refused to believe that God would permit either of them "to be banished from off the face of the earth." [7] In 1780, on this

---

[4] See Michael Kraus, *The Writing of American History* (Norman, Okla., 1953), 70–73, for a brief summary of the findings of O. G. Libby at the turn of the century.

[5] Benjamin Trumbull, *A General History of the United States of America; From the Discovery in 1492, to 1792: or, Sketches of the Divine Agency, in Their Settlement, Growth, and Protection; and Especially in the Late Memorable Revolution* (New York, 1810).

[6] Quoted in Baldwin, *New England Clergy and the American Revolution,* 133n.

[7] John W. Thornton, *The Pulpit of the American Revolution; or, the Political Sermons of the Period of 1776* (2d. ed., Boston, 1876), 311.

same occasion of the annual election, the Rev. Simeon Howard declared: "Our contest is not merely for our own families, friends, and posterity, but for the rights of humanity, for the civil and religious privileges of mankind." [8] Dr. David Ramsay, speaking at Charles Town, South Carolina, in 1778, was inspired to the same eloquent affirmation by nothing more, apparently, than the flattering attention of Europe, where an influential body of opinion had agreed to hail the Revolution as the beginning of a new age in human history.[9]

And this was a view that was destined to enjoy even wider popularity among the American people after their independence had been established. Indeed, there is reason to believe that such an interpretation of the American Revolution did not gain its fullest popularity until after 1789, when the coming of the French Revolution promised for many Americans the fulfillment of Dr. Ramsay's prophecy in 1778 of a widespreading conflagration that would wipe tyranny off the face of the earth.[10] With others, and especially in New England, the reaction against the French Revolution came promptly to lend, as I suggested in the preceding lecture, a new emphasis to the idea that our own Revolution had been fought simply in defense of the "ancient ground" seized by the liberty-loving first settlers. But not even in Federalist New England did this reaction rob the American example of its special significance as "the world's *best* hope," if I may borrow a phrase from Mr. Jefferson's inaugural of 1801 that seems clearly to have

[8] *Ibid.*, 391. See also *ibid.*, 454–55, where Ezra Stiles in 1783 describes the recent war as having been fought not only for the liberties of America "but the liberties of the world itself," and David Tappan's statement that same year that the Revolution "tends to wake up and encourage the dormant flame of liberty in all quarters of the earth." Moore, *Patriot Preachers of the American Revolution,* 300.

[9] David Ramsay, *An Oration on the Advantages of American Independence: Spoken Before a Publick Assembly of the Inhabitants of Charlestown in South Carolina, on the Second Anniversary of that Glorious Aera* (Charlestown, 1778).

[10] *Ibid.*

been used for the assurance of his Federalist opponents.[11]

Nowhere is the emphasis on the Revolution more apparent than in our national observances. Not until the Civil War would there be a national holiday commemorating an event associated with the original settlement of the country. There were, it is true, certain usages of the colonial period that made an early bid for national acceptance. Thus the Continental Congress on several critical occasions during the War for Independence set special days of prayer and fasting in accordance with a long-established custom in the New England colonies. The Congress also called upon the people to observe special days of thanksgiving, not the modern and annually recurring fall festival but a thanksgiving when there was something special to give thanks for, as for the French alliance in 1778 and for a victorious peace in 1783.[12] Both Washington and Adams followed these precedents on occasion, but when the Presbyterian divine, Samuel Miller of New York, proposed that a day of prayer be proclaimed in 1808, Jefferson argued that the separation of church and state under the constitution must be considered absolute, so much so as to prohibit even the recommendation of any kind of "religious exercise" by the president.[13] Madison, during the unhappy course of the War

[11] It will be recalled that this famous statement of the American mission falls in the passage devoted to the proposition that "we are all Federalists, all Republicans." After reading a good deal of New England oratory which had emphasized the difference between "the rank luxuriance of natural licentiousness" and "the corrected sweets of civil liberty," I have thought it worth suggesting that Jefferson intended here to indicate his own indorsement of a theme especially popular with the New England Federalists. The quotation given immediately above is taken, incidentally, from John Phillips's Fourth of July oration of 1794 (Boston, 1794), an oration that can hardly be described as hostile to the French Revolution.

[12] W. deLoss Love, *The Fast and Thanksgiving Days of New England* (Boston and New York, 1895) provides full detail in an appendix, pp. 464–514, with references to the preceding text. For the text of the first Congressional resolution in June, 1775, see Ford, *Journal of the Continental Congress,* II, 87–88.

[13] Ltr., Jefferson to Miller, Washington, Jan. 23, 1808, in Princeton University Library. In the same place, see also Miller's statement of 1833 "Respecting Mr. Jefferson's Letter of Jany 23, 1808."

of 1812, called the people to their knees on three separate occasions, and when the peace came he urged that they humble
themselves once more in a spirit of thankfulness. But the practice lapsed after 1815, except for occasions so rare and so extraordinary as to leave no excuse for speaking in terms of a
national custom.

Meanwhile, the Fourth of July had promptly become *the*
national holiday. Dr. David Ramsay may have delivered, as he
claimed, the first Independence Day oration, at Charles Town
in 1778,[14] but there were in any case earlier celebrations. Some
informal celebration marked the first anniversary at Philadelphia in 1777, and in Boston on that day William Gordon
delivered a special sermon before the General Court of Massachusetts on "The Separation of the Jewish Tribes." [15] Boston
already had its annual patriotic address in the oration delivered in commemoration of the Boston Massacre each spring
from 1771 through 1783.[16] When in this last year it was decided
to substitute an annual celebration of Independence Day, the
decision conformed with the custom then rapidly developing
throughout the country.

Though the early Fourth of July orations have many things
in common with their modern sequels, they were in one fundamental way quite different. Coming so soon after the proclamation of independence and at a time when the nation still
faced critical problems that were consequent upon the decision
in favor of independence, these orations had to be directed

[14] See note 9 above and, for his claim to priority, *An Oration Delivered
on the Anniversary of American Independence, July 4, 1794, in Saint Michael's Church, to the Inhabitants of Charlestown, South Carolina* (London:
By Citizen Daniel Isaac Eaton, Printer and Bookseller to the Supreme
Majesty of the People, 1795).

[15] Moore, *Patriot Preachers of the American Revolution*, 159–85; and,
for a brief discussion of the early celebrations of the Fourth, Merle Curti,
The Roots of American Loyalty (New York, 1946), 136–41.

[16] These orations are conveniently consulted in Hezekiah Niles, *Republi-
cation of the Principles and Acts of the Revolution in America* (New York,
Chicago, and New Orleans, 1876), 17–30, 34–79, 490, where they are reprinted
from an edition by Edes. In 1776 the oration was delivered at Watertown.

chiefly toward the illumination of contemporary questions. No mere panegyric on the virtues of a bygone generation could have met the need. Some historical introduction seems to have been favored, and in this the orator, especially if a New Englander, might dip far back into the stream of American history. But the very occasion tended to pull his attention forward to the crisis that had precipitated the Revolution, a subject usually treated with brevity and often presented with an apology for any review of events so well remembered by all and in which so many of those present had themselves played a distinguished part. A tribute to the sacrifices of the Revolutionary soldier and to the leadership of Washington offered an easy transition into the main body of the text, not to mention the opportunity for an oratorical passage or two. The chief topic of discussion varied according to time and place, and the discussion was often distinctly partisan in its tone, but it usually focused attention on some problem of the union that had been achieved, however imperfectly, in 1776. And this remained a natural focus through the long years of continuing debate over the form that union should take and the purposes it should serve.

But this very great and overshadowing interest in the Revolution served also as a powerful stimulant to the study of colonial origins. It was generally agreed among those who had fought the Revolution that the most remarkable thing about it was the fact that in 1776, as John Adams later put it, "thirteen clocks had struck as one." [17] The modern American, who takes the union for granted, has some difficulty in recapturing a sense of how impressive to this earlier generation of Americans was the simple fact that in 1775 a Virginian had gone to the defense of Boston. The Declaration of Independence was to them as much a declaration of union as of independence and from it they dated the existence of the union itself, as also did Lincoln at Gettysburg in 1863. Indeed, among a people who even today can recall only with difficulty the exact date on

[17] Ltr., Adams to H. Niles, February 13, 1818, in *Works*, X, 282–84.

which their constitution was officially adopted, "the spirit of '76" was destined to remain a slogan calling first of all for unity and, from the first, the question of the sources of this original union has naturally loomed large in any national history.

The answer given to that question was shaped in part by the very incompleteness of the union achieved in 1776. Since no formal constitution or treaty of alliance existed for several years thereafter, it was easy to assume that the union rested basically upon a community of "principles and feelings," if I may quote John Adams in his old age, and that the explanation must be "sought in the history of the country from the first plantations in America." [18] Adams did not live to read Timothy Pitkin's *History of the United States,* published in 1828, but he would have agreed fully with Pitkin's assertion that the "unexampled unanimity of sentiment against the stamp act, . . . was not the work of a day or a year." [19]

A closely related question was the question of the national character. It could be agreed that the Revolution had demonstrated the characteristic features of the American people—such as their tendency to view the powers of government jealously while recognizing the necessity for order in any society, a strong sense of the right to property as the reward of labor, or a feeling for the tolerance that should be shown for differing opinions and convictions, especially in the field of religion. But whence came these characteristic qualities? To answer such questions was the very function of history itself in the contemporary view, as is suggested by the justification given by William Robertson, the Scottish historian, for discussing the early history of Virginia and New England in his unfinished *History of America.* "It will exhibit a spectacle no less striking than instructive," Robertson wrote, "and presents an opportunity, which rarely occurs, of contemplating a society in the first moment of its

[18] *Ibid.*

[19] Timothy Pitkin, *A Political and Civil History of the United States of America, from the year 1763 to the Close of the Administration of President Washington , , ,* (New Haven, 1828).

political existence, and of observing how its spirit forms in its infant state, how its principles begin to unfold as it advances, and how those characteristic qualities, which distinguish its maturer age, are successively acquired." [20] However lacking in color the story of the first settlements may have seemed to some, its pertinence to problems of the most compelling interest could not be disputed.

John Marshall devoted a full volume of his well-known biography of Washington to a summary history of the colonies, an allotment of space he justified on the ground that Washington's life was so much the history of his country that any biography of him could only be regarded as incomplete without some attempt to explain the genius, character, and resources of the people he led.[21] Jeremy Belknap and Ebenezer Hazard undertook in the 1790's an American biographical dictionary so ambitiously conceived that the two volumes that were published did not get beyond the seventeenth century.[22] John Sanderson in the 1820's felt the same compulsion as had Marshall to preface his *Biography of the Signers to the Declaration of Independence,* a work completed in nine volumes, with an introductory volume devoted, except for the thirty-eight pages given John Hancock, to a review of colonial history.[23] Similarly, David Ramsay had prefaced his history of the Revolution with a review of the colonies' settlement that was shamelessly paraphrased from Chalmers' *Political Annals.*[24] The

[20] William Robertson, *The History of America. The Tenth Edition. In which is included the Posthumous Volume, containing The History of Virginia, to the year 1688; and of New England, to the year 1652* (London, 1803), IV, 182–83.

[21] John Marshall, *The Life of George Washington* (5 vols., Philadelphia, 1804–7), I, xi–xii.

[22] Jeremy Belknap, *American Biography: or, An Historical Account of those Persons Who Have Been Distinguished in America, as Adventurers, Statesmen, Philosophers, Divines, Warriors, Authors, and Other Remarkable Characters* ... (Boston, 1794–98).

[23] John Sanderson, *Biography of the Signers to the Declaration of Independence* (Philadelphia, 1820–27).

[24] David Ramsay, *The History of the American Revolution* (2 vols., Philadelphia, 1789), Chap. 1.

point he sought to establish in this preface received a more succinct statement in an oration delivered by Ramsay at Charleston on July 4, 1794. "From the first settlement of this country," he declared, "everything concurred to inspire its inhabitants with the love of liberty: the facility of procuring landed property, gave every citizen an opportunity of becoming an independent freeholder. Remote from the influence of KINGS, BISHOPS, and NOBLES, the equality of rights was inculcated by the experience of every day." [25]

No doubt mention should also be given to a growing sense of the national destiny that served, while broadening, to deepen the interest in American history. The new recognition given by citizens of the Republic to Christopher Columbus—especially in the use that was made of the poetic form of his name for the designation of places, educational institutions, and even the nation itself—betrayed a new sense of identification with the great work he had begun in America.[26] It is not without significance that Columbus became an early choice for presentation by the talented pen of Parson Weems, or that Washington Irving's life of Columbus, published in 1828, won an instantaneous and enduring popularity. Abiel Holmes in his *Annals of America,* first published in 1805, made a more serious effort than theretofore had been made to fill in the background of English colonization by attention to the activity in North America of other European peoples. As his foreword explained, a "New World" had been discovered and a "new empire" had arisen to provide "a theatre of great actions and stupendous events." That the origins and development of the United States, which now promised to dominate the later stages of the great adventure begun by Columbus, should take precedence over still broader interests was only natural. Even in the second edition of the *Annals* in 1829 Holmes concentrated on the story of English settlement after 1607, but he called attention to the new interest recent additions to the territory of the United

[25] See n. 14 above.
[26] See George R. Stewart, *Names on the Land, A Historical Account of Place-Naming in the United States* (New York, 1945), 171–72.

States had lent to the detail on European activity before Jamestown.[27]

It may seem to some of you that any effort to establish national reasons for an interest in colonial origins is somewhat unnecessary in view of the very simple explanation that is offered by the strong provincial pride of the several states. Not only was the most solid achievement of American historical scholarship in the first years of the Republic represented by such works as Belknap's history of New Hampshire or Trumbull's history of Connecticut,[28] but such institutions as existed for the encouragement of historical study were overwhelmingly provincial in their identification. An American Academy of Arts and Science was founded at Boston as early as 1780, but it had no such influence as did the Massachusetts Historical Society established in 1791. The American Philosophical Society, the oldest and most influential of national institutions for the promotion of scholarly interests, did not establish its committee for literature and history until 1815. The American Antiquarian Society, organized in 1812, directed its chief attention during the first years to Indian relics in Ohio.[29] A short-lived American historical society marked the years of Peter Force's activity in the 1830's, but the present American Historical Association was not established until 1884.

Meanwhile, a growing interest in American history found its chief encouragement through the organization of state historical societies modeled, more or less, after the pattern of the Society of Antiquaries of London and the more recently established

[27] Abiel Holmes, *American Annals; or, A Chronological History of America, from Its Discovery in 1492 to 1806. With Additions and Corrections by the Author* (2 vols., London, 1813). The second edition, with a continuation to 1826, was issued at Cambridge, Mass., in 1829.

[28] Jeremy Belknap, *The History of New Hampshire* (3 vols., Boston, 1784–92); Benjamin Trumbull, *A Complete History of Connecticut, Civil and Ecclesiastical* (2 vols., New Haven, 1818).

[29] See especially Julian P. Boyd, "State and Local Historical Societies in the United States," *American Historical Review*, XL (1934), 10–37; and Leslie W. Dunlap, *American Historical Societies, 1790–1860* (Madison, 1944).

Royal Society of Antiquaries of Scotland. As would be expected, the Massachusetts Historical Society was the first. The New-York Historical Society came next in 1804, and the establishment of similar societies in other states followed—for Rhode Island in 1822, Pennsylvania in 1824, Connecticut in 1825, Indiana in 1830, Ohio and Virginia in 1831, to mention only the earlier ones. The first societies gave testimony in their plans to a broad interest in the whole of American history.[30] With provision at times for a corresponding membership, these societies identified themselves with the ideal of an active communication among scholars in all parts of the country. But practical considerations, together with provincial pride, served quickly to narrow the actual fields of activity, and in so doing to focus attention on the particular rather than the general.

It would be easy, however, to misinterpret this natural emphasis on provincial origins. The very pride that now stimulated a new interest in state history was in no small part a product of the new nationalism, as is clearly indicated by the competitive spirit in which state historians laid claim to the special honors belonging to their own provinces. It may be helpful also to bear in mind the peculiar character of the new nationalism. James Wilson labored in his lectures on law to demonstrate that the distinguishing feature of the American system of government was the federal principle which had called into existence a new loyalty to the whole of America without requiring the sacrifice of an older loyalty to one's state. To accept this proposition one had to assume, as did Wilson, that so natural a division existed between the functions of state and nation that little room was left for conflict and thus for competing claims on the citizen's loyalty.[31] It is an assumption

[30] For example, The New-York Historical Society announced a purpose "to discover, procure, and preserve whatever may relate to the natural, civil, literary, and ecclesiastical history of the United States in general, and of this State in particular." The New-York Historical Society *Collections,* I (1811), 1.

[31] See Andrews, *Works of James Wilson,* especially I, 318.

the modern American, in view of the country's more recent history, has difficulty in accepting, but there can be no question of its influence on the writing of American history during these earlier years.

The competition among the states might show at times excessive zeal and not a little ill will. It was difficult for those who lived outside New England, in view of the dominant influence she had already exerted on the shaping of a national tradition, not to feel that the main task in the writing of American history was to demonstrate that New England had no exclusive claim on the founding of the country—a task to which much paper and ink has since been devoted. In making the point, certain old grudges—as old perhaps as the memory of the execution of the Quakers in seventeenth-century Massachusetts—might have their influence.[32] Some Americans found it hard to overlook the contrast between the actual record of the Puritan fathers and the heavy emphasis New England's tradition had come to place on religious liberty, and this was made more difficult by the reluctance shown by both Massachusetts and Connecticut after the Revolution to adjust their actual practice to the national standard of a true separation of church and state.

The impulse to draw contrasts unfavorable to the Puritans seems to have been especially strong in New York. Discussions of American history in the meetings of The New-York Historical Society began quietly enough. Samuel Miller entertained the Society in 1809 with a factual discourse in commemoration of Henry Hudson's explorations. Hugh Williamson, the historian of North Carolina, talked the next year on the benefits of "Civil History" with particular attention to the broad interest of American history, especially in its more recent chapters.[33] But Gouverneur Morris, addressing the Society in 1812, struck a different note by dwelling on the peculiar glories of Dutch

[32] Belknap in his first volume of the *History of New Hampshire* (the 1792 reprint at Boston, p. 99) urged that the memory of old grievances not be kept alive for the reproach of fellow countrymen.

[33] The New-York Historical Society, *Collections*, I, 19–40; II, 23–36.

history and of New York's Dutch ancestry. He labored to demonstrate the priority of the Dutch in fighting for the very principles that New England had made its chief boast, and dwelt on the good fortune of New York in having escaped England's control through years in which hypocrisy and crime, or impiety and vice, had been the characteristic features of English life.[34]

Gulian C. Verplanck's anniversary discourse in 1818 made New England herself the more immediate target. Though conceding the love of liberty that had inspired the first settlers of the eastern states, he found in their history "an incongruous and unaccountable mixture of the gigantic and the childish— of glorious truth and miserable prejudice." He praised Roger Williams and Lord Baltimore for having given to America the "glory of having first set an example of a practical and extensive system of religious freedom." Verplanck also boasted, despite the shortcomings of the Fundamental Constitutions of Carolina, that John Locke had been among the "original legislators of this country," and saw in Oglethorpe a "benign legislator and magistrate, who had rivalled" William Penn "in the arts of peace and in acts of mercy," but he saved the highest praise for the Dutch. New Yorkers, Verplanck affirmed, had "no cause to blush" for any part of their descent, "and least of all" for their Dutch ancestry, because New Amsterdam had been founded at a time when Holland led all Europe in the glorious struggle "against civil and religious tyranny." [35]

Perhaps it was the proximity of New York to New England, and the sense men had of a long-standing rivalry between the two communities,[36] that explains the inclination to build New York's case upon a critical view of the Puritan. Perhaps the emphasis belongs rather to the fact that the Dutch were the first non-English group to demand recognition for a significant contribution to the founding of the nation, and that they naturally

[34] *Ibid.*, II, 127.

[35] *Ibid.*, III, 54, 56, 63, 68, 83–84.

[36] A subject discussed in an earlier series of the Phelps Lectures by Dixon Ryan Fox in *Yankees and Yorkers* (New York, 1940).

felt a compulsion to state their case in the strongest possible terms. Perhaps the derogatory remarks on New England's founding deserve less attention than does the praise for Baltimore and Penn, men on whom New Yorkers had no claim except that belonging to all Americans. In any case, there is evidence enough that many were willing merely to claim honors equal to those admittedly belonging to New England.

For example, there is the claim advanced in behalf of Virginia by John Daly Burk in a remarkable three-volume history of the state that was published early in the nineteenth century. Burk was an expatriated Irishman and a devotee of Jeffersonian republicanism who undertook to counter the "universally received opinion, arising from the want of an authentic history," that Virginia had been distinguished "for her invariable loyalty, and her submission and tractable temper, during the greater part of her colonial existence." In his view, it had too long been a custom to contrast Virginia's "yielding policy with the sturdy patriotism of New-England."[37]

In the very first pages of his work Burk conceded a large part of his case by warning his readers that the real glory of Virginia's history had been crowded into the last thirty years of the eighteenth century. He confessed that he found the early history of the colony dull by expressing the hope that when he came to "events of real dignity" he might present a more interesting text.[38] Even so, he devoted the whole of his first volume to the years before 1619, apparently for no better reason than that the beginning of American settlement demanded close attention, however uninteresting that story might be. To the story itself, as previously presented by Smith, Beverley, and Stith, Burk added literally nothing, except for an interpretation

[37] John Burk, *The History of Virginia from Its First Settlement to the Present Day* (3 vols., Petersburg, Va., 1804–5), II, 233. Burk's death terminated his study at the year 1775, but a fourth volume was added in *The History of Virginia Commenced by John Burk and Continued by Skelton Jones and Louis Hue Girardin* (Petersburg, 1816).

[38] Burk, *History of Virginia*, I, 5–6. See also *ibid.*, I, 297–98.

nowise dependent upon the record. His own contribution came in repeated references to hardy adventurers, cut off from the world and "embosomed in the forest," who carried the germ of a mighty nation promising to "eclipse the glory of Rome and Athens." Typical of the whole text is the author's treatment of the abandonment of Jamestown in 1610. As the sorely tried survivors of a dreadful winter destined to be remembered as the "starving time" drop down the river in a desperate gamble that they might reach England by way of Newfoundland, Burk invites his audience to consider the fateful significance of the providential arrival of Lord Delaware in time to turn them back to Jamestown. "This little fleet," he wrote, "carried with it the altars and destinies of liberty: The germ of human happiness is on board: Unconscious of the invaluable treasure they possess, the wretched colonists carry with them the sacred fire, which shall bless their posterity, and animate the world. The vestal flame lives unnoticed amongst them, without the care of a priestess or an altar. The time is yet to come, when their descendants, enflamed with a holy enthusiasm, shall build temples, and raise altars, for its preservation." [39] It is difficult to read this and other such passages without feeling that Burk was badly in need of two or three Puritan settlers who understood the great work to which they were committed.

When Burk reached the critical question of Virginia's relations with Cromwell, he went beyond both Bland and Jefferson to claim that the colonists at the time had been overwhelmingly devoted to the principles of republicanism, no less so than the people of New England. For support of this view he offered no evidence at all, and he managed to execute a difficult transition to the restoration of Charles II in 1660 by resorting to the simple device of charging an act of usurpation to a Cavalier minority.[40] Not until he reached Bacon's Rebellion did Burk find a fully satisfactory case to support his main thesis. In the effort to rescue Bacon from the discredit and oblivion into

[39] *Ibid.*, I, 160.
[40] *Ibid.*, II, 75–76, 119–20.

which he had so early fallen, Burk for a change even did some
research. He included a special appendix of documentary evidence on the subject in addition to a full discussion of the
rebellion in the text, where Bacon became, I think it safe to
say, for the first time a forerunner of the Revolution.[41]

If Nathaniel Bacon has found no fixed place in the national
tradition, it is partly because the Virginians themselves have
shown some reluctance to back his claims to recognition. Robert Beverley, the colony's first historian, had been the son of one
of Berkeley's supporters. Neither Bland nor Jefferson had
shown any marked interest in the opportunity Bacon's career
offered. John Marshall, in his life of Washington, dismissed
Bacon as a man of uncertain motivation and judged his rebellion to have accomplished no good for the colony.[42] Edmund
Randolph, writing in an unpublished history of Virginia, took
strong exception to Burk's attempt to put a "historical gloss"
on the true character of the rebellion.[43] The subsequent popularity of the Cavalier thesis as to Virginia's origins naturally
limited the usefulness of Bacon.

There is no reason to doubt, however, that Burk's history enjoyed real popularity for a time after its publication. Among
its other influences must be included the decision to celebrate
Virginia's bicentennial in 1807. As the bicentennial year approached, the editor of the *Virginia Apollo* was reading Burk's
history. He had also taken note of the recent revival at Plymouth of more or less annual celebrations of the Pilgrims' landing
in 1620. Accordingly, he recommended to his fellow Virgin-

[41] *Ibid.*, II, 246–74.

[42] Marshall, *Washington*, I, 198 ff.

[43] In an unpublished history commonly cited as Randolph's Manuscript
History of Virginia and currently in possession of the Virginia Historical
Society at Richmond. See pp. 94–98. Randolph was in full agreement with
Burk, however, on the dullness of Virginia's early history. "It must be confessed," he wrote, "that the portion of our history, which is least capable
of being rendered interesting," was that part extending from the first settlement to the dissolution of the Virginia Company in 1624. *Ibid.*, 17.

ians an appropriate observance of the coming bicentennial at Jamestown.[44]

Since Jamestown itself had long since been abandoned as a town site, no local committee could take the initiative as was done at Plymouth. Instead, committees were established in several of the leading towns of the state to sponsor a pilgrimage to Jamestown on May 13, 1807. When that day arrived no less than thirty-two vessels had found anchorage in the river off the old town site, and residents who rode in from the surrounding countryside brought the attendance to an estimated 2,000 people. Hawksters had pitched their tents to give the occasion a carnival atmosphere, and Norfolk provided a company of artillery to lend the dignity of military salutes, beginning at sunrise. All of those in attendance found place in the procession that formed at midday for a solemn march to the old churchyard where the venerable Bishop Madison led in prayer. Afterwards, the band struck up a lively tune as the people marched to a nearby residence for dinner. The meal was delayed while two students from the College of William and Mary delivered orations, the one speaking on the settlement of Virginia, the other on the character of republican institutions. The evening was given over to dancing. It was a matter of special comment that everyone behaved well. As the printed report explained,

[44] See *Report of the Proceedings of the Late Jubilee at James-Town, In Commemoration of the 13th May, the Second Centesimal Anniversary of the Settlement of Virginia; . . . Reported by the Select Committee* (Petersburg, 1807). Contrasting the previous neglect of Virginians with the practice in New England, the *Apollo* declared: "It is not so in New England: the sagacity of that intelligent people would not permit them to omit an occasion calculated to produce such effects upon the minds and principles of their descendants: they knew that it would afford *fresh oil to the lamp* of their patriotism, and accordingly the era of their debarkation at Plymouth is celebrated by annual festivals; but in the ancient dominion of Virginia, which may be called the principal fountain of American population, not the slightest notice is taken of an event in which the whole world is interested." See *ibid.*, 6. Also for attendance, the report in *The True American* of Trenton, N. J. (VII, June 8, 1807).

all the pilgrims "seemed to think themselves in the presence of
the awful fathers of their nation, and this idea . . . had the
effect to chasten and purify their language and deportment." [45]
Additional solemnity was lent to the proceedings by the death
of one of the pilgrims from "too free use of Ice in Cyder, having
been violently heated." On the 14th a second procession to the
graveyard ended in the burial of this unfortunate victim of an
indiscreet use of ice by the side of the fathers of his country,
apparently with a good deal more pomp than he had been entitled to expect.

The surprisingly good conduct of the Virginians on the occasion of the bicentennial is of less moment than is another point.
Though the celebrants expressed the special pride they felt as
Virginians, much of their satisfaction seems to have come from
a feeling that Virginia no longer lagged behind New England
in paying honor to those to whom honor belonged. Of jealousy
for New England and for her claims to recognition I recall no
trace at all. A large part of the company in attendance accepted
the invitation of nearby Williamsburg to stay over for festive
celebrations of the anniversary of the meeting in that town of
the Virginia convention of May, 1776, that had so largely influenced the American decision for independence.[46]

As this story suggests, the really remarkable thing about these
first years is how much good will was shown. Those who wrote
state histories wrote in the firm belief that they were contributing importantly to the history of the nation, a belief generously
confirmed by all who undertook some broader summary of the
full story. The best of the state histories were written by men
who were also noted for their efforts in the larger field of our
national history. Though evidences of a competitive spirit are
not wanting, the competition can be accurately described as a
competition for national honors. Invariably, the demand was

[45] *Ibid.*, 44.

[46] *Ibid.*, 46–48, records the eighteen toasts drunk at a public dinner in the
Raleigh Tavern on May 15, among them toasts to "our Irish Brethren" and
to the oppressed of all nations.

for recognition of founding fathers as worthy as any of those already recognized, and there were no disputes at all as to the standard by which any of the fathers should be judged. For that standard had been fixed by the national ideal.

There may even be some advantage in considering the whole effort as an attempt by a new nation to find for itself a suitable group of national heroes. No nation can get along without its heroic figures. Our own nation, it is true, was especially fortunate to find in Washington a man who could serve the need in his own lifetime. And let me say in passing that no one can do the reading I have been doing in recent months without being appalled to discover the extent to which Washington was deified, as a symbol of national unity, while he still lived. Beyond dispute, and despite the criticism he received during the term of his presidency, he was the first of our national institutions to be securely established. The nation also made good use, as James Wilson's introductory remarks show, of other military leaders, especially those who had died for the Revolutionary cause. Ben Franklin helped, for as the only truly elder statesman of the Revolution he died early in the postwar era. But the rest of the great leaders of the Revolution, those we have agreed in later years to honor, lived on and fought on as active participants in our political life. In other words, they were not yet available for deification.

The time of their canonization is not too difficult to fix in general terms. John Adams, in the preface to his *Defense of the Constitutions of the United States* in 1787, declared: "It will never be pretended that any persons employed in that service had interviews with the gods, or were in any degree under the inspiration of Heaven." [47] But his grandson, Charles Francis Adams, felt it necessary in 1841 to preface his collection of the *Letters of John Adams . . . to His Wife* with this warning: "We are beginning to forget that the patriots of former days were men like ourselves, acting and acted upon like the present

[47] Adams, *Works of John Adams,* IV, 292.

race." [48] Meantime, the first to win special honors were the common run of patriots, those who had followed rather than those who led. Before 1800 apologies for the review of familiar events in Fourth of July orations were being replaced by tributes to "our fathers" for their courage and their sacrifice. Lyman Butterfield has recently suggested that the emotional outburst which all across the country greeted the news that John Adams and Thomas Jefferson both had died on the Fourth of July, 1826, marks the point at which the American people came to remember the Revolutionary fathers for what they had agreed upon rather than for their disputes with one another.[49] Whatever specific date one might wish to choose, it lies well forward in the nineteenth century.

In the meantime, how were the heroic figures of our first settlement called to the nation's attention? For the purpose of illustration, let me use the examples of William Penn, Roger Williams, and the Pilgrim Fathers. It should be noted, first of all, that none of these was in any sense a new discovery. Each of them had been the object of special veneration before the Revolution, and the interests that then had sponsored their claims to recognition stood ready to press those claims even more vigorously now.

The question of sponsorship is an important one, as may be illustrated by the case of Lord Baltimore. His claim to high honors had been pressed with special vigor by George Chalmers, perhaps because Chalmers had been a resident of Maryland, and James Wilson had given to Baltimore a place beside Penn and Franklin in the American temple of fame. But John L. Bozman, the first native of Maryland to write a history of its founding, had doubts about Lord Baltimore. In his *History of Maryland,* a two-volume work published posthumously in

[48] Charles Francis Adams, ed., *Letters of John Adams Addressed to His Wife* (2 vols., Boston, 1841), I, xiii–xiv.

[49] L. H. Butterfield, "The Jubilee of Independence, July 4, 1826," *Virginia Magazine of History and Biography,* LXI (1953), 119–40.

1837,[50] Bozman was impressed by the fact that Calvert, though a Catholic, seemed to have gotten along with Cromwell almost as well as with Charles I. Was Maryland's statute of religious tolerance drafted to please Cromwell and thus to protect Lord Baltimore's charter? Was the statute written for the purpose of attracting into Maryland the Puritan settlers of Virginia who were having trouble with the Anglicans of that province, or for some other such self-serving end? These are questions that do credit to Bozman as a historian, but the raising of them denied to Lord Baltimore the support he might have received from a less discriminating student of the state's history.

Perhaps mention should also be given to the disadvantage Lord Baltimore suffered as a Catholic. I dislike to suggest that Bozman may have been subject to such a prejudice, for no one can read his history without having respect for it, and it is evident enough that his strongest prejudices were directed against the Puritans. It must be noted, however, that Bozman was an Episcopalian and that he offered evidence in dispute of the common tendency to describe Maryland's famous statute as a Catholic measure.[51] Certainly, the rising tide of anti-Catholic sentiment in the nineteenth century cannot be ignored in any attempt to trace the declining fortunes of Lord Baltimore as a national hero.[52] He continued to be useful to those who would berate the Puritan. State pride and a denominational interest, moreover, have repeatedly raised up for him many champions.

[50] Bozman published *A Sketch of the History of Maryland, During the Three First Years after Its Settlement* at Baltimore in 1811, and left at his death in 1823 the manuscript of *The History of Maryland, from Its First Settlement, in 1633, to the Restoration, in 1660 . . .* (Baltimore, 1837).

[51] Samuel A. Harrison, *A Memoir of John Leeds Bozman, the First Historian of Maryland* (Baltimore: Maryland Historical Society Fund Publication No. 26, 1888).

[52] Peter Guilday in his *John Gilmary Shea* (New York: U. S. Catholic Historical Society, 1926), x, 27, offers an interesting example of this decline in the contrast between the treatment of Calvert in Bancroft's early and later editions.

But he has never quite recovered the position assigned to him in the first flush of our enthusiasm for the ideals of the Revolution.

William Penn still suffers perhaps from the fact that he was more an Englishman than an American. But he was an English Whig who held some of the most important convictions we cherish as to the rights of a subject, or perhaps I should say the rights of the citizen. Those convictions had generously shaped the fundamental charters under which the Quakers made their settlements in New Jersey and Pennsylvania, and to a generation of Americans busily engaged in the writing of constitutions he was a natural choice as the great lawmaker of our history. Since this choice depended somewhat upon the willingness of Pennsylvania to back his claim, it was a fortunate circumstance that the Revolution had resolved the previously debated issues of the Penn proprietorship. There was thus no bar to the enthusiastic endorsement of William Penn to which the Pennsylvania Historical Society immediately dedicated a large share of its energies. Still more important perhaps was Penn's Quakerism, for this gave him an indisputable identification with the cause of religious freedom and with a social ideal depending upon the hope that men of differing convictions can live together in peace. His leadership in the Quaker movement also guaranteed the sponsorship of a religious group that had developed out of its peculiar experience a well-established historical tradition of its own.

Penn had the additional advantage of having won the favorable attention of influential groups outside America, a fact that encouraged Americans to claim him as their own.[53] Among others who had promoted Penn's reputation was Benjamin West, who in 1772 made "Penn's Treaty with the Indians" the subject of one of his most famous paintings. This somewhat romanticized view of Penn's relations with the native inhabit-

[53] See especially William I. Hull, *Eight First Biographies of William Penn in Seven Languages and Seven Lands* (Swarthmore College Monographs on Quaker History, 1936).

ants of his province not only caught the imagination of Europe intellectuals but of the American people, who have ever been periodically subject to an impulse to do justice to the Indian and who at the time of their conflict with Britain had found in the evidence of purchases from the Indians by the first settlers additional support for the argument that the Americans' title to America did not depend on the gift of the English government. Parson Weems displayed his unerring instinct for choice of subject by devoting one of his earliest biographical efforts to Penn and his keen sense of the theme that should be emphasized by underscoring Penn's friendship for the Indian.[54] Weems's vogue passed with time, but such has been the continuing popularity of West's picture that Penn's treaty with the Delawares has remained as indelibly impressed on the American mind as has Washington's crossing of the Delaware.

Although the distinction of being Penn's first American biographer has been assigned to Parson Weems,[55] the honor might just as well have gone to Robert Proud, author of the earliest published history of Pennsylvania. Proud was an English schoolmaster who had come under the influence of Quakerism and who wrote most of his history during the course of the Revolution. Its two volumes, first published in the 1790's, emphasized the biography of Penn and the peculiar character of the first Quaker settlers, as do most of the histories of early Pennsylvania that have been written since then.[56] Proud gave notice to the early activity of the Dutch and the Swedes on the Delaware, but this was by way of introduction to a story of settlement by men who were principally English and Quaker. In the second volume, devoted to a description of the country, he undertook to identify the several German sects settled in Pennsylvania, but he gave them no real place in the history of the province and he virtually ignored the Irish settlers of the back country.

[54] *Ibid.*, 13–27.   [55] *Ibid.*
[56] Cited above, Chapter II, n. 57.

These omissions raise a question of why Pennsylvania, which certainly had as good an opportunity as any other of the original thirteen states to present itself as the prototype of what America was becoming, did not emphasize at the very beginning the cosmopolitan character of its population. Gouverneur Morris, speaking in behalf of New York's Dutch forebears, advanced such a claim for that state as early as 1812, when he commented on the cosmopolitanism of its population and resultant advantages for its inhabitants that other people could enjoy only at the cost of expensive travel.[57] In Pennsylvania the non-English and non-Quaker elements of the population were by no means lacking in organizations that might have demanded that such a theme be placed at the very heart of the state's history. From very early days, emigrants have shown an inclination to join together for social intercourse and celebration of the glories of their native land. In London by 1685 Scottish immigrants had found a helpful justification for their meetings by organizing for the aid of indigent Scotsmen in their midst, and well before the American Revolution St. Andrew's Societies flourished in various parts of America, including Philadelphia. St. Patrick's Day was also celebrated in colonial Philadelphia, and the German settlers of Pennsylvania, aroused by the treatment their fellow countrymen received at the hands of unconscionable shipmasters, had organized immigrant aid societies as early as 1765.[58] But to meet periodically for the sober or drunken glorification of the original homeland, or for the promotion of a worthy charity, is not enough. Somewhere in the group there must be a volunteer antiquarian who is less concerned with ancient glories than with the place of his fellows in a newly forming tradition, for in this country each group must look out for its own ancestors. No one else is likely to bother.

[57] The New-York Historical Society *Collections*, II, 128–29.
[58] See especially Erna Risch, "Immigrant Aid Societies before 1820," *Pennsylvania Magazine of History and Biography*, LX (1936), 15–33.

Within a few years the clergymen of the Presbyterian Church would vigorously demand correction of Proud's oversight, and later in the nineteenth century the Germans would insist upon recognition of the part their fathers had played in the founding of the nation. But meanwhile, William Penn and the Quakers provided assurance enough that Pennsylvania would not be overlooked in the writing of our national history. The assurance, at any rate, was good enough for the gentlemen who enjoyed membership in the Pennsylvania Historical Society, an organization that had its headquarters in Philadelphia and whose activity naturally reflected interests appropriate to that location.

The denominational interest is especially apparent in the case of Roger Williams. Though the Baptist faith had been only one of the stations at which Williams paused on his way to becoming a Seeker, the Baptists became his chief champions. This championship, no doubt, owed less to the fact of Williams' brief identification with that denomination than to its need in eighteenth-century America for the protection of the principle of religious freedom for which Williams had stood. The Rev. John Callender, a Baptist minister of Newport who reviewed the history of Rhode Island in a centennial sermon of 1738, had even expressed a doubt that Williams had ever been a Baptist.[59] Morgan Edwards, while compiling his "Materials for a History of the Baptists in Rhode Island," found satisfying evidence, with the aid of Hutchinson's *History of Massachusetts*, that Williams had in fact been baptized.[60] But that fact counted not so much as did the proposition, as phrased by Governor Hopkins of Rhode Island on the eve of the Revolu-

[59] John Callender, *An Historical Discourse, on The Civil and Religious Affairs of the Colony of Rhode-Island and Providence Plantations, in New-England, in America, from the First Settlement, 1638, to the End of the First Century* (Boston, 1739), in Rhode Island Historical Society *Collections*, IV, 110.

[60] See Rhode Island Historical Society *Collections*, VI, 302–3.

tion, that Roger Williams had been "the first legislator in the world that fully and effectually provided for and established a free, full, and absolute liberty of conscience." [61]

It was to the establishment of this "absolute liberty" that the Rev. Isaac Backus devoted his remarkable energies during and after the Revolution. His contributions to the cause were many and varied but by no means least was the three-volume *History of New England, with Particular Reference to the Denomination of Christians Called Baptists* that he published between 1777 and 1797.[62] Here one finds the promise that in time Roger Williams would cast a shadow over all his contemporaries in seventeenth-century America. In the fulfillment of that promise the Baptists continued to be aggressively active,[63] but they did not have to work alone. As Governor Hopkins' proud boast indicates, the name of Williams had become a gratifying stimulant to state pride, a pride that found prompt and repeated expression in the proceedings of the Rhode Island Historical Society from 1822 forward.[64] And the name of Williams was useful to still others, if only for the purpose of berating the Puritans.

Even so, Williams was relatively slow to win national recognition. Though destined to be the subject of more biographical studies than any other leader in seventeenth-century America, he was noticeably omitted from the first attempt at an American biographical dictionary, that of Jeremy Belknap in the 1790's.[65] There is no reason whatsoever to assume that this

[61] Quoted by Edwards, *ibid.*, 319.

[62] See especially Alvah Hovey, *A Memoir of the Life and Times of the Rev. Isaac Backus* (Boston, 1859).

[63] Henry M. Dexter, *As to Roger Williams and His "Banishment" from the Massachusetts Plantation; With a Few Further Words Concerning the Baptists, the Quakers, and Religious Liberty* (Boston, 1876) conveniently summarizes much of this activity.

[64] The first volume of the Rhode Island Historical Society *Collections* (1827) was devoted to a reprint of Williams' *Key into the Languages of America* with an unsigned prefatory sketch of the author's life.

[65] See n. 22 above.

omission reflects distaste on Belknap's part for a policy of religious freedom. His *American Biography* included a very favorable chapter on William Penn and treated generously the three Calverts most actively identified with the settlement of Maryland. Belknap's history of New Hampshire, moreover, vigorously repudiated the intolerance of early Massachusetts and paid high tribute to Rhode Island for a record free of religious persecution.[66] The trouble, quite obviously, was with Williams and not with his policy.

A suggestion as to the source of this difficulty is provided by George Chalmers, who described Williams as a man "always fruitful in religious frenzies" and thus identified him with "the dark fanaticism" of his time.[67] Such a view was naturally prejudicial to Williams' reputation in the "Age of Reason," as is indicated by the fact that James Wilson left him out of a hall of fame that included both Penn and Calvert and omitted all reference to him in an oration that hailed the establishment of religious freedom as one of the chief glories of America.[68] As late as 1818, a speaker before The New-York Historical Society could demand that the humorous naïveté of Williams' religious enthusiasms not be allowed to obscure his title to high honors.[69]

The belief that Williams had been too much the religious zealot to be grouped among the prophets of "genuine principle," if I may borrow James Wilson's phrase, had of course a solid historical foundation. Indeed, there was perhaps more truth in this view of the man than in the popular assumption today that Williams in his advocacy of the separation of church and state thought ahead of his age and thus should be honored as one of the forerunners of the eighteenth century. As Perry Miller has recently demonstrated, it is difficult for the modern mind to follow the route that led Williams to his conviction

[66] Belknap, *History of New Hampshire,* I, 89–99.

[67] Chalmers, *Political Annals,* 156.

[68] See above, pp. 67–68.

[69] The New-York Historical Society *Collections,* III, 56.

that church and state should be separated, so far removed was it from the way which Jefferson followed to the same conclusion.[70] But the compulsion to make Williams over into the likeness of the eighteenth-century man was great, and he did not have to wait long for admittance to the highest honors the nation had to bestow.

If descendants of the Bay Colony Puritans had some difficulty in accepting the new verdict, it was not because their own historical tradition had been wholly unfavorable to Williams. In fact, the New England tradition had always shown a certain tolerance for his aberrations while recognizing that he had many merits, something that cannot be said in the case of Mrs. Hutchinson or of the Quakers. That tradition, moreover, had long since embraced the ideal of religious freedom, and no one now showed any real difficulty in conceding the whole case against the Puritans when the Puritans had been clearly in the wrong, as in the execution of the Quakers, an act Belknap described without qualification as "disgraceful." [71] The case of Roger Williams' expulsion from Massachusetts was different, for there was after all something to be said for the Puritans in this instance, and Belknap could have been influenced by loyalty to his forebears. But it would be easy to overemphasize the significance of his omission of Williams from the *American Biography*. Not only had James Wilson made a comparable estimate of Williams' importance, but Benjamin Trumbull soon treated him generously in his history of the United States and George Bancroft probably had more influence on Williams' ultimate ranking among the worthies of America than did any other single writer.[72]

In the adaptation of their own tradition to new requirements the descendants of the Puritans were greatly helped by the Pilgrim Fathers, who now acquired an importance they had never

---

[70] Perry Miller, *Roger Williams, His Contribution to the American Tradition* (Indianapolis, 1953).

[71] Belknap, *History of New Hampshire*, I, 91, 99.

[72] See his *History of the United States*, I (1834), 397–414.

before known. I do not mean to suggest that they had ever been ignored, for they had always received in New England the special honors reserved in this country for first settlers. The appealing story of their flight from persecution, first to Holland and then to America, no doubt had helped in earlier years of the eighteenth century to fix a popular belief that New England had been founded for the purposes of religious freedom. But the focus of attention, as John Adams' "Dissertation on the Canon and Feudal Law" makes unmistakably clear, had remained on the Bay Colony Puritans. What occurred after the Revolution was perhaps basically nothing more than a shift of the focus onto the Pilgrims, with a transfer of all the virtues traditionally associated with the Puritan fathers to the more acceptable Pilgrims.

The shift was not difficult to make, and the persuasion to do so was strong. There were differences between the Plymouth Separatists and the nonseparating Puritans of Massachusetts Bay which may or may not count, depending upon the purpose one has in mind. Both groups were Puritan, but the Puritans of Plymouth had compiled no such record of persecution in the New World as had their neighbors to the north. They had not driven Roger Williams into the wilderness, or expelled Mrs. Hutchinson. They had executed no Quakers; nor had they hounded Anabaptists through their streets. A simple folk, their faith, their courage, and their triumph over adversity made of their story, as a large body of our popular literature testifies, one that was especially well suited to the need of a new nation to understand itself. More than that, Plymouth itself, unlike Jamestown, had lived to take the initiative in keeping alive the memory of the Pilgrims.

The town's annual celebration of the landing at Plymouth had been dropped after 1780, but it was revived in 1793 and again in 1798. Forefathers' Day in 1799 fell so close to the planned ordination of a new minister that a separate celebration was dispensed with, but from 1800 to 1811 the anniversary was celebrated each year. After a lapse during the war years, the annual celebration was re-established, beginning with 1815.[73] Since 1800, the orator of the occasion had been as frequently as not a layman. When J. Q. Adams served as orator in 1802, he directed special attention to the Mayflower Compact. More important, he listed Raleigh, Smith, Winthrop, Calvert, Penn, and Oglethorpe as men who "excite in our minds recollections equally pleasing, and gratitude equally fervent with those of Carver and Bradford." [74] Meanwhile, Boston had taken some notice of Forefathers' Day as early as 1798, and thereafter the practice grew in other parts of New England. When the New England Society of New York was formed in 1805 on the model of older immigrant aid societies for the assistance of such sons of New England in the city as may have forgotten the thrifty precepts of their fathers, or been abandoned by providence, it picked Forefathers' Day for its annual celebration. The term "Pilgrim," first used by Bradford himself, came to be fixed in its special identification with the Plymouth settlers as early as 1799. In 1807 it was proposed to organize at Plymouth a Pilgrim Society with membership limited to 101, the number of the first settlers, and with responsibilities appropriate to the name. But this was not actually accomplished until 1819, the needed stimulus to action being then provided by the approaching bicentennial of the Pilgrims' landing.

Like the earlier bicentennial at Jamestown, this one became a pilgrimage for hundreds of people from outside Plymouth. The Massachusetts Historical Society sent an official delegation.[75] President Kirkland of Harvard led in a prayer of eighteen minutes' duration, and then came the orator, who this time

[73] Albert Matthews, "The Term Pilgrim Fathers and Early Celebrations of Forefathers' Day," Colonial Society of Massachusetts *Publications,* XVII, 293–391; *New England Historical & Genealogical Register,* I (1847), 114–25; *Records of the Town of Plymouth,* III, 457–58; appendix to Webster's speech of 1820 as cited below, n. 77.

[74] John Quincy Adams, *An Oration, Delivered at Plymouth, December 22, 1802, at the Anniversary Commemoration of the First Landing of Our Ancestors, at that Place* (Plymouth: Republished by Joseph Avery, 1820).

[75] Massachusetts Historical Society *Proceedings,* I, 289.

was no college student. Instead, Daniel Webster spoke for better than two hours and with such eloquence as to make his speech a plague to schoolboys for a generation to come.[76] As published, the address covered 102 printed pages.[77] Even so, Webster could find time, as he explained, for no more than a "brief remembrance of the causes which led to the settlement of this place; some account of the peculiarities and characteristic qualities of that settlement, . . . ; a short notice of the progress of New-England in the great interests of Society; with a few observations on the principles upon which society and government are established in this country." He credited the Pilgrims with the introduction into this country of the principle of religious freedom, which he described as transcending in importance all others, and attributed to them all the familiar Puritan virtues—a strong adherence to the right of self-government, a firm belief in education, the rejection of feudal concepts of land-holding, and the conviction that society must be founded on morality and religious faith. As he approached the end of his address, Webster gazed into the future to see a people who, like the Pilgrim Fathers, believed in God and had the courage that comes from conviction, and whose destiny it was to plant the standards of civilized man in the remotest corners of the North American continent. "Advance, then, ye future generations," began his peroration. "We greet your accession to the great inheritance we have enjoyed."

It would be a mistake to describe this as being in any real sense a national celebration. It belonged first of all to the town of Plymouth and then to New England. The chief obligation falling upon the day's orator was to give appropriate expression to the natural pride his hearers felt for the contribution their fathers had made to the founding of the nation, but

[76] *Proceedings of the Celebration by the Pilgrim Society at Plymouth, December 21, 1870, . . .* (Cambridge, 1871), 126.

[77] Daniel Webster, *A Discourse, Delivered at Plymouth, December 22, 1820. In Commemoration of the First Settlement of New-England* (Boston, 1821).

Webster was careful to point out that the Plymouth settlement had not been the first European establishment within the present United States. He asserted only that it had been so peculiar in its causes and character, and had been followed by consequences so significant as to give it a high claim to lasting commemoration—considering the occasion, a modest statement indeed. If he wasted no time on tributes to Jamestown, he also drew no invidious comparison of the type later speakers on that same platform were to make. He referred to the "contamination" of slavery in the country but limited his exhortation to the hope that all would make their pledge "upon the Rock of Plymouth" to destroy any survival of the slave trade.

I do not mean to suggest that the American people by 1820 had as yet achieved a common tradition. I have tried only to suggest, with the omission of many topics which might have been discussed, that by this date they were well on the way toward that achievement. More than ten years remained before Bancroft would begin his great history of the United States, but I hope this discussion may have suggested a basic reason for its extraordinary success. Given the literary skill he possessed and his willingness to let love of country illuminate the text, he had only to identify the principles of the Revolution with the first founding of the colonies, to be generous in the apportionment of credit (especially on the issue of religious freedom or on the question of the determination men had shown in the defense of their political liberties), and thus to point the text from the beginning toward a revolution that could be viewed as so grand and climactic a defense of human liberties as to have taught the American people the true basis of their union. Certainly this was the national history toward which the American people, acting in their own several communities and each with its own historical problem, were moving in the years before Bancroft took up his pen.

Certainly, too, there should be no difficulty in understanding the central importance we have since given the Pilgrim Fathers in our national history. Penn, Baltimore, and Williams, like

Washington and Franklin, have been honored for their leadership, but the Pilgrim Fathers have represented the people themselves. Have we not seen in them what we like to think we are —men of faith and men of courage, men who are free and men who are tolerant?

CHAPTER IV

Pride of Ancestry

THE years roughly bracketed between the centennial in 1832 of Washington's birth and the celebration of the hundredth anniversary of American independence in 1876 are difficult to bring under any one heading for the purposes of these lectures. These are years we immediately identify with the vigorous nationalism of Bancroft's *History of the United States,* a work brought to completion only in 1876, or with the varied activities of Jared Sparks in the field of our common history. These are years we also mark for the beginning of Francis Parkman's great studies of the Anglo-French conflict for the possession of North America, or of Joseph Sabin's great *Dictionary of Books Relating to America,* and it would be easy to offer other examples in proof of a broadening concept of American history appropriate to the nation's extraordinary expansion during this period. But this nationalism and this breadth of view have seemed to me not so representative of the forces shaping the popular interest in American history as are sectionalism, provincialism, and other forms of localism and particularism, including pride of family and loyalty to one's church. My choice of caption for this lecture may give undue weight to a newly developing interest in genealogy, but certainly the local antiquarian and the church historian through these years had as much influence on the popular concept of American origins as did the national historian, perhaps even more.

An especially impressive development of the period was a growing interest in local history. Continued progress in the organization of state historical societies brought the South and the West abreast of the northeastern states,[1] and in all parts of the country an active interest in state history stimulated the pride of lesser communities. The earliest local historical society seems to have been that organized at Salem, Massachusetts, in 1821.[2] Others followed, as did also the first of the church historical societies with their encouragement to an interest in the history of individual congregations,[3] and a new type of genealogical society for the promotion of studies that naturally found their sharpest focus on local records. By the beginning of our own century, T. L. Bradford and S. V. Henkels would require no less than five volumes for their *Bibliographer's Manual of American History, Containing an Account of all State, Territory, Town and County Histories.*[4]

As I undertook to suggest in the preceding lecture, the fact that most students of American history gave their closest attention to some part of the story that was peculiarly their own counts for little. We must read with sympathy and understanding John L. Bozman's statement in the introduction to his *Sketch of the History of Maryland* in 1811. "A native of the American States, will always feel an interest in the affairs of any one of them," he declared, "but contracting the circle of his patriotic sensations to a smaller compass, he finds that the individual state, of which he is a citizen, nay indeed, the county and neighborhood of his nativity, will more particularly claim both his affection and his attention."[5] It must be recognized

---

[1] See n. 29 in preceding chapter.

[2] Dunlap, *American Historical Societies*, 168–69.

[3] See below, pp. 121 ff., and especially source cited in n. 52.

[4] Published at Philadelphia, 1907–10. The fifth volume was devoted to a general index by town, county, and state.

[5] Bozman, *The History of Maryland,* vii.

also that before large segments of the record had been put in print for common use, an undertaking that had only its beginning in this period, most of those who turned to the study of our history were necessarily restricted to the source materials immediately and easily available to them. But much depends upon the spirit in which one interprets his own part of the larger story, and it has seemed to me that that spirit spoke as frequently in these years of the things that divided us as of the things that united us.

The Fourth of July continued to be celebrated according to now well-established conventions—with the firing of guns from early in the day, either by plan or spontaneously by enthusiastic citizens, with the gathering of the people from the surrounding countryside, and with the parade to the town or courthouse square, where the Declaration was read and the oration was delivered, indoors or outdoors according to circumstance. To many people, however, the national holiday seemed to be losing something of its former meaning. In 1835 a New England author could write a cruel description of the annual celebration as he pictured the orator laboring through worn-out themes before an audience held in place by no more than a sense of duty, and the older men of the town dutifully pounding their canes at the public dinner and then going home with a disturbing sense of dissatisfaction.[6] Part of the trouble was suggested by Hugh Caperton of Virginia when he opened a Fourth of July address at Georgetown College in 1840 with this observation: "Long since have I despaired of advancing anything original on this old and almost exhausted theme." [7]

Discontent with the manner of celebrating the Fourth was in some instances obviously related to a growing temperance sentiment, and to the resulting distaste for having to leave the final rites of the day to those who had not yet come to appreci-

[6] [Jacob Abbot], *New England and Her Institutions* (Boston, 1835), 149–57.

[7] Hugh Caperton, *Address Delivered before the Philodemic Society, of Georgetown College, . . .* On the 4th July 1840 (Washington, 1840).

ate the evils of liquor. It is noticeable that the temperance societies increasingly sought and found a place in the line of march on the Fourth, partly no doubt because of the common inclination of political organizations to turn patriotic occasions to their own advantage and partly in an effort to restore respectability to the national celebration.[8] The casualties each Fourth of July exacted as a result of an indiscreet mixture of gunpowder, liquor, and patriotism became the subject of unfavorable comment. The editor of the Harrisburg *Chronicle* in Pennsylvania compiled available statistics in 1839 to show no less than forty-one deaths and almost half as many maimings as the cost of that year's celebration. He estimated that complete statistics would show figures four times as high.[9] By 1857 the *North American Review* was looking for a suitable substitute for the Fourth, which was considered to have degenerated into such a show of rowdyism as to serve chiefly for the annoyance of physicians and fire companies. The editor proposed that a solemn celebration of Washington's birthday be substituted.[10]

But not even in 1832 had the leaders of the country been able to bring off a celebration appropriate to the centennial of Washington's birth and to the sense of unity his name was supposed to evoke. The story, as it has been told by Charles Warren, has today its humorous aspects, although at the time J. Q. Adams saw in it the promise that the union itself might not last five years.[11] The Congress had adopted a joint resolution shortly after Washington's death in 1799 for the erection of a marble monument in the capital city. The plan, to which Martha Washington gave her consent, was to rebury the general at its base, but nothing more was accomplished before the cen-

[8] See, for example, *Niles National Register,* L (July 10, 1841), LII (July 9, 1842), LXXII (July 10, 1847), where the Sons of Temperance are described as being out in full force and having "a delightful day of it."

[9] Reported in *Niles National Register,* LVI (July 27, 1839).

[10] *North American Review,* LXXXIV, 334–63.

[11] Charles Warren, "How Politics Intruded into the Washington Centenary of 1832," in *Massachusetts Historical Society Proceedings,* LXV (Dec., 1932), 37–62.

tennial year approached. It was then proposed to transfer the body from Mount Vernon for reinterment in a special crypt under the rotunda of the capitol building, and to have Chief Justice John Marshall, who was Washington's biographer, deliver a special address before the Congress. Unhappily the centennial year was one of marked discord in our political life. The proposal was adopted in Congress only after strong opposition had been expressed by some of the Democrats, Southerners, and especially the Virginians, who disliked the idea of removing the body from Virginia for reasons that included the possibility of a later secession from the union. When it became apparent that President Andrew Jackson had not been invited to the ceremonies by the committee in charge, of which Henry Clay was the moving spirit, the House undertook to rectify the oversight by special resolution, but the Senate, describing the procedure as extraordinary, refused to concur. John Augustine Washington put a final stop to the plan by refusing to allow the body to be moved, and the Chief Justice found that his health made it impossible for him to deliver the proposed address. In the end, the ceremonies at the capitol building were reduced to a divine service from which the President ostentatiously absented himself for the purpose, as he publicly announced, of reading the Farewell Address.

When the centennial of independence came in 1876 the nation had not yet completed a monument to Washington. The fiasco in 1832 had been followed by the organization during the next year of a Washington National Monument Society, which managed to raise $56,000 by 1848, when the cornerstone of the present monument was laid.[12] Thereafter, the work continued slowly until 1856, as voluntary subscription made the necessary funds available. And then construction stopped for the lack of funds, leaving the monument to stand unfinished through many troubled years as a fitting symbol of the nation's disunity.

A people who could not agree on an appropriate memorial to Washington naturally had raised no other monuments except such as were made possible by local pride. Such a monu-

12 *Ibid.*

ment was that begun at Bunker Hill in 1825 and completed in 1842.[13] Local interest had also rescued Independence Hall from demolition in 1816, but it had been a close call. The Pennsylvania state legislature, then located at Harrisburg, had proposed that the old statehouse yard be broken up for sale as building lots. Though this proposal evoked no storm of popular protest, the legislature first offered the premises to Philadelphia for $70,000 and fortunately the city accepted the offer. In the negotiations, the now cherished Liberty Bell remained "an unmentioned fixture." [14] It may be that the spirit of republicanism was partly to blame. Certainly, it provided the excuse with which Americans met the patronizing sneers of Europeans at the absence, to quote the *North American Review* in 1822, "of those costly structures, which have been piled up in the old world by caprice, by luxury, by superstition, or by pride, at the expense of unutterable misery on the part of an oppressed people." [15] But one suspects that all this was mainly an excuse.

That J. Q. Adams should have been so disturbed by the miscarriage of plans for the Washington centennial in 1832 was natural enough, for this was a time when the people of New England were giving many successful demonstrations of the observances appropriate to a centennial occasion. After the great celebration of the bicentennial at Plymouth in 1820, it had been Salem's turn and then Boston's, and after Boston's celebration in 1830 had come the turn of lesser communities. Emerson delivered a historical discourse before the assembled citizens and their guests on the occasion of Concord's bicentennial in 1835. In 1836 Harvard pointed the way to a custom from which no self-respecting educational institution seems now able to escape. Leonard Bacon was soon appropriately honoring the bicentennial of the First Church of New Haven with thirteen discourses. Noah Webster, the schoolmaster to

[13] George W. Warren, *The History of the Bunker Hill Monument Association* (Boston, 1877).

[14] Hampton L. Carson, *History of the Historical Society of Pennsylvania* (2 vols., Philadelphia, 1940), I, 35–36.

[15] *North American Review*, XV (1822), 22.

America who had now grown old, spoke at Hartford in 1840 in commemoration of the Fundamental Orders of Connecticut, or, as he put it, of the state's first constitution. J. Q. Adams delivered an oration on the New England Confederation in 1843 before the Massachusetts Historical Society, which was remarkably faithful in the attention it gave to significant anniversaries. And in the next year, the descendants of Richard Haven gathered at Framingham on August 29 to celebrate the "Second Centennial Anniversary of his landing in New England," with an orator from Boston.[16]

These were occasions on which no one could dispute the right of local or some other special pride to dominate the proceedings. The spirit in which the celebrations were conducted is perhaps best illustrated by reference to the Rev. William Allen's discourse on the occasion of Northampton's bicentennial in 1854. Northampton was a western town, as distances are calculated in Massachusetts, and the orator dwelt heavily on the adventurous spirit that had carried the first settlers so far west in 1654. "It is no great affair, at the present day," he affirmed, "to emigrate to Minnesota, or Kansas, or even to California: there are thousands of fellow countrymen to be found as protectors." [17] It may be that Mr. Allen, like so many of us on the east coast today, had no real feeling for the vast reaches of the west, but a more likely supposition is that he was merely trying to live up to the requirements of the occasion. Perhaps we who live today under the influence of a highly developed tradition of western pioneering might well pay respectful attention to his suggestion that the pioneer settlers at Northampton had had only God to protect them.

For many of those attending the town's bicentennial the occasion was primarily a homecoming. In the nineteenth century a heavy and continuing migration, not only from the older

[16] See again Albert Matthews on centennials in Colonial Society of Massachusetts *Publications*, XXVI, 419–26; *North American Review*, L (1840), 162; Massachusetts Historical Society *Proceedings*, especially I and 2d ser., II.

[17] William Allen, *An Address, Delivered at Northampton . . . on the Evening of October 29, 1854. . . .* (Northampton, 1855), 10–11.

to the newer areas of settlement but from the town to the city, greatly increased the number of Americans who lived away from the old family home and who experienced the nostalgia common to all emigrants. Indeed, I think it worth suggesting that this nostalgia contributed substantially to the growing interest in state and local history. Certainly, it helped to swell the attendance at bicentennial and other such celebrations. Mention should also be given to the railroad and other improvements of transportation facilities that now gave the American population still greater mobility. It was becoming easier each year to get back home, or simply to indulge a natural desire for participation in a great event. When the two hundred and fiftieth anniversary of the Pilgrims' landing was celebrated at Plymouth in 1870, the railway station served not only as the point of debarkation for most of the guests but as the hall best suited to the great banquet that climaxed the proceedings.[18]

The influence of nostalgia for one's native country is suggested by the activity of a growing number of New England societies. I have made no effort to determine just how many of these societies there were in this period. The oldest was that organized in New York in 1805 by a group of immigrants from the more eastern states who found an excuse for their organization in the need for charitable assistance to fellow immigrants. In Charleston, South Carolina, a New England Society flourished from 1819 until late in 1860.[19] In Cincinnati the date of organization was 1845,[20] in San Francisco 1852. In Philadelphia, the date fell somewhat later, in 1880. As this

[18] *Proceedings at the Celebration by the Pilgrim Society at Plymouth,* December 21, 1870, . . . (Cambridge, 1871).

[19] William Way, *History of the New England Society of Charleston,* South Carolina, . . . 1819–1919 (Charleston, 1920).

[20] *New England Historical and Genealogical Register* I, 100, reported its organization "to cherish the memory and perpetuate the principles of the original settlers of New England, to collect and diffuse information respecting New England and New England emigrants to other parts of the country, especially to the West, and to extend charity to the needy of New England descent."

incomplete listing indicates, the New England societies speak partly of the special opportunities for social intercourse provided by the modern city. I do not have to belabor the point while speaking in a city which annually views with characteristic tolerance the celebrations of any number of such societies, including the Southern Society, and where New York University in the 1890's persuaded the Ohio Society to contribute several thousand dollars and a name for its athletic field.[21]

In the mid-nineteenth century the New England Society of New York customarily held its dinners at Delmonico's, where in the midst of every comfort the members celebrated the austerity endured by their forefathers. Of the many toasts, the one most certain to bring a hearty laugh was the toast spotted late in the evening to modesty as a special Puritan virtue. But the occasion was not altogether one of fun. The main event of the evening might be a serious historical address of such length as to appall any modern student. And if the orator had recently enjoyed the privilege of a trip to Europe and could report on his own emotions as he stood in Leyden, or Scrooby, or on the wharf at Old Plymouth, the evening might become a memorable one for all who were privileged to be present.[22]

The number of those who could make the pilgrimage to Leyden, or to Scrooby and to Plymouth in Old England, was still few, but there were enough within reach of the New World's Plymouth to make a tourist's guide to the town a worth-while publishing venture as early as 1846.[23] In the first half of the nineteenth century the term "pilgrim" had a general and special popularity with those who sought to pay appropri-

[21] James H. Kennedy, *History of the Ohio Society of New York, 1885–1905* (New York, 1906), 140–44; Theodore F. Jones, *New York University, 1832:1932* (New York, 1933), 159–60.

[22] C. and E. W. Brainerd, eds., *The New England Society Orations* (2 vols., New York, 1901). It was the custom of the Society to publish full accounts of each anniversary celebration including the oration, toasts, and responses.

[23] William S. Russell, *Guide to Plymouth, and Recollections by the Pilgrims* (Boston, 1846).

ate honors to their forebears. Some 2,000 pilgrims spent another day at Jamestown in 1834, and for all I know the years after 1807 had been marked by several such occasions.[24] In 1842 the Philodemic Society of Georgetown College became the sponsor of a pilgrimage to the site of Lord Baltimore's first settlement at St. Mary's.[25] And for those who could not make pilgrimages of this sort there was the state or the local history provided by the devoted labors of some volunteer antiquarian.

The antiquarian is not easy to describe, especially in the effort to distinguish between him and the historian. Both of these scholars follow the same rigid standards. Neither of them will admit a point not supported by evidence and on this the antiquarian may be more of a stickler than the historian, who recognizes that imagination has an appropriate part to play in any attempt to reconstruct the past. The difference between the two reflects chiefly perhaps a difference of perspective. The historian seeks to depict the larger picture, the antiquarian to make sure that that picture in all its detail is faithful to the facts. The antiquarian, I think it may be said, has a sense of the importance of the unimportant. "He stands before us," as the eulogy to one of the earlier librarians of the American Antiquarian Society described him, "wrapt in admiration of the ancient volume, delighted with the faded manuscript." [26] Because of this delight, he will tolerate no deviation from the faded manuscript, as more than one historian has known to his sorrow.

Those who seek an especially good example of the antiquarian in the nineteenth century will do well to look at James Savage, who served as president from 1841 to 1865 of the Massachusetts Historical Society, of which he was a member through the sixty years that preceded his death in 1873. He was a colorful character, a man of strong convictions and vigorous opinions, the master of a sharp tongue, and a persistent investi-

---

[24] *Niles Weekly Register,* XLVI (June 28, 1834).
[25] *Niles National Register,* LXII (May 21, 1842).
[26] American Antiquarian Society *Proceedings 1835–54,* Oct. 23, 1835, p. 3.

gator whose enthusiasm carried him "into the smallest incidents of history." [27] As a youth he had become a Federalist with a strong distaste for the violence of the French Revolution and for Napoleon and throughout life he remained a staunch conservative in politics. He was "a good hater," and he hated no one quite so much as he did Cotton Mather, whose *Magnalia* he discovered could not always be trusted. He came to dislike John Hancock, whom he regarded as a pompous fraud, but his veneration for Washington was almost idolatrous. His dislike of Cotton Mather owed much to the work he did as the editor of John Winthrop's journal, which Savage published in 1825 and 1826 as *The History of New England,* with footnotes that are still worth reading for their caustic comment on the shortcomings of his Puritan forebears.[28] His extraordinary energies were subsequently devoted to the completion of a four-volume *Genealogical Dictionary of the First Settlers of New England,* a compilation covering the years ending with the second Massachusetts charter and published between 1860 and 1862.[29] He enjoyed an acquaintance with the leading antiquarians of England and, like most historians of his day, he did not teach school for a living. He had been the founder in 1817 of the Provident Savings Bank of Boston, in whose affairs he remained active until 1862. He had been trained as a lawyer.

Savage's *Genealogical Dictionary* represents the new interest in genealogy at its best. It was a development that had deep roots in the antiquarian movement and like so much else that must be described as new it was not altogether new. Nor can it be considered as an isolated phenomenon of American life. In Europe, where society had for so long been organized on the

[27] The following sketch of Savage's career depends chiefly upon Charles Deane's tribute before the Massachusetts Historical Society in 1873 and a memoir by G. S. Hilliard, both in Massachusetts Historical Society *Proceedings* (1871–73), 438–42; (1878), 117–53.

[28] *The History of New England from 1630 to 1649 . . . with Notes . . . By James Savage* (Boston, 1825–26).

[29] At Boston, 1860–62.

basis of distinctions between families that were of the most far-reaching economic, social, and political significance, heraldic or genealogical records had a fundamental importance. Nowhere perhaps is that importance better illustrated than in the accommodating attitude of the College of Heralds in England toward the needs of a newly rising aristocracy in the sixteenth and seventeenth centuries. So many were the accommodations made to family need during this period—and incidentally this is the critical period for American families who have also sought some lineage tracing back to William the Conqueror—that Blackstone could observe on the eve of the American Revolution that the common seal of the College of Heralds would not be admitted in evidence in any court of law in the United Kingdom.[30] The antiquarian interest that had developed apace with the aristocracy of modern England by its very standards of simple honesty lent encouragement to a serious study of genealogical records, as in the work of Dugdale in the seventeenth century, but Bishop Stubbs could comment two centuries later on "the expansion and extension of genealogical study" as "a very remarkable feature of our times," as indeed it was.[31] Of the heavy dependence of the American interest upon the contemporary interest in England every genealogical publication of nineteenth-century America bears its eloquent testimony.

In America, as in England, the basic need upon which this interest fed was old. From the earliest days the American-born settler had displayed a natural curiosity as to his Old World origins and some inclination to preserve the memory of his forebears' settlement in this country. Indeed, the first settlers themselves had shown a remarkable concern for the record of their Old World background, as any number of suits for slander eloquently testify. Judge Samuel Sewall in 1720 recorded

[30] See especially J. Horace Round's essay on "Historical Genealogy" in *Family Origins and Other Studies* (ed. with memoir and bibliography by William Page, New York, 1930), 1–12.

[31] *Ibid.*, 4.

for his son the main facts regarding the family and its migration to America in a letter which begins thus: "You have often desired that I would give you some account of the family of which you are." [32] In the introduction to his autobiography Benjamin Franklin observed: "I have ever had pleasure in obtaining any little anecdotes of my ancestors." [33] When in England before the Revolution, Franklin found time to check the parish registers and to visit the graves of his ancestors, just as has many a modern tourist. The colonists had also been quick to seek an Old World sanction for positions they had won in the New World. William Fitzhugh in Virginia had accumulated enough acres and enough slaves by the later years of the seventeenth century to order a set of plate from a London merchant with instruction to use his coat of arms for its embossment.[34] Thomas Hancock, who made the fortune John Hancock threw away, in 1739 instructed his London agent "to Look into the Herald Office & take out my Arms." [35]

Whatever was new in the nineteenth-century interest in genealogy undoubtedly had its base in the rise of the middle class and in the growth of democracy. Many of those who now embraced the democratic philosophy of life seem to have felt some inner compulsion to preserve a distinction between themselves and the common herd of men. Nothing of course was better suited to the need than pride of family, which is something most of us feel enough of to pardon the excesses of which others may be guilty.

It had never been the intention of those who fostered the study of genealogy that the effort should depend so largely as it did upon family pride. Those who first undertook serious genealogical studies were active in the accumulation or dissemination of a variety of useful information. The man often hailed

[32] *New England Historical and Genealogical Register,* I (1847), 111–13.

[33] Smyth, *Writings of Benjamin Franklin,* I, 226.

[34] *Virginia Magazine of History,* II (1893–94), 267, 269, 271, 272.

[35] W. T. Baxter, *The House of Hancock* (Cambridge, Mass., 1945), 69.

as the father of genealogical studies in New England was John Farmer, who helped to found the New Hampshire Historical Society in 1823, who published that same year a *Gazetteer of the State of New Hampshire,* who had compiled in the preceding year *A Compilation of Rules and Regulations for the Use of the Militia,* who edited from that year through 1838 *The New Hampshire Annual Register and United States Calendar,* and who issued *A Catechism of the History of New Hampshire . . . for Schools and Families* in 1829, *The Concord Directory* in 1830, and a new edition of Belknap's history in 1831.[36] He worked frequently with the careless haste of an invalid confined to his own residence, but the range of his publications has a certain significance.

So also does Samuel Hazard's plan for the *Register of Pennsylvania,* a weekly publication beginning in 1828 that was "devoted to the Preservation of Facts and Documents, and Every other Kind of Useful Information Respecting the State of Pennsylvania." As the editor explained, the materials he presented were intended to be "permanently useful, rather than to be merely amusing for the present moment." Contents of the periodical were to include, and practice conformed with the announcement, "Facts and Documents relative to the early settlement and progressive improvements of the state"; records of Indian history; tables of finance, commerce, and agriculture; topographical descriptions of towns and counties; biographical memoirs of Pennsylvanians; reports on internal improvements and of benevolent, scientific, literary, and religious societies; important legislative proceedings of state and city; legal decisions of major importance; meteorological tables and other information pertinent to the natural history of the state; and a chronicle of important events and developments. In the field of politics the editor promised that he would eschew

[36] A memoir of Farmer in *New England Historical and Genealogical Register,* I (Jan., 1847), 9–20.

all controversy and include only such facts as were necessary to a complete history of the state.[37]

The new science of genealogy, as its leaders were fond of describing it, was confidently expected to open up a new approach to the study of man.[38] But this promise depended upon the opportunity to employ the newly developing techniques of statistical science and that meant that family records would be required in quantity. Hence the temptation to invite in the amateur, and to build the whole structure on the uncertain foundation of family pride. Through journals that were the first historical periodicals in this country to be marked by any measure of permanent success, the genealogist made an effort to teach proper methods of research and compilation. But the army of investigators of which the leaders were fond of speaking actually included all too many recruits whose interest did not go beyond a desire to find evidence of distinction in their own family lines.

The point in time at which the genealogical interest may be said to have acquired a distinct existence of its own is conveniently marked for us by the emergence of a new kind of historical and genealogical society. First of these was the New England Historic-Genealogical Society, organized in 1844 and chartered in the next year. Two years later, in 1847, the society began the publication of the *New England Historical and Genealogical Register,* earliest periodical of its type in the United States.[39] As is true of many other organizations, the society owed much in its origins to the zeal of one man, Samuel G. Drake, a bookseller and author of historical works whose motivation came in no small part from the fact that he was never elected to the exclusive company of the Massachusetts

[37] *The Register of Pennsylvania,* I (Jan.–July, 1828) , especially the lead article of explanation in No. 1 of Jan. 5, 1828.

[38] See, for example, the anniversary address by President Henry R. Stiles of the N. Y. Genealogical Society in 1871, *New York Genealogical and Biographical Record,* II (1871), 71–98.

[39] *New England Historical and Genealogical Register,* I (1847), preface and appendix.

Historical Society.[40] Although not all the older historical societies had been so markedly exclusive as was the original one in Boston, the newer historical and genealogical societies were avowedly and actually much more democratic than were their predecessors. Due form seems to have been observed on questions of admission to membership, but it was never really hard to get in. The response, indeed, never quite kept up with the need. As late as 1861, Drake was complaining of the "miserable support" his *Register* received from no more than 500 subscribers.[41] As the frequent tendency of the genealogists to defend their efforts suggests, many persons seem to have regarded the whole business as contrary to the true spirit of democracy and most of them, as since, remained indifferent.

Nevertheless, the new interest was a growing one. New York followed Massachusetts with the organization of a society in 1869 which began the issuance of the *New York Historical and Biographical Record* in 1870.[42] In most parts of the country, however, the genealogists did not find it necessary to seek a separate organization. Instead, they became a main prop for newly established state historical societies, as every student who has had occasion to consult the state magazines of history and biography well knows.

In 1856 the *North American Review* took notice of the increasing number of separately published volumes on the genealogy of particular families. From this article it would appear that the earliest such volume in the United States was published in 1816. The *Review* identified a total of ten such

[40] See especially George W. Wolkin's article on "The Prince Society," another venture of Drake, in Massachusetts Historical Society *Proceedings,* LXVI, 223–54, recounting an undignified scrap between Drake and the M.H.S. over an unsuccessful effort in 1858 to change the name of the Historic-Genealogical Society. Also *Proceedings,* VIII, 266–70, and *New England Historical and Genealogical Register,* IX (1855), 9–12, on origins of the sponsoring society.

[41] *Ibid.,* XV (1861), iii–vi. See also *ibid.,* XII (1858), 94, 103–4.

[42] Which was preceded by a *Bulletin,* in December, 1869, setting forth the details of the Society's organization.

volumes that had been published by 1845 and noted no less than 70 that had received publication since that year.[43] In the twenty-fifth anniversary discourse before the New England Historic-Genealogical Society in 1870, the Rev. E. F. Slafter claimed the publication of 365 family histories since the society's organization as against only 25 theretofore, a total that probably included all those published by the *Register*. But the orator warned that the time for a boastful relaxation of effort had not yet come. He estimated that a total of 15,000 distinct families had settled in New England before 1776 and argued that all of them should be traced down.[44]

Of more interest than his estimate of the work yet remaining to be done is the choice of the year 1776 as the terminal point, for the society at the time of its first organization had expressed an interest only in families settling before 1700.[45] The forward shift of dates is doubtless to be explained in part by the need for subscribers, but I suspect that there were more fundamental influences than that. From an early date after 1776 the close linking of the first settlement of the country with the defense of its liberties at the time of the Revolution had prepared the way for an assumption that anyone who settled before the Declaration of Independence could be counted among the nation's founders. By 1870, moreover, the country had already witnessed many indications that this assumption would be used to fix a standard for the exclusion of more recent immigrant groups.

It would be easy to overestimate the influence of the genealogists, for their numbers have never been large, and at the same time it is possible that their significance may be too much discounted. Those who would understand a growing sense of kinship with Britain in the modern age may be well advised to pay attention to those among us whose primary concern has been with their kin. Well before the middle of the nineteenth

[43] *North American Review*, LXXXII (April, 1856), 472–73.

[44] *New England Historical and Genealogical Register*, XXIV (1870), 225–49.

[45] *Ibid.*, I (1847), iii.

century references to the superiority of the Anglo-Saxon race
had made their appearance in discussions of our national origins. Now was the time, too, for countless researchers, most of
them pathetically amateurish in their methods and uncritical
in their approach to the record, to find confirmation for William Stoughton's assertion in 1671 that God had sifted a whole
nation to provide choice grain for the American wilderness.
The record itself was not too enlightening, but it was easy with
the guidance of a now well-defined legend of America's founding to find a quick association of the bare details of that record
with qualities of character so well remembered in "grandpa."

The genealogists had a way of concluding their studies with
general observations on family characteristics that tell us more
about nineteenth-century America than they do about the adventurous souls who first settled the country. All the founding
fathers seem to have had a highly developed acquisitive instinct
and to have become men of property through the honor they
paid to precepts of thrift. For a country that probably had had
more godless men and unchurched women than any other in the
modern age the number of clergymen, deacons, and elders who
turned up in the family tree is impressive. It was still not appropriate through much of the nineteenth century to seek
public office, but one's ancestors had often been called to it in
tribute to their marked sense of public responsibility. Another
source of pride was longevity, a significant indication of the
many hazards that still beset life in nineteenth-century America.

The record, it is true, was not lacking in embarrassing detail.
Many of the early colonists had come as indentured servants
and not a few as transported convicts, escaping the hangman's
noose by becoming founders in America. But there were ways
around this difficulty as the people of Australia, a country that
owes its origins to a convict colony established as one of the by-
products of the American Revolution, have independently discovered.[46] Not only did the convicts have an accommodating
way of not turning up in one's own family tree, except for an

[46] See W. K. Hancock, *Australia* (New York, 1931), 37 ff.

occasional political prisoner, but the whole lot of them in an age of legal and prison reform gained an acquittal the eighteenth-century American, in his bitterness over convict transportation, had been unwilling to give. Among the readers of American history it became a well-known fact that the unreformed laws of Old England had been viciously severe, and why apologize for the victim of an unjust law, especially if he belonged to a neighbor's family and not your own? Had it been remembered that the transported criminals actually represented the more serious offenders rather than innocent victims of the law, perhaps we would have discovered, as have the Australians, that a criminal can be so vicious as to be incapable of having descendants. The American distaste for servitude in any form has been so strong that the indentured servant could have been a bother, but it was soon discovered that the indenture was used on occasion for the migration of skilled craftsmen and even for schoolteachers. So why bother? Obviously the obscure ancestor who turned up in the court records with an indenture could have been a man of letters.

It would be quite misleading to leave the suggestion that only the genealogists showed concern for the reputation of their fathers. Indeed, it was a subject of some concern to the whole nation, for there were those in Europe, and especially in England, who suggested that the settlers of this country had been nothing better than the refuse of the Old World.[47] John Sanderson undertook to answer the charge in the introduction to his *Biography of the Signers to the Declaration of Independence* in 1820. He had little historical evidence to go upon as yet and so he resorted frankly to logic. Obviously, those who had dared to cross the Atlantic and to risk the dangers of settlement in the wilderness had been men of stern qualities—the stronger and not the weaker elements of Europe's population.[48]

[47] See, for example, Robert Walsh, Jr., *An Appeal from the Judgments of Great Britain Respecting the United States of America* (Philadelphia, 1819).

[48] See also Robert J. Breckinridge, *A Discourse on the Formation and Development of the American Mind*, Baltimore, 1837.

The American was easily persuaded that the settlement of his country represented a process of natural selection that had indeed made of his forebears choice grain.

If he had any doubts, his minister stood ready to reassure him. The clergyman's purpose was quite different from that of the genealogist, for he sought not to encourage a vain pride of family but to set before his congregation the example of men who had known and followed the ways of God. At the same time, however, he was moved by a strong sense of denominational loyalty, and that loyalty, given the way in which so many of our denominations owed their origins in this country to some particular phase of the earlier migrations to America, often tended to find identification with a pride of ancestry based on associations not wholly religious.

The most interesting example that I have found time to follow is provided by the Presbyterians. The Presbyterian Church in this country has consistently, and not without some justification, claimed descent primarily from the Scotch-Irish immigrants who in the eighteenth century became an increasingly important element of the colonial population. Thus, the *Biblical Repertory,* a Presbyterian organ, in April, 1847, declared that nine tenths of the membership of the Presbyterian Church, including all its branches and divisions, traced their ancestry to the Scotch-Irish.[49] This term "Scotch-Irish," I know, has since that date become the subject of bitter controversy, to which I shall refer in the next lecture. But let me use it here as a commonly accepted designation for a people whose original home had been the lowlands of Scotland, who in the earlier part of the seventeenth century had migrated in large numbers to northern Ireland, and whose descendants in the eighteenth century migrated in still larger numbers to the North American colonies, where they settled chiefly on the backside of the provinces reaching southward from Pennsylvania to South Carolina. There they became one of the more vigorous elements in an increasingly mixed population. Their continued identification

[49] *Biblical Repertory,* XIX (April, 1847), 281.

with the Presbyterian faith owed much to the evangelical zeal stimulated by the Great Awakening of the mid-eighteenth century, a movement in which the Presbyterians were especially active. This evangelicalism also brought within the folds of the Presbyterian Church many non-Scottish people, as is suggested by the care Presbyterian orators usually observed to bring virtually all the non-English elements of the American population into their historical discussions.[50] But a decent courtesy having been observed, the speaker commonly saved his warmest tributes for the Scotch-Irish.

I have no intention of suggesting that the Presbyterian interest in the history of the church had no other purpose than to serve this pride of ancestry. Like other denominations, the Presbyterians after the Revolution had made adjustment to the facts of political independence and national union by the organization of an independent American church, and with time the church faced constitutional and doctrinal questions on which historical evidence had of course a fundamental bearing. There was, moreover, the interest and pride that any institution tends to find in its past, an interest that in this country has received additional stimulation from a public policy leaving the area of man's spiritual life open to the free competition of differing sects. These were years that saw the publication not only of Charles Hodge's *Constitutional History of the Presbyterian Church* in 1839,[51] and the organization of the Presbyterian Historical Society in 1852,[52] but Francis L. Hawks's collection, on special commission from the Episcopalian Church, of the materials relating to the history of that denomination,[53] and the organization of the Protestant Episcopal His-

[50] As in Breckenridge, n. 48 above.

[51] Charles Hodge, *The Constitutional History of the Presbyterian Church in the United States, Part I, 1705 to 1741* (Philadelphia, 1839).

[52] See statement and charter of the Society in Richard Webster, *A History of the Presbyterian Church in America, from Its Origin until the Year 1760* . . . (Philadelphia, 1857), 695–700.

[53] See preface to his *Contributions to the Ecclesiastical History of the United States of America,* I (New York, 1836), x.

torical Society in 1850.[54] Nor should it be assumed that the interest in church history at this time was in any way bounded by a narrow sectarianism. For these were also the years in which William Henry Foote ranged far south from his native New England to lend fame to such apostles of eighteenth-century evangelicalism as Samuel Davies of Virginia and Princeton,[55] when William B. Sprague compiled his monumental biographical dictionary that was published in nine volumes as the *Annals of the American Pulpit*,[56] when John W. Thornton brought out his *Pulpit of the American Revolution,* and Frank Moore his no less useful *Patriot Preachers of the American Revolution*.[57]

My investigations in this area of our historical literature have been necessarily limited, but they have gone far enough to suggest to me the advantage of some fuller investigation. The pulpit obviously still retained its ancient function as a chief medium of instruction for the people on the essentials of their historical tradition as well as on questions of faith.

The Scotch-Irish, like so many other groups who have contributed to the building of this nation, needed a sponsor. As settlers for the most part of the backwoods, they had gained for themselves an early reputation that suggested few parallels between them and the earlier fathers of the country. The judgment of the Rev. Charles Woodmason—an itinerant Anglican minister in the Carolina back country who on the eve of the

[54] A. P. C. Griffin, *Bibliography of American Historical Societies* (American History Society Report for 1905, Washington, 1907), p. 741. There was a Historical Society of the American Lutheran Church as early as 1848.

[55] William Henry Foote, *Sketches of Virginia, Historical and Biographical* (2 vols., Philadelphia, 1850–55), and his *Sketches of North Carolina, Historical and Biographical, Illustrative of the Principles of a Portion of Her Early Settlers* (New York, 1846).

[56] *Annals of the American Pulpit, or Commemorative Notices of Distinguished American Clergymen of Various Denominations from the Early Settlement of the Country to the Close of the Year Eighteen Hundred and Fifty-five* (New York, 1857–69).

[57] Both in 1860, with a second edition of Thornton's work in 1876. Full citations in Chapter II, above, n. 25 and III, n. 7.

Revolution described the Scotch-Irish as "the lowest vilest crew breathing" and "the worst Vermin on Earth" [58]—undoubtedly should be considered an extreme example. Nevertheless, his uncomplimentary references are indicative of opinions that easily and naturally found their way into the tradition and that, by their very exaggeration, help to explain the excessive enthusiasm of those who sought to correct the popular impression. When the Rev. John Leaman published his short history of the Cedar Grove Presbyterian Church of Lancaster County in 1854, the backwoods settlers so castigated by Woodmason and others as the refuse of Europe's peoples had become "on the contrary, the choicest of her subjects, the refined, the learned, with the word of God in their hands and His spirit in their hearts"—in short, worthy examples for Mr. Leaman's congregation to follow.[59]

There was need for sponsorship on still another count, for the Scotch-Irish had been late comers, so late indeed that Proud's history of the state in which they had principally settled, which was Pennsylvania, could be written with hardly more than an incidental reference to their presence.[60] In protesting this neglect and the tendency to mention the Irish only in a critical way, Presbyterian divines, like the advocates of the Dutch in New York, showed a marked inclination to argue that their own ancestors had been ahead of the English in their resistance to tyranny. The Presbyterians also showed some

[58] Richard J. Hooker, ed., *The Carolina Backcountry on the Eve of the Revolution; The Journal and Other Writings of Charles Woodmason, Anglican Itinerant* (Chapel Hill, 1953), 14, 50.

[59] John Leaman, *History of the Cedar Grove Presbyterian Church and Congregation, of East Earl Township, Lancaster County* (Philadelphia, 1853). [George Chambers], *A Tribute to the Principles, Virtues, Habits and Public Usefulness of the Irish and Scotch Early Settlers of Pennsylvania* (Chambersburg, Pa., 1856), helpfully records the chief items in the indictment of the Scotch-Irish settlers to which their descendants objected—which were those brought generally against all backwoodsmen and which can be itemized by the simple device of reading in the negative the more recent tributes to the Scotch-Irishman's virtues.

[60] See above, p. 91. Chambers complained as vigorously of the slighting of the Scotch-Irish as he did of aspersions upon their character.

inclination to find identification with the first settlement of
the country, as in Charles Hodge's claim that the Puritans of
Massachusetts Bay originally had been Presbyterian.[61] But
the case for the Scotch-Irish rested chiefly on their record at
the time of the Revolution.

The evidence was impressive enough for a Presbyterian audience. In Mecklenburg County of North Carolina, in Hanover
County in Virginia, and in resolutions adopted by the New
York synod in 1775, Presbyterian investigators found proof
that their fathers had been the very first to declare for independence of Britain. The Pennsylvania constitution of 1776,
the most democratic of the early state constitutions, became a
document written by Presbyterians. The Presbyterians also
received credit for overthrowing the Anglican establishments
in Virginia and South Carolina, with results that guaranteed
the nation's dedication to the principle of a separation of
church and state. More than that, it was claimed that the federal union itself had been built on principles deep rooted in
the policy of the Presbyterian Church.[62] Little wonder that the
Rev. John C. Smith could declare in Washington on July 4,
1844, that there was "no denomination more dreaded by the
enemies of America than Presbyterians," [63] or that an audience
assembled at Pittsburgh in 1875 to celebrate the centennial of
Presbyterianism in western Pennsylvania listened to a vigorous
refutation of the popular notion that the Whisky Rebellion
had been inspired by nothing more than "a hatred of government and a love of whiskey." [64] Charles Woodmason and Robert

[61] Hodge, *Constitutional History,* 68; and Webster, *History of the Presbyterian Church,* 45.

[62] See, for example, "Presbyterianism, The Revolution, The Declaration,
and the Convention," a reprint of a review article appearing in the *Southern Presbyterian Review,* n.d. but c. 1847, and found in Princeton University Library, call no. 1066.999.

[63] In *The Religion and Patriotism of '76. A Discourse Delivered in the
City of Washington, on the Fourth of July, 1844* (Washington, 1844), 13.

[64] *Centenary Memorial of the Planting and Growth of Presbyterianism
in Western Pennsylvania and Parts Adjacent, . . . Held in Pittsburgh,
December 7–9, 1875* (Pittsburgh, 1876), 394.

Proud to the contrary notwithstanding, the Presbyterians had found their place among the founders of the country. So certain were they of this that they rarely bothered to criticize the Puritans, perhaps in part because they held much in common with the New England Congregationalists.

The strong compulsion so many Americans felt to add an inch or more to the stature of their fathers was of little help to the nation in meeting one of the more difficult of its current problems. A mounting tide of immigration—stimulated by the dislocations of Europe, by the economic opportunities of America, and doubtless by the invitations extended by some of the more flamboyant of our past orators to the oppressed in all the world—had presented us with the problem of an immigrant who somehow failed to measure up to the standard presumably set by our first immigrants. They had been giants and these men were merely mortals, so much so as to suggest that many of them might be indeed the refuse of Europe. The legend of the founding fathers, not yet fully subject to the influence of a democratic philosophy, had tended to stress the high social station many of the founders had enjoyed in the Old World, the better to emphasize the sacrifice they had made for the principles in which they believed. Unhappily, many of the newer immigrants obviously had suffered in the Old World the penalties of an inferior social status. The founding fathers, moreover, had been men devoted to learning, men who on reaching America had promptly looked to the establishment of schools and colleges. In contrast, these newcomers often seemed ignorant, not only of letters but of the ways of self-government, an area of human activity in which all the founders had excelled. Too often also these newcomers seemed lawless, whereas the first fathers, for all their love of liberty, had never lost sight of the advantages of law and order. Such, at any rate, was the image on which their descendants had come to depend.

That image was especially helpful to those who feared the growing number of Catholic immigrants but disliked to base their objections on religious grounds. The legend of the founding fathers had taught the American people to believe that they believed without qualification in the principle of religious freedom, but it had also taught them to equate the growth of religious liberty with the growth of Protestantism and thus to view the right itself as something wrung from the unwilling hands of the Catholic Church. In other words, the very tradition that supported the principle of religious freedom made it difficult for many Americans to accept the prospect of a large Catholic population and no less difficult to express freely the fundamental reason for their fear of the Catholic immigrant. In that dilemma, it was comforting to note how sharp in other ways was the contrast between this immigrant and the heroic figure of the founding father.

It probably would have helped had the American people been more prompt than they were to recognize the role of a continuing immigration in the development of their country. If one may judge by Franklin's famous essay on population, written in the middle of the eighteenth century, and by Jefferson's *Notes on Virginia,* published just after the Revolution, even the more astute observers of the extraordinary growth of population in the American colonies were inclined to attribute it to nothing more than the natural increase of an original stock.[65] Such an assumption had some justification in the experience of New England, but it is a remarkable fact that a Pennsylvanian and a Virginian should have talked in these terms. The Revolution brought with it a new emphasis on the concept of America as a refuge for the oppressed and so pointed the way to an interpretation of American history that was broad enough to embrace all those who had sought a refuge here. But the Revolution, as we have seen, also encouraged a sharp focus in the study of American history on the earliest years of settlement to the neglect of subsequent chapters in our colonial history. And more recently, a sharpening contest for the special recognition of particular groups was having the effect of divert-

[65] Ford, *Writings of Jefferson,* III, 484–88; John Bigelow, ed., *The Works of Benjamin Franklin* (12 vols., New York, 1904), II, 338–50.

ing attention all too frequently from the larger picture. Even today, while our library shelves are loaded with books testifying to the contribution of this or that group of immigrants, the number of books that testify simply to the role of the immigrant himself remains relatively small.

It would be misleading to suggest that a developing interest among Catholics in the history of their church in America represented nothing more than an attempt to combat the tendency at the time of the Know-Nothing movement to exclude Catholics from any possessory right in the American tradition. The work of so distinguished a scholar as John Gilmary Shea, who has been justly described as the "Father of American Catholic History," or of so devoted an antiquarian as Edmund B. O'Callaghan of New York, has too obvious a relation to the interests that inspired American historians in the age of Francis Parkman to permit any such suggestion. And yet I think there may be some advantage in viewing Shea's studies of Catholic missions in the United States, of the early exploration of the Mississippi Valley, and of the history of the Catholic Church in the United States from "the earliest settlement of the country," together with his editions of the Jesuit narratives,[66] as literature falling in the general class of that which sang the praise of the Scotch-Irish or of Roger Williams as the Baptist founder of Rhode Island.

Certainly, Shea helped to point the way to recognition and acceptance as Americans for other groups who were neither Protestant nor English. There is tragedy in John Shea's life as an American historian. He could write a child's history of the United States that left no suspicion that its author was a Catholic, except perhaps for its emphasis on the early explorations.[67] But in his old age, when the United States was celebrating the

[66] See Peter Guilday, *John Gilmary Shea, Father of American Catholic History* (New York: U. S. Catholic Historical Society, 1926), which includes a bibliography of Shea's works.

[67] John Gilmary Shea, *A Child's History of the United States* (2 vols., New York, 1872).

discovery of America by Columbus, he felt compelled to remind his coreligionists that it had been a Catholic who discovered America, Catholics who first explored its coastlines, Catholics who made known the opportunities of the Great Lakes and the Mississippi, Catholics who founded the oldest cities in the United States, and Catholics who first undertook to bring the native Indian to a knowledge of Jesus Christ.[68] It is a remarkable fact that the American who finds himself rejected as an American quarrels not so much with the test by which he is rejected as with the proposition that he cannot meet the test.

No less remarkable is the evidence during the period we have under discussion of uncertainty as to whether or not the claim to recognition had been accepted. It would be easy by turning to Bancroft and other authors who dealt with the national story to demonstrate an inclination on their part, in the interest of national unity, to concede some recognition to all those who demanded recognition. But somehow this concession seemed to be not enough. Again and again men were apparently guided by a suspicion that the recognition conceded to them represented no more than a courtesy.

When the *Southern Literary Messenger* directed its readers' attention in 1835 to George Bancroft's first volume, the reviewer summed up an attitude by no means wholly peculiar to the South in these words: "We did indeed find what was intended to be a favorable account of our ancestors. Yet we were disappointed." The disappointment in this case was aggravated by a fundamental disagreement with Bancroft's nationalist interpretation. "What Mr. Bancroft gives as praise, we cannot accept as praise," the reviewer continued, "and, what is worse, we cannot help suspecting, in all such cases, that a sneer, or something more mischievous, is intended." All that Bancroft had done was to credit the seventeenth-century Virginians with a purpose primarily to protect their own legislative independence against Cromwell—a good Jeffersonian interpretation that served well to establish a helpful similarity in the aims of the

[68] Guilday, *John Gilmary Shea*, 33–34.

Virginia and Massachusetts colonists. But the Richmond reviewer would have none of this. He suspected a purpose to
imply "that the people of the colonies, all together, formed one
body politic before the revolution," and preferred to believe
that the Virginia settlers had been distinguished by an un-
swerving loyalty both to Charles I and Charles II. His discussion once more almost suggested that Virginia had not been
founded until midway in the seventeenth century, for he spoke
of Virginia's fathers as men who at home had "withstood the
usurpation of Cromwell while resistance was practicable," and
who then, "driven from their native country," had "bent their
steps toward Virginia, as that part of the foreign dominions
of England, where the spirit of loyalty was strongest." In short,
the forefathers of Virginia had been a band of exiled Cavaliers, chivalrous, generous, and, like all Virginians, "ever ready
to resist the strong, to help the weak, to comfort the afflicted,
and to lift up the fallen." [69]

This romantic notion, which probably owed as much to the
novels of Sir Walter Scott as to any other influence, is a truly
significant development of the nineteenth century, for it marks
Virginia's rejection of an interpretation of its origins that
could have served to strengthen her ties with the union. I have
no time to explore the question fully and no desire to enter
into dispute as to the validity of the Cavalier thesis but perhaps you will find some interest in its genealogy. The Cavaliers
had been in the picture for some time. Robert Beverley, without trying to make any special point of the fact, had noted the
presence in Restoration Virginia of some of the king's old supporters. George Chalmers, depending on Beverley, had used the
Cavaliers to ridicule the argument of Bland and Jefferson that
the colonists at the time of Cromwell had been primarily concerned to protect their legislative independence. John Daly
Burk had found in the Cavaliers a convenient escape from a

[69] *Southern Literary Messenger,* I (June, 1835), 587–91.

historical problem—that of interpreting the Restoration of 1660—arising largely from his own enthusiasm for the idea that the seventeenth-century Virginian had been no less a republican than was his New England compatriot.[70] In short, the Cavalier already had proved useful enough to both Tory and Republican as to have found a place of some importance in the state's history.

Such evidence as I have found time to check suggests that his elevation to the place of first importance among the founders of the Old Dominion was not the work of the very able historians who served antebellum Virginia. William W. Hening's *Statutes of Virginia,* a compilation that ranks with the more important achievements of American scholarship in the first half of the nineteenth century, lent strong support to the Jeffersonian view of the state's history by substantial additions to the record of Virginia's legislative history during the middle years of the seventeenth century.[71] Conway Robinson, whose dedicated labors did so much to round out Virginia's historical records, drew new attention to the earliest years by finding the proceedings of the first assembly of 1619, a document that had escaped both Stith and Hening.[72] Charles Campbell's *History of the Colony and Ancient Dominion of Virginia,* while recognizing that "some royalist refugees had been driven hither by the civil war," argued that republicans had also found a refuge in Virginia and vigorously challenged the popular notion that Virginia had been the first to restore Charles II.[73] George Tucker's well-known *History of the United States* devoted only a brief introduction to the colonial period, but in that intro-

[70] See above, pp. 82–84.

[71] William W. Hening, ed., *The Statutes at Large, Being a Collection of All the Laws of Virginia from the First Session of the Legislature, in the Year 1619* (13 vols., Richmond, 1810–23).

[72] See comment by H. B. Grigsby in 1854 in *The John P. Branch Historical Papers of Randolph-Macon College,* IV (1916), 416.

[73] Published at Philadelphia, 1860. See also his *Introduction to the History of the Colony and Ancient Dominion of Virginia* (Richmond, 1847).

duction he emphasized the common qualities that had characterized the original members of the union.[74] Joseph Martin in
his *Gazetteer of Virginia,* published at Charlottesville in 1836,
presented an interpretation of the colony's seventeenth-century
history that was distinctly democratic in its emphasis.[75] And
Hugh Blair Grigsby, best known for his studies of the Revolutionary period in Virginia, was almost violent in his repudiation of the Cavalier thesis. To his friend, Henry S. Randall,
the biographer of Jefferson, he announced in 1856 a purpose
to prove "that the Colony of Virginia was settled by thousands
of Cromwellians" and to "make it plain, altho' I strip every
jack daw of his borrowed plumes." [76]

   There is no time for exploration of the intriguing question
of the failure of Virginia's historians to control the development of popular tradition. Grigsby, in a letter to another friend
in 1854, offers an interesting suggestion as to a part of the
difficulty the historian faced by expressing his distaste for
attempts to "borrow" the "motives and views" associated with
the Pilgrim settlement at Plymouth. It had to be admitted, he
said, that the Jamestown settlement had been "essentially a
trading venture" having little in common with the "grand and
noble achievement" of the Pilgrims.[77] Perhaps he had Burk in

[74] George Tucker, *The History of the United States, From Their Colonization to the End of the Twenty-sixth Congress, in 1841* (4 vols., Philadelphia, 1856–57). The introductory chapter acknowledges the author's
indebtedness especially to George Bancroft.

[75] Joseph Martin, *A New and Comprehensive Gazetteer of Virginia and
the District of Columbia* (Charlottesville, 1836), where Martin (p. 594)
boasted that Virginia was the first state in the world whose government
was organized on the principle of universal suffrage, and where (p. 595) he
described Virginia in 1660 as a "nearly independent democracy." Martin's
history was reprinted in Henry Howe's *Historical Collections of Virginia*
(Charleston, 1852).

[76] Frank I. and Frank W. Klingberg, eds., *The Correspondence between
Henry Stephens Randall and Hugh Blair Grigsby, 1856–1861* (Berkeley and
Los Angeles, 1952), 76.

[77] *Branch Historical Papers,* IV, 415–17.

mind, and perhaps the Virginian in his choice of the Cavalier as an ancestor should be credited with some sense of the superficiality of Burk's interpretation of the early history of Virginia.

Certainly, many Virginians were guided by a strong desire to repudiate a New England influence that now served so frequently to bring indictment of the South. When the *North American Review* was indiscreet enough to discuss in 1837 the evidences of New England's unpopularity in the nation, the *Southern Literary Messenger* leaped at the opportunity offered by a conclusion that the explanation was basically political. In an article on "The New England Character," the *Messenger* suggested that instead a much more fundamental cause was the New Englander's descent from the Puritan fathers. Affirming the Virginian's descent from the Cavaliers, "the enemies and persecutors of those old puritans," the author suggested that in Richmond men entertained, "perhaps unwittingly, something of an hereditary and historical antipathy against the children for their fathers' sake." [78]

Though Webster had been circumspect in his remarks on slavery at Plymouth in 1820, others soon showed less care. A commentator on Cooper's *The Spy* in the *North American Review* of July, 1822, drew a contrast between "the Virginia colony importing into the country a cargo of negroes, to entail the curse of slavery on their remotest posterity, in the same year that our first fathers were founding the liberties of America on the Plymouth rock," and made what was undoubtedly intended as an irreverent reference to Captain John Smith "who had challenged a whole Ottoman army in his youth, . . . and who was now solacing his riper years . . . in the arms of the renowned Pocahontas." [79] In 1831, while commenting on Grahame's history of the colonies, a significant work by a British author, the review identified the true spirit of the Cavalier with Governor Berkeley's thanks to God that there were

[78] *Southern Literary Messenger,* III (1837), 413.
[79] *North American Review,* XV (July, 1822), 255–57.

neither schools nor printing presses in Virginia, a quotation destined to be repeated *ad nauseam* over the years to come.[80] It is evident enough that the Virginian's position was in more than one way a defensive one.

At the same time, the New Englander also found himself on the defensive, and not just from attacks on his ancestry by the Southerner. No Southerner went further than did Job R. Tyson in his summation of the case against New England in a paper delivered before the Pennsylvania Historical Society in 1842. Tyson struck vigorously at the pretension, as he put it, "conveyed in every form which fond reverence or local partiality can assume," that New England had "originated the free principles which followed our independence, as a political society, by sowing the seeds which gave them birth." He conceded to the New England settlers a leadership in the founding of schools, a firmness of character that had been useful in the settlement of a new country, and the idea of union represented by the New England Confederation in 1643. But he quoted John Cotton to prove New England's early repudiation of democracy and defined the distinguishing quality of the American political system as "the freedom of the state from all the trammels of ecclesiastical restriction." He denied the validity of the common excuse that the Puritan belonged to his own age—citing in support of his position the record of Roger Williams, Lord Baltimore, and William Penn—and he linked the Puritan treatment of the Quakers with "the fires of Smithfield, the dungeons . . . of the Inquisition, the massacre of St. Bartholomew, and the penalties of the Star Chamber." His addition of a stricture on account of the witchcraft hysteria at Salem made the case complete.[81] Even so he failed quite to get into his paper the full venom that John Pennington had man-

[80] *Ibid.*, XXXII (Jan., 1831), 181–82.

[81] *Discourse Delivered before the Historical Society of Pennsylvania, February 21, 1842, on the Colonial History of the Eastern and Some of the Southern States* (Philadelphia, 1842). Also in the Society's *Memoirs,* IV, Pt. II, 5–64.

aged to crowd into a single sentence before the same audience two years before. The Puritans, Pennington had declared, "never scourged, mutilated, or hung a Baptist, or Quaker of either sex; they never destroyed in cold blood Indian prisoners of war . . . without quoting chapter and verse as their warranty." [82]

Meanwhile, the Baptists continued to push the claims of Roger Williams, with the stout assistance of the Rhode Island Historical Society and to the applause of still others. It is difficult to see how George Bancroft could have been more generous than he was in his treatment of Williams, and Bancroft's interpretation, it should be noted, governed our school textbooks for two generations. But somehow the impulse to correct the earlier wrong still survived. In May, 1860, an unhappy year in our history, it was decided to exhume the remains of Williams and his wife in Rhode Island, with results that included an offer by the Rev. E. M. Stone of Providence to present to the Massachusetts Historical Society certain mementos of the occasion, including a stone, some earth from Williams' grave, and a nail from his lady's coffin, an offer the society somewhat stuffily rejected. [83]

When residents of Sturbridge, Massachusetts, submitted to the state legislature meeting in 1874–75 a petition calling for formal revocation of the original order of banishment against Williams, Henry M. Dexter, a Congregationalist clergyman who had previously published a volume on *The Church Policy of the Pilgrims* and would devote two other studies to their history, decided that the time had come to set the record straight. In a closely argued study entitled *As to Roger Williams and His "Banishment" from the Massachusetts Plantation; with a Few Further Words Concerning the Baptists, the*

[82] Historical Society of Pennsylvania *Memoirs*, IV (1840), Pt. I, 135–37. In this same place Pennington pokes fun at the Virginians, especially those claiming descent from Pocahontas, and goes on to jeer at the exaggerated claims by New Yorkers for their Dutch ancestry.

[83] Massachusetts Historical Society *Proceedings*, V (1860–62), 46–47, 51.

Quakers, and Religious Liberty,[84] Dexter flatly denied that rights of conscience had had anything to do with Williams' expulsion. Mr. Dexter showed more than a little feeling toward the Baptists, whom he charged with having "canonized" Williams, and still more feeling toward Quaker writers he accused of having suppressed the full facts on the experience of their coreligionists in New England. His indignation became especially strong while relating the resort of Quaker women to nudism as a form of protest.[85] His indignation owed something perhaps to the necessity he faced to admit that the Puritan fathers, for all their resourcefulness, had not known what to do about a naked woman in the meetinghouse at the hour of worship.

I do not mean to leave the impression, however, that Dexter's work is fully representative of New England's reaction to criticism of the Puritans. It would be difficult to find any sharper criticism of the Bay Colony founders, for instance, than that presented by James Savage in his notes on Winthrop's journal. Writing in the 1820's, Savage's comments reflected not only his own rigid standards of scholarship but deep currents in the intellectual and spiritual life of New England that made of the Puritan a real bother to his nineteenth-century descendants. It is worth noting that Dexter later accused the Unitarians of having been too harsh in their treatment of the Puritans.[86]

Savage, when issuing his second edition of Winthrop's journal, left the notes unchanged,[87] but it cannot be said with assurance that others among his contemporaries would have done so. Perhaps it was because of the round of bicentennial celebrations that began in 1830, perhaps it was because other Americans joined too enthusiastically in the criticism of the Puritan—whatever the reason, a change occurred after the 1820's. While preparing his bicentennial address for Salem in 1828, Justice Story wrote half humorously to a friend that he had been struggling with his Puritan ancestors and happily

---

[84] At Boston by the Congregational Publishing Society, [1876].

[85] *Ibid.*, especially 134–35.   [86] *Ibid.*, 105n.

[87] Two vols., Boston, 1853.

had made a final peace with them on these terms: that their faults had been no worse than those of their age, and that for all their faults they had been men of courage and principle.[88] In this spirit all New Englanders could enter heartily enough into the bicentennial celebrations that followed, and that not unnaturally encouraged a reviving filial piety.

As the enthusiasm of the bicentennial decade waned, it seems to me that a more sophisticated attitude tended to develop, an attitude that is represented at its best by John G. Palfrey's *History of New England*.[89] This work, of which the first of five volumes was published in 1859, is frequently described today as filio-pietistic, which it was. But it was not the filio-piety of a New England society address or of the orator who labored to meet the requirements of some other significant anniversary. Palfrey brought to his effort, which was marked by intensive investigation of the sources on both sides of the Atlantic, a superior scholarship resulting in a work justifiably hailed as a landmark in American historiography. If he showed too much of a tendency to defend the Puritan, it must be said that the Puritan at the time needed a defender, and it can be said that little of substance has been added since that time to the defense he provided. With Palfrey having entered the lists, and with the attention of New England increasingly focused on the difficult problems of the nation, it seems to me that the descendants of the Puritans entered into the period of our Civil War with a relatively relaxed and confident feeling about their ancestry. In other words, I am inclined to view Henry M. Dexter primarily as a Congregationalist minister who had let the Baptists and the Quakers get under his skin.

Before closing, let me say that this discussion can be misleading. It may be that the wide popularity enjoyed by Washington Irving's five-volume biography of George Washington, published between 1855 and 1859, is much more representative of

[88] William W. Story, *Life and Letters of Joseph Story* (2 vols., Boston, 1851), I, 543–51.
[89] John Gorham Palfrey, *History of New England* (5 vols., Boston, 1859–90).

the popular interest in American origins than anything I have discussed. It may be that I have discounted too much the many other evidences of a national sentiment that might have been mentioned, including the textbooks for our schools. Perhaps the time could have been more profitably spent in comment on Edward Everett's famous address on "The Character of Washington," an oration delivered first in Boston and then in many different parts of the country for the purpose of preserving Mount Vernon as a historical monument. Perhaps I should have paid more attention to the little books written by the Rev. Joseph Banvard that in the mid-nineteenth century offered instruction to our youth on the Romance of American History, with attention impartially divided among the stories of the French Huguenots in Florida, of Captain Smith and Pocahontas at Jamestown, or of the Pilgrim Fathers at Plymouth. Perhaps I should have stressed Sarah Hale's not unsuccessful campaign to make of Thanksgiving, as a harvest festival celebrated in memory of the Pilgrim Fathers, a national holiday, and more especially the fact that as late as 1855 the governor of Virginia issued the desired proclamation.[90] Perhaps I should have talked of Benson J. Lossing's *Pictorial Field-Book of the Revolution,* with its artistic and immensely popular representations of the Revolutionary battlefields Lincoln later recalled so effectively to the nation's memory. Perhaps the whole lecture belonged to Lincoln, who certainly understood the role that a common memory of the Revolution might play in preserving the Union.

But I have been impressed, possibly too much, by the evidences that we were a nation lacking as yet a common view of our origins.

[90] Merle Curti, *The Roots of American Loyalty,* 135–36; Ruth E. Finley, *The Lady of Godey's, Sarah Josepha Hale* (Philadelphia, 1931), 195–98; Isabella W. Entrikin, *Sarah Josepha Hale and Godey's Lady's Book* (Philadelphia, 1946); articles on "Thanksgiving Day" and "Fast Days" in *Dictionary of American History.*

CHAPTER V

Differing Descendants

AS the year 1875 approached, the calendar in itself was enough to draw the attention of the American people chiefly to those chapters of their history which reminded one and all of a common heritage. Ahead lay the centennials of Lexington, of the Declaration of Independence, of the victory at Yorktown, and of the Constitutional Convention of 1787, to mention only the more important. Not only had the centennial observance of historic events become too characteristic a feature of American folkways to permit those occasions to pass without special notice, but the need to use them for their healing effect upon the wounds of a recent civil war could not be ignored. Just as in years past the bicentennial celebration of events associated with the original settlement of America had served to evoke the patriotism of locality, so now did a long series of centennial years help to stimulate a new nationalism.

No one was more alert to the special opportunities of the centennial years than were the publishers. There were books for the young and books for the old. Some sought to instruct, others primarily to entertain. Especially popular were studies pointing up the contrast in the conditions of life at the beginning and at the close of the nation's first century, studies lending emphasis to the theme of national achievement that domi-

nated the whole centennial celebration.[1] No less representative
was John Fiske's immensely influential *Critical Period of American History,* a work that lent the full sanction of history to a
growing veneration for the federal constitution as the supreme
accomplishment of the Revolutionary fathers. The completed
volume did not reach the public until a year after the centennial of the constitution, but much of its vigorous argument
had been presented over the two preceding years in the pages
of the *Atlantic Monthly*.[2]

Periodical literature exploited the widest range of interests,
but the more serious journals showed preference for summary
reviews of a century of progress in particular areas of our
national life. Thus, the *North American Review* devoted the
entire issue for January, 1876, to comprehensive surveys in the
fields of religion, politics, science, economics, law, and education.[3] *Harper's Magazine* began in the fall of 1874 a series of
articles on "The First Century of the Republic" that in the next
year gave emphasis to progress in such fields as the mechani-
cal arts and agriculture.[4] Religious periodicals took the opportunity for review of a century of religious activity or examined
the record of their own denomination, as in John Gilmary
Shea's article for the *American Catholic Quarterly Review* in
January, 1876, on "The Catholic Church in American History." [5] A people whose appetite for military memoirs and
history had been whetted or dulled by the flood of literature
on the Civil War quite evidently found now a new interest in
the campaigns of the Revolution.

[1] As in Edward Abbott's *Revolutionary Times: Sketches of our Country,
Its People and Their Ways, One Hundred Years Ago* (Boston, 1876).
Abbott was also the author of *A Paragraph History of the United States*
(Boston, 1875) and *A Paragraph History of the American Revolution* (Bos-
ton, 1876), short accounts for instruction of the lay reader or the school
child.

[2] *Atlantic Monthly,* Vols. LVII–LX.

[3] *North American Review,* CXXII (January, 1876).

[4] *Harper's New Monthly Magazine,* XL (1874), 861 *et seq.*

[5] See bibliography in Peter Guilday, *John Gilmary Shea,* 164.

Though public observances of the more important centennial occasions got under way in 1874 and 1875 with special ceremonies at Carpenters' Hall in Philadelphia and at Lexington and Concord in Massachusetts, with Boston's tribute to the heroes of Bunker Hill, and with the commemoration at Cambridge of Washington's assumption of the command of the Continental Army, *the* centennial year was of course 1876. For most Americans the centennial of independence offered nothing more unusual than the traditional ritual of the Fourth, enlivened perhaps by more bunting, a longer or smarter line of march, and the opportunity the orator had in a centennial year to say a few things that could not have been said before.[6] There were millions of the country's citizens, however, who enjoyed during the summer and fall of 1876 the special privilege of attending the great centennial exposition at Philadelphia.

This was the first of the international expositions that have become familiar to modern Americans. The idea was borrowed from Europe, where Prince Albert had sponsored at London in 1851 the Great Exhibition that was destined to be remembered chiefly for its Crystal Palace. Others had followed: at London in 1862 and 1871, at Paris in 1855 and 1867, and at Vienna in 1873—all of them built around some plan for an international competition in the fine and industrial arts and all of them dedicated to the ideal of international understanding. It had occurred to more than one American observer that such an exposition might be an especially appropriate way of marking the centennial of independence. Some of them reluctantly concluded that our federal system of government forbade any hope

[6] A joint resolution of Congress on March 13, 1876, recommended that each county or town celebrate the centennial with a historical address on the history of the county or town, and that copies be forwarded to the Library of Congress "to the intent that a complete record may thus be obtained of the progress of our institutions during the First Centennial of their existence." Reports of the President, Secretary, and Executive Committee in *United States Centennial Commission, International Exhibition, 1876* (11 vols., Washington, 1880), II, App. C, 116.

that the prerequisite of governmental support could be provided. But others persisted and more especially some of the leading citizens of Philadelphia, to which history had given an advantage as the choice for the site of the exposition. It was believed that an exhibition featuring the natural resources of the country, with special recognition for each of the several states, might be combined with an international competition affording an opportunity to compare the achievements of the United States "in those arts which benefit mankind" with the progress of the older nations of Europe.[7] In the end this faith proved to have been justified.

There was much truth in the boast of the Centennial Commission in its final report that the success of the exposition represented a triumph for the principle of voluntary organization. The Franklin Institute of Philadelphia, taking the initiative in 1870, demonstrated its understanding of the American political system by first getting assurances that the City of Philadelphia would co-operate. Next the question was cleared with Harrisburg, and the stage was thus set for a special committee to try its hand in Washington, with the aid of the Pennsylvania congressional delegation.[8] It took a full year to get action out of Congress, where many of the members seemed to feel that their own constituents stood to gain little if anything from the proposed exposition at Philadelphia. When Congress finally acted in March, 1871, it did so with no evident generosity of spirit. It authorized the appointment of a centennial commission representing each state and territory of the

[7] The chief sources used in the following discussion of the exhibition are the official published reports of the United States Centennial Commission, cited immediately above. See also J. S. Ingram, *The Centennial Exposition* (Philadelphia, 1876), and *Our National Centennial Jubilee* (New York, 1876), and more especially, James D. McCabe, *The Illustrated History of the Centennial Exhibition Held in Commemoration of the One Hundredth Anniversary of American Independence* (Philadelphia, Chicago, and St. Louis, n.d.).

[8] See especially the Secretary's report, *ibid.*, II, 107 ff.

Union, the issuance of a proclamation of the exposition by the president on receiving assurance from the governor of Pennsylvania that provision had been made for the necessary buildings, and the communication of this notice to interested foreign governments. But the act also specified that the United States government would bear no part of the cost.[9]

The Commission, after being organized, had first to face the fact that it not only lacked funds but even the power to raise them. Congress was persuaded in 1872 to pass a second act providing for a Board of Finance with authority to secure subscription of capital stock up to $10,000,000.[10] President Grant issued the formal proclamation of the forthcoming exhibition in July, 1873, a document that commended the enterprise to the attention of both the American people and foreign states which might wish to participate. When a dozen or more of these states accepted the President's "invitation," as they had read it, Secretary of State Fish felt compelled, in the interest of international understanding, to send out a circular indicating that no invitation had been issued by the United States government. This circular naturally had an unsettling effect on the plans of the Commission, as did also the panic of 1873. The Congress turned down an urgent request for $3,000,000 in the spring of 1874, but it did appropriate a fund of some $600,000, enough to permit the federal government to become one of the exhibitors. More important still, Congress now agreed in lieu of the requested funds that the president might *invite* foreign governments to participate.[11] As the centennial year opened, the Board of Finance was in serious difficulty, but the response of foreign states to the president's invitation had been most encouraging. As a result, the board managed to convince Congress that the honor of the United States had been engaged— to the extent, at least, of $1,500,000, the total of an appropria-

[9] *Ibid.*, II, App. C, 101–2.   [10] *Ibid.*, II, App. C, 102–9.

[11] *Ibid.*, II, 9–12; App. C, 110–15, for other documents relating to the government's role.

tion that the Supreme Court subsequently held to have been only a loan.[12]

If this record suggests something less than the outpouring of patriotic sentiment that usually features the brief statement accorded the centennial exhibition in our textbooks, the response outside Congress nevertheless was in the end gratifying enough. All told, twenty-four of the American states accepted the invitation to provide some state building on the exhibition grounds. Not counting the separate representation for several members of the British Empire, twenty-six foreign nations contributed exhibits, and nine of them erected special buildings of their own, as did also many American business firms. The more important of the exhibits were arranged in capital buildings devoted to art, mining, manufacturing, horticulture, agriculture, and so forth. When the exhibition was opened on May 10, 1876, approximately 284 acres of Fairmount Park had been inclosed. Buildings large and small covered roughly 70 acres. The Pennsylvania Railroad had run a special line to a newly constructed depot close at hand to the main entrance, where one could board the narrow-gauge steam railway that offered the advantages of rapid transit through the exposition grounds.[13] The whole arrangement stirred expressions of pride in the special aptitude of Americans for the management of large enterprises.

President Grant opened the exhibition in ceremonies that also featured a centennial march written on commission by Richard Wagner, a hymn by John Greenleaf Whittier, and a cantata by Sidney Lanier.[14] The ceremonies on July 4 were transferred to Independence Square, where in the absence of President Grant the Emperor of Brazil was the ranking head of state, and where William M. Evarts of New York delivered the major address after a reading of the Declaration by Richard

[12] *Ibid.*, II, 12; App. C, 115–16.

[13] See especially the statistical summary in report of Director-General, *ibid.*, I, 297–305; and report of the Bureau of Transportation, 312 ff.

[14] *Ibid.*, II, 27–38.

Henry Lee of Virginia. Stung perhaps by sharp criticism of his absence on the Fourth, the president returned to Philadelphia on November 10 for the formal closing of the exposition.[15]

Meantime, every device had been exploited for swelling the attendance. Particularly helpful was the proclamation of special state days, on which the featured parts of the program were usually a parade and an address by the state's governor.[16] Fraternal and other organizations received encouragement to hold their annual conventions at Philadelphia that summer; arrangements were made for excursion trips by thousands of school children within reach; the Italian citizens of the United States found help in the erection and dedication of a monument to Christopher Columbus; the Catholic Total Abstinence Beneficial Society got the featured spot at the exposition grounds on July 4 for the dedication of an ice-water drinking fountain. As a result of these and other promotional devices, the public response was such as to persuade most of the railroad companies that they could safely drag their feet on proposals for special excursion rates.[17] The final totals showed 9,910,966 admissions from May to the close of the exhibition on November 10, of which number over 8,000,000 paid their way in.[18] It was a source of national pride that only at Paris in 1867 had attendance at such an exposition come anywhere close to these figures.[19]

It might have been expected that the American people would then relax in the confident assurance that they had staged the greatest of all the international expositions. But the accomplishment belonged chiefly to Philadelphia, and other cities were now alert to their own special opportunities. In 1884 came New Orleans' Cotton Centennial Exposition, in 1893 Chicago's Columbian Exposition, in 1901 Buffalo's Pan-American Exposition, in 1904 St. Louis' Louisiana Purchase Exposition, and in

[15] *Ibid.*, II, 41–76, 93–103.

[16] *Ibid.*, II, 24; and in I, 444 ff., the table on admissions, especially 488.

[17] *Ibid.*, I, 345–46.   [18] *Ibid.*, I, 438–39.

[19] McCabe, *Illustrated History of the Centennial Exhibition,* 888.

1907 the Jamestown Exposition at Norfolk. In giving his endorsement to the last named of these projects, Grover Cleve-
land commented, and not without reason, on "the surfeit of
expositions" that had "somewhat afflicted" the country in recent years.[20]

Meanwhile, celebration of the national centennial continued.
In view of the tremendous success of the Philadelphia exposition, later observances could have been viewed as somewhat
anticlimactic, but each occasion in its turn had some special
importance for one community or another. There were ceremonies at Saratoga, Trenton, Brandywine, Germantown, Valley Forge, Monmouth, Stony Point, Camden, Charleston,
Cowpens, Savannah, and Eutaw Springs.[21] The commemoration
of Revolutionary events reached an appropriate conclusion
with celebrations at Yorktown in 1881 that were financed by a
federal appropriation.[22] Of greater interest was the dedication
of the Washington Monument in 1885, a date determined simply by the fact that only then, after half a century of effort and
with the aid of a new enthusiasm stimulated by the centennial,
had the nation managed to complete a fitting memorial to the
father of the country.[23] Two years later it was again Philadelphia's turn.

Perhaps because of the city's expenditure of effort in 1876,
the initiative this time was left to others. The New Jersey assembly in June, 1886, adopted a resolution proposing that the
governors and other representatives of the thirteen original

[20] Cuyler Reynolds, *New York at the Jamestown Exposition* (Albany,
1909), 129.

[21] See Hampton L. Carson, *History of the Celebration of the One Hundredth Anniversary of the Promulgation of the Constitution of the United
States* (2 vols., Philadelphia, 1889), I, 297.

[22] The *Official Program of the Yorktown Sesquicentennial . . . 1931*
(Richmond, n.d.) carries a brief description. The federal appropriation
included the cost of the Yorktown Monument.

[23] *The Dedication of the Washington National Monument, With the
Orations By Hon. Robert C. Winthrop and Hon. John W. Daniel, February 21, 1885* (Washington, 1885).

states meet in Philadelphia the following September 17 to consider a national celebration of the centennial of the constitution. This proposal having met with a cordial response, the conference in September resulted in the establishment of a Constitutional Centennial Commission representing the several states and territories.[24] A hurried Congress failed to take final action on a bill for the appropriation of $100,000 for the proposed celebration, but the state of Pennsylvania contributed $75,000 and the citizens of Philadelphia another $50,000 by private subscription. Several of the states bore the cost of their own participation, as did many private organizations taking a part in the three-day festival of parades, banquets, receptions, and orations extending from the 15th through the 17th of September.[25] President Cleveland and other dignitaries from Washington were present for most of the ceremonies.

Once again, as in 1876, the emphasis fell heavily on the evidences of material progress. The ceremonies at Philadelphia in 1887 were opened with a great civic and industrial parade featuring such contrasts as that between the Conestoga wagon and the modern locomotive and also featuring, it might be added, the names of the manufacturing firms that had contributed the floats.[26] The chief marshal, in reporting his efforts to provide for "the people" a valuable lesson on the "Progress of a Century under Constitutional Government," indicated that he had experienced not a little difficulty in preventing "the degeneration of the display into a mere medium for advertising." He had found it difficult to awaken a public spirit without appealing to the desire for gain and that desire had more than once threatened to override the public interest. But he recorded his ultimate satisfaction in having been able to provide "legitimate advertisement" for participating firms without obscuring the larger object the display was intended to serve.[27]

This experience calls perhaps for comment on the fact that

[24] Carson, *op. cit.*, I, 261–78.   [25] *Ibid.*, I, 278–91.
[26] Report of chief marshal in Carson, *op. cit.*, II, 1–194.
[27] *Ibid.*, II, 5–6.

the staging of the more important centennial observances had been left chiefly in the hands of leading citizens in the industrialized northeastern states. Despite an evident care to give special recognition to the Southern states, the extent of their participation was disappointing, and the part taken by the Western states was often more formal than real.[28] I have no reason for believing that a sponsorship more truly national in character would have resulted in a different choice of theme, for the theme of progress, with emphasis on the material evidences of national achievement, was congenial to the time. I seek only to suggest that the indifference of the federal government to its own opportunities for leadership left the national observances peculiarly dependent upon the resources of particular communities, and that history gave the greater opportunities to that section of the country that had been most highly industrialized. If the business community there, in lending the sanction of its achievement to the Revolution and the constitution, gained thereby some additional sanction for itself, it was only natural.

The chief marshal in 1887 complained that proposals to educational institutions for demonstration of the progress of a century in the field of education had met with indifference.[29] As a result, his great parade was dominated by the military, the patriotic order, and the industrialist's float. It is not surprising that the orator on September 17, Justice Miller of the United States Supreme Court, stressed doctrines well suited to the views of those whose public spirit had made the occasion possible. The Constitution, he found, had been intended to establish a truly national government, a government, for example, having the power to protect commerce from unwarranted interference by the states.[30] As he approached the end of his address, Justice

[28] *Ibid.*, I, 315, for a listing of states not participating in 1887. More important is the evidence throughout the record of the commission that the real responsibility was carried by local residents. On the disappointment over the Southern participation in 1876, see McCabe, *Illustrated History,* 895.

[29] *Ibid.*, II, 9.   [30] *Ibid.*, II, 262–90.

Miller gave testimony, as had so many before him during the centennial years, that George Bancroft had finally become the historian of the American people.

Bancroft had finished his great history, begun in 1834, just in time for the centennial of independence in 1876. More recently, he had added two volumes on the Constitution.[31] His ultrapatriotic and nationalistic interpretation of our history had run counter to some of the strongest forces at play in American life before the Civil War, and he was soon to be repudiated by those who accepted the standards of a new and more objective scholarship. But before that rejection came, Bancroft had his day in the celebration of the national centennial, so much so that those who wish to recapture the spirit of that centennial can do no better than to read Bancroft's history. From him Miller quoted the famous description of the last hours of the Constitutional Convention. "The members were awe-struck at the results of their councils," Bancroft had said, "the Constitution was a nobler work than any one of them had believed possible to achieve." [32]

Such fulsome expressions of veneration for the Constitution, and for those who gave shape to it, were by no means a new feature of our national life, as the successive volumes of Bancroft's history eloquently testify. But there can be no question that the settlement of certain constitutional issues that had divided the American people before the Civil War, together with the opportunity provided by the national centennial for celebration of the unity they had known at the time of the Revolution, encouraged a new emphasis in the interpretation of our national origins upon the years which had given birth to the Republic. In other words, the Revolutionary fathers now took a distinct step toward becoming *the* founding fathers. I think it may be suggested also that this was the time at which their chief claim to glory first tended to become the drafting

[31] George Bancroft, *History of the Formation of the Constitution of the United States of America* (2 vols., New York, 1882).

[32] Carson, *op. cit.*, II, 288.

of the Constitution rather than the signing of the Declaration. To the development of this forward shift of emphasis there were many contributing factors, among them the fact that some of the newer groups within our society, like the Scotch-Irish before them, found it easier to gain an identification with the Revolutionary period than with the earlier years of settlement.

But it would be a serious mistake to assume that the Revolutionary fathers enjoyed as yet anything approaching a monopoly of the honors. Not only had George Bancroft taught us, as had John Adams and James Wilson before him, that the roots of the great American experiment must be traced back to the seventeenth century, but this was an age much inclined to view institutions as the product of an evolutionary development. Nowhere was this more apparent than in the newly developing universities, where the professional historian was beginning to exert a new influence on the interpretation of our history. The outcome of the Civil War, while assuring the perpetuation of the union the Revolutionary fathers had created, had neither destroyed the states nor denied freedom of play to that provincial pride which so frequently in the past had received stimulation from every advance of national sentiment. No less representative of the age than Bancroft's description of the closing hours of the Constitutional Convention is Alexander Johnston's claim for Connecticut's leadership in the development of democracy and constitutional government. "It is on the banks of the Connecticut," said he in 1887, "that we drew the first breath of that atmosphere which is now so familiar to us. The birthplace of American democracy is Hartford." [33] And there were other birthplaces. One of them, and one that draws attention especially to a new emphasis on constitutional government, was the *Mayflower*. The Pilgrims themselves, and not the ship on which they had chanced to cross the Atlantic, had heretofore been the object of chief interest, but

[33] Alexander Johnston, *Connecticut; A Study of a Commonwealth-democracy* (Boston and New York, 1887), 73.

the vessel itself, presumably because it had provided the stage
on which the Mayflower Compact was drafted, became now an
object of the closest scrutiny by antiquarian and patriot.[34]

Still another birthplace was Jamestown. The claims now
made in behalf of Jamestown have a special interest, if only because they mark the heaviest emphasis any generation of Virginians, either before or since, has placed upon the colonial
origins of that state. These were the years in which Alexander
Brown and Philip Alexander Bruce, both of them concerned
primarily with questions of colonial origins,[35] were the dominant figures in the writing of Virginia's history.

Of the two, Brown is the more interesting. He became active
in the study of Virginia's history late in life and as a result of
a growing controversy over the veracity of Captain John Smith.
It was a controversy that had been touched off in 1859 by
Charles Deane of Massachusetts in his edition of Edward Maria
Wingfield's "Discourse," an item of early Virginiana that unmistakably called into question the story of Smith's rescue by
Pocahontas—a story that had lent romantic interest, as did the
character of Smith himself, to a period of Virginia's history
that all students had found complex and that some had frankly
considered to be otherwise dull. As the debate broadened out
to include students on both sides of the Atlantic, it naturally
became somewhat warm and was enough in itself to stimulate

[34] The Society of Mayflower Descendants, organized in 1894, explained
that its purpose was not so much to honor the individuals who landed at
Plymouth as rather the principle for which they had become exiles. Consequently, the compact, "drafted and signed on the *Mayflower*," a document to be viewed as "the germ of the American Constitution," became
"the key-note of our association, and its date our anniversary day." *The
General Society of Mayflower Descendants* (Published by order of The
General Congress, 1901), 4.

[35] So far as the earlier years of his career are concerned, perhaps the same
could be said of Lyon Gardiner Tyler. See especially his *The Cradle of the
Republic; Jamestown and James River* (Richmond, 1900 and 1906); *England in America, 1580–1652* (New York, 1904); *Narratives of Early Virginia*
(New York, 1907); *Williamsburg, the Old Colonial Capital* (Richmond, c.
1907).

a new interest in the colony's first years.[36] Having determined
to study the question for himself, Brown was led first into an
intensive search for new sources that he published in a two-
volume work in 1890 entitled *The Genesis of the United
States*.[37] Eight years later, he followed up with *The First Republic in America,* and in 1901 he published his *English Politics in Early Virginia History*.[38] In these last two works he
developed to the fullest possible extent the claim that the glory
of Virginia lay, first of all, in the service of the early colony to
the cause of political freedom in England and in America. It
was a theme depending upon the special significance of the first
representative assembly at Jamestown and the argument that
this institution had been established by the parliamentary opponents of James I as an integral part of their struggle against
Stuart absolutism.

This was by no means a novel view. Indeed, it had received
some measure of support from most of Virginia's historians
during the first half of the nineteenth century.[39] Generally
speaking, however, they had shown an inclination to let the
central issue in Virginia's early history turn on the critical question of interpreting the middle years of the seventeenth century,
in part no doubt because of the public's unmistakable attachment to the Cavalier thesis. In the years after the Civil War,
the defensive psychology of the South continued to lend popularity to the notion that a Cavalier migration had largely
shaped the pattern of life in old Virginia. Not until 1910, when
Thomas J. Wertenbaker published his *Patrician and Plebeian*,[40]
did any Virginia historian attack the Cavalier thesis with any-

[36] A subject discussed briefly in my *Dissolution of the Virginia Company*
(New York, 1932), 12–14.

[37] Boston and New York, 1890.

[38] *The First Republic in America* (Boston and New York, 1898); *English
Politics in Early Virginia History* (Boston and New York, 1901).

[39] See above, pp. 131–32.

[40] Thomas Jefferson Wertenbaker, *Patrician and Plebeian in Virginia, or,
The Origin and Development of the Social Classes of the Old Dominion*
(Charlottesville, 1910).

thing approaching the hostility Grigsby had shown toward it before the Civil War.[41] The picture of colonial society presented by Philip Alexander Bruce could have jarred no one who remained dedicated to the idea that Virginia owed much of its essential character to its Cavalier settlers. The difference after the Civil War was that the Virginian, for all his attachment to the Cavalier thesis, wanted no less to be known for his early contribution to the development of self-government in America.[42]

Such is the evidence, at any rate, offered by Virginia's historians. Such, too, is the conclusion indicated by the attitude of northern historians who sought, in the best spirit of a reviving nationalism, to give the South its proper place in the history of the nation. Alexander Brown's propositions met resistance from the beginning, some of it resting simply on the view that the first republic in America obviously had had a more northerly location.[43] But John Fiske, whose very readable volumes probably had a wider influence than those of any other historian of the day, accepted the substance of Brown's interpretation in his *Old Virginia and Her Neighbors,* published in 1897.[44] Thereafter it tended to become in some degree or other the standard interpretation.

When Virginia proposed to celebrate in 1907 the tercentennial of Jamestown as the birthplace of the American nation,

[41] See above, p. 132. Earlier expressions of hostility to the Cavalier thesis can be found, however, as in the *Virginia Magazine of History and Biography,* I (Oct., 1893), 213–22; or in *The Lower Norfolk County Virginia Antiquary,* III (1901), where, in the introduction to the volume, the editor warns that Americans should "stop wasting their time and fooling away their money in ridiculous searches after noble and royal ancestors, almost invariably the result of vanity and almost invariably ending in failure."

[42] Philip Alexander Bruce, *Social Life of Virginia in the Seventeenth Century* (Richmond, 1907). See John Esten Cooke, *Virginia, A History of the People* (Boston, 1883), especially 160–62.

[43] A point made clear enough in the volume on *English Politics in the History of Virginia.*

[44] John Fiske, *Old Virginia and Her Neighbors* (2 vols., Boston and New York, 1897).

the proposal met with a generous response despite the fact that
the idea of a great exposition had been somewhat overplayed
in recent years. Even the Congress, which twice had refused
requested aid to Philadelphia for celebrations of much more
obvious national significance, came through with relatively
handsome appropriations, including one for a permanent monument at Jamestown.[45] It is reported that the Virginia delegation
which first brought the question before Congress was more than
a little disturbed to discover that many congressmen had never
heard of Jamestown, but happily the committee was able to
explain the historical connection between the Virginia House
of Burgesses and the United States Congress.[46]

These were years that also brought significant developments
in New England. Even before the last volume of Palfrey's great
history appeared in 1890, Brooks Adams scandalized "all the
reputable historians" in the state of Massachusetts, as he later
put it, by publishing in 1887 his *Emancipation of Massachusetts*.[47] It was the story of Massachusetts' escape from its original
bondage to an ecclesiastical oligarchy, a story whose significance
Adams summarized in these words: "the struggles and the
agony by which this poor and isolated community freed itself
from its gloomy bondage, the means by which it secularized its
education and government, won for itself the blessing of free
thought and speech, and matured a system of constitutional
liberty which has been the foundation of the American Union,
rise in dignity to one of the supreme efforts of mankind." [48]
Though not inclined to set up new idols while tearing down
old ones, Adams dealt sympathetically with Mrs. Hutchinson,
the Quakers, the Anabaptists, and other victims of Puritan
intolerance who by their sacrifice had helped to establish "our

[45] Cuyler Reynolds, *New York at the Jamestown Exposition* (Albany,
1909), 129–31.

[46] *Ibid.*, 127.

[47] Brooks Adams, *The Law of Civilization and Decay, An Essay on History* (New York, 1943), 6, where Charles A. Beard by way of introduction
to a new edition quotes the author.

[48] *The Emancipation of Massachusetts* (Boston and New York, 1887), 43.

perfect liberty of thought and speech." For the "learned clergy-men who have been the chief historians of the Puritan commonwealth," or as Adams described them in another place, "the reverend historians of the theocracy," he showed a sharply phrased contempt. Admitting that the Quakers had been enthusiastic and extravagant, he declared: "The question at issue is not their social attractiveness, but the cause whose consequence was a virulent persecution." [49]

To this attack on the filio-pietists by Brooks, his brother Charles Francis Adams added his own hardly less sensational efforts. After his *Chapters of Erie* had won him fame in 1871 for their revelations as to railway finances, the younger Charles Francis Adams became interested in the study of history as a result of an invitation in 1873 to deliver the oration on the occasion of the 250th anniversary of the settlement of Weymouth.[50] The address led to his election to membership in the Massachusetts Historical Society, of which he was president for the twenty years following 1895, and to an interest in historical studies that brought him in time the presidency of the American Historical Association. In 1893 he published a small volume entitled *Massachusetts: Its Historians and Its History,* which presented to the public some iconoclastic ideas he had previously tested on the students of Professor Channing's class in American history at Harvard.[51]

Adams began his discussion by quoting two inscriptions prepared by President Eliot of Harvard for the Water-Gate at the Chicago Exposition of 1893. The one hailed civil liberty as "The Means of Building Up Personal and National Character," the other toleration in religion as "The Best Fruit of the Last Four Centuries." Adams asked Channing's students, and

[49] *Ibid.*, 135, 140.

[50] *Charles Francis Adams, 1835–1915, An Autobiography, with a Memorial Address Delivered November 17, 1915, by Henry Cabot Lodge* (Boston and New York, 1916), 179–82.

[51] Charles Francis Adams, *Massachusetts: Its Historians and Its History, An Object Lesson* (Boston and New York, 1893).

then his readers, to accept these propositions as a standard for judging the history of the state. He then went on to find that "the record of no community" in the development of civil liberty was "more creditable, more consistent, nor, indeed, more important than that of the community composing the Commonwealth of Massachusetts." Its godfathers had been Hampden, and Milton, and Cromwell, and from "the days of settlement, through the Revolutionary troubles, down to the fall of slavery, so far as the principles of civil liberty and human rights are concerned," according to Adams, Massachusetts had "always been at the front." But on the question of religious freedom, he declared, her record could be viewed as "scarcely even creditable." The province had faced the issue as early as 1637 and had decided it so wrongly that her historians had "wriggled and squirmed" in the presence of the record ever since. If Massachusetts did not go to the rear of the advancing column of mankind, it had taken its position well toward the rear and there it had remained until others had settled the issue. Even at the time of the Revolution, the concessions made to a new spirit of tolerance had been incomplete and were grudgingly made at that. So far was Massachusetts from leadership in man's struggle for religious freedom that her record was "in degree only less discreditable than that of Spain."

In these views, though they were sharply attacked in Massachusetts,[52] one finds a promise that the nation might soon reach agreement on some of the historical issues that had theretofore sharply divided it.[53] Especially significant was the concession on the issue of religious freedom, for this had long been a chief bone of contention. If it could be admitted that the settlers of Massachusetts, like those at Jamestown, were to be credited chiefly for their contribution to the establishment of self-government in this country, then would the way be open for

[52] See Robert C. Winthrop's attack in the Massachusetts Historical Society *Proceedings*, 2d ser., VIII, 378–82.

[53] Among other places, the book received a warm welcome in Rhode Island. Rhode Island Historical Society *Publications,* II, 29.

assignment of the highest honors in the development of religious freedom to Rhode Island, to Maryland, to Pennsylvania,
and to the Revolutionary fathers who finally had made of this
ideal one of the cardinal principles of our national union. I
speak of this as a promise simply because a good deal of bickering of the sort that had been so characteristic of the earlier
years of the nineteenth century continued. In the very years of
Virginia's tercentennial celebrations, there were some in New
England who felt compelled to argue that the first republic in
America had been a Yankee invention.[54] The Rhode Island
Historical Society seems to have been not yet satisfied that Roger
Williams had been given the recognition rightfully belonging
to him.[55] But there were also evidences that the old issues were
losing something of their former interest. For example, influential members of the Massachusetts Historical Society were
now arguing that the time had come for closer attention to the
national period of our history and for less emphasis on questions of colonial origins.[56] The Pennsylvania Historical Society,
though losing none of its interest in William Penn, was now
encouraging attention to the role of the German and Irish
settlers in the history of the state.[57] I think there is good reason
for saying that many of the old interests were becoming antiquarian in the sense that only antiquarians were interested in
them.

But with this promise that the older type of rivalry might
disappear there came also new evidences of division. In this
new division provincial boundaries counted for little. Instead,
the contest now featured the efforts, on the one hand, of a growing number of so-called patriotic societies having some special

[54] See, for example, Morton Dexter's "Some Differences between Plymouth and Jamestown," Colonial Society of Massachusetts *Publications*, XII,
256–70.
[55] As in Zachariah Allen's presidential address of 1882, Rhode Island
Historical Society *Proceedings*, 1881–82.
[56] Massachusetts Historical Society *Proceedings*, 2d ser., XII, 296.
[57] As in the *Pennsylvania Magazine of History and Biography*, II (1878),
117.

genealogical qualification for membership and, on the other
hand, of a new type of historical society dedicated to the purpose of establishing beyond dispute the contribution to our
founding that had been made by some ethnic group of settlers.
These later years of the nineteenth century witnessed the organization of the Sons of the Revolution, which usually gives 1876
as its date of origin, the Sons of the American Revolution in
1889, the Daughters of the American Revolution and the Colonial Dames of America in 1890, the Daughters of the Revolution in 1891, the Daughters of the Cincinnati and the Colonial
Order of the Acorn in 1894, the Children of the Revolution in
1895, the Colonial Daughters of the XVIIth Century, the Order
of the Descendants of Colonial Governors Prior to 1750, and
the Order of the Founders and Patriots of America in 1896,
the Society of American Wars of the United States and the Society of Mayflower Descendants in 1897, the Daughters of the
Founders and Patriots of America in 1898, and there have been
others, among them the Society of Colonial Wars and the
Colonial Society of Massachusetts. The Huguenot Society was
organized in 1883, the Holland Society in 1885, the Scotch-
Irish Historical Society in 1889, the American Jewish Historical
Society in 1892, and the American-Irish Historical Society and
the German-American Historical Society in 1897.[58] This listing
is representative, not complete.

The patriotic order was of course by no means a new feature
of American life. As is well known, the officers of the disband-
ing Continental Army in 1783 had organized the Society of the
Cincinnati, and later wars had produced such organizations as
the Aztec Club of 1847 or the Military Order of the Loyal
Legion of the United States established in 1865. Though a vet-

[58] Frederick A. Virkus, ed., *The Abridged Compendium of American
Genealogy* (Chicago, 1925), 999–1007, provides a convenient listing of patriotic orders; A. P. C. Griffin, *Bibliography of American Historical Societies* is helpful in identifying the other organizations. See also Wallace E.
Davies, *Patriotism on Parade; The Story of Veterans' and Hereditary Organizations in America, 1783–1900* (Cambridge, Mass., 1955), a study published since these lectures were delivered.

erans' organization in the first instance, this type of society had followed the practice of opening membership to the sons of the original members and time only was required to bring any one of the orders to a primary dependence upon some special pride of ancestry. The era of the Know-Nothing movement had produced a variety of professedly patriotic organizations, most of which had not survived the Civil War, but one of them, The Patriotic Order Sons of America, not only survived the war but grew thereafter to such strength as to hold the place of honor at the head of the first division in the great parade that opened the centennial observances at Philadelphia in 1887.[59] Only in the multiplication of such organizations, all of them dedicated to the same general purpose, in the increasingly prominent part taken by women's organizations, and in the very marked tendency to identify patriotic responsibilities with descent from a colonial ancestry does one find anything new in these developments of the late nineteenth century.

It may be that my classification of these new organizations is oversimplified. Perhaps I should have drawn some distinction between societies like the Sons and Daughters of the Revolution, and such organizations as the Colonial Dames or the Society of Mayflower Descendants. There is some difference if only because the latter group has focused its attention on the colonial as distinct from the Revolutionary period. I have made no exact check, but it has also seemed to me that the colonial societies, if I may designate them thus for convenience, have shown greater concern for the collection, preservation, and publication of historical materials pertaining to their special province than has the other group. The Mayflower Descendants published their own historical and genealogical magazine for over thirty years and served thus to bring to light additional minutiae, sometimes useful, on the history of the Pilgrims and of the *Mayflower*.[60] The Colonial Society of Massachusetts had

[59] Carson, *op. cit.*, II, 20.

[60] *The Mayflower Descendant; a Quarterly Magazine of Pilgrim Genealogy and History* (34 vols., 1899–1937).

until more recent years the usual genealogical qualification for membership but more than one of Harvard's professors have been able to meet the test, and their influence has helped to make of the Society's serial publications a frequently valuable source of information for the student of American history. But there would seem to be little reason for drawing fine distinctions. All these societies established some special genealogical qualification for membership, and all justified their establishment by a need to protect the principles upon which the country had been founded.

In any discussion of the patriotic societies, the first thing that should be said is that they ought not be taken too seriously. We are notoriously a nation of joiners and the patriotic order, like the fraternal order, has served primarily perhaps to provide one more outlet for the extraordinary energies the modern American is inclined to devote to his organizations. Whatever may be the worthy purpose given in justification for the organization's existence, participation in its activity, whether in the meeting of the local chapter or in the larger assembly of its national congress or convention, is valued very largely for the social opportunities provided. When such opportunities can be identified with some suggestion of social exclusiveness, they seem to become all the more valued by the American, and since an ancient American lineage had become one of the tests of social standing, the patriotic society had this special attraction to offer. But before labeling such societies as undemocratic, one should bear in mind that any organization basing its primary requirement for membership on the accident of birth has made a fundamental concession to democracy. On the several occasions on which I have agreed to address some patriotic society, it has been my impression that a major attraction for many members must be the opportunity for fraternal association with those few who are unmistakably the elite of the town.

It should also be observed that a very large part of the energies of such societies has been given over to the simple task of keeping the organization going. This seems to have been especially true of those societies that occupied what may be described as a marginal position in the larger movement, no doubt because they were superfluous to any real need that might be admitted. The incomplete list I have already given is enough to suggest that a certain ingenuity was required at times to discover some distinctive basis of membership that would justify the organization of a new society. Thus when the Order of The Founders and Patriots of America was organized in 1896, the field was already filling up with hereditary societies for descendants, on the one hand, of Revolutionary patriots and, on the other, of the first settlers. But it had been noted by several gentlemen that a man of unimpeachable colonial ancestry might acquire membership in a patriotic society—that is, one of the colonial orders—even though his ancestors had been Tories at the time of the Revolution, just as a man might qualify for the Sons of the Revolution without any special distinction in his pre-Revolutionary ancestry. Consequently, the new order found justification for its organization by requiring proof of descent in the male line of father or mother from a colonist settled in America within fifty years of the founding of Jamestown (specifically, before May 13, 1657) and further proof of descent in the same line from a patriot at the time of the Revolution.[61] It hardly needs to be added that this was an idea good enough to save the new order from the risks of a marginal position, for this society became one of the more exclusive.

The purposes of the organization, as announced in its charter, are representative—to "associate" men of a similar ancestry, to teach reverent regard for the founders and the patriots, to preserve historical records and monuments, to commemorate appropriate historic events, and to serve other historical and patriotic purposes.[62] In the type of organization adopted by such societies one finds little variation, except in

[61] *The Order of the Founders and Patriots of America; Register: 1902* (published by authority of the General Court, 1902, n.d.), 9–25.

[62] *Ibid.*, 14–25.

terminology, from a pattern shaped basically by our federal system of government. Most of them sought some national organization and functioned in addition through state and local units. The colonial orders showed a preference for terminology associated with pre-Revolutionary government in America, as in the use of "court" to designate assemblies of the membership. Once again, the growth of the patriotic order provides occasion for comment on the special opportunities and the special needs for social intercourse in our urban communities.

That the internal politics of the movement itself absorbed much time and energy is indicated by the contests dividing the two orders devoted to perpetuating the memory of the Revolutionary patriots—the Sons of the Revolution and the Sons of the American Revolution. The story is complex, and I offer the following brief account with apologies for any error that may have resulted from incomplete research. In 1875, it appears, a group of gentlemen in San Francisco had organized as "The Sons of Revolutionary Sires," with a provision in their constitution for affiliation with auxiliary societies that might be organized in other states. In 1883, certain gentlemen in New York City organized an independent society described as the Sons of the Revolution, with a similar provision for auxiliary branches in other states. But when the Sons of the Revolution were organized in Philadelphia in 1888 it was decided that the society would not be auxiliary to New York, and in that same year some of the members of the New York society who were residents of New Jersey, while making plans for a state society of their own, seem to have found a comparable objection to the idea of an auxiliary status. At any rate, they took the lead in promoting the organization of independent societies in other states with a view to their association on a coequal basis in a national society. The hope apparently was to bring effective pressure upon New York for modification of its auxiliary provision, but not even a meeting of representatives from eighteen state societies held in the hallowed surroundings of Fraunces

Tavern in 1889 could resolve the differences. With the New York and Philadelphia societies abstaining, the convention then proceeded to establish the Sons of the American Revolution.[63] Subsequently, the Sons of the Revolution were organized into a national society, and the sons of our Revolutionary fathers have remained divided to this day, despite several efforts to effect a union. Similarly, the daughters have been divided. But the DAR, organized in 1890, as a result of the SAR's refusal to admit women to membership, took an early lead over the Daughters of the Revolution, organized in the next year.[64]

I have made no attempt to check membership totals, for they could be easily misleading as a result of the very evident and considerable duplication of membership among the several societies. The typical American at this time was a man who belonged to many different organizations and devoted his energies to more than one worthy cause.[65]

For the purpose of making a check on the early activity of the patriotic societies, I have selected the Daughters of the American Revolution. Perhaps I should say that this choice has been influenced in part by the remark of a colleague at lunch one day—he is a Democrat—that it probably could be proved that the DAR had supported every reactionary cause that has flourished in this country since its organization. I thought I might look into the question, and here is what I found.

[63] See Louis H. Cornish, ed., *National Register of the Society of the Sons of the American Revolution* (New York, 1902), 10–14. Also, Charles W. Ferguson's unfriendly account in *Fifty Million Brothers* (New York, 1937), 263–65. Cf. Davies, *Patriotism on Parade*, 50–53.

[64] See report of D.A.R., Sen. Doc. 164, 55th Cong., 3d Sess. (Washington, 1899), which contains the constitution and gives a history of the society's origins.

[65] Thus Admiral Meade of the American-Irish Historical Society died in 1897 as a member of the Order of the Founders and Patriots of America, the Society of Colonial Wars, the Military Order of Foreign Wars, the Military Order of the Loyal Legion of the United States, the Grand Army of the Republic, the California Pioneer Society of New York City, and the New England Society of New York. See memorial in *Journal of the American-Irish Historical Society,* I (Boston, 1898), 55–57.

It is very clear from the early records of the DAR, as it is of other patriotic societies I have had time to investigate, that a major inspiration, perhaps the chief inspiration, for its organization came from the fears that had been stirred by what was currently described as foreign immigration. And yet, if I may judge by the official action of the national congresses, the DAR refused to identify itself with the cause of immigration restriction. Like other patriotic societies, it defined its function as strictly nonpolitical and abstained from efforts to advise the government on questions of public policy. Even in 1898, a national congress meeting in Washington one week after the *Maine* had been sunk voted down proposals, described in the record as somewhat hysterical, that the society advise the government on the action it should take. Instead, it was decided that attention should be directed toward preparation for those emergencies of camp and hospital "which womanly foresight assured us would call for womanly assistance" in the event of war. The chief action taken, therefore, was an offer of help to the surgeon-general in the recruitment of nurses and an effort to alert local chapters to opportunities for welfare work among the troops and their families.[66]

On the question of immigration, the DAR interpreted its function to be that of educating the immigrants, and more especially the adults, in the principles of the American government and the glories of our history. It must be admitted, I believe, that the vast numbers of non-English-speaking immigrants who were crowding together in the slums of our cities had stirred a genuine fear that the principles of that government might be subverted in time through what was described as a blotting out of the memory of the Revolution in the common mass of the people. The blame for this prospect, so far at least as official statements may be accepted as the evidence, was not attached to the immigrant. The fault was attributed instead to the failure of older American stocks to do what they

[66] Report of D.A.R. for 1897–98, Sen. Doc. 425, 56th Cong., 1st Sess. (Washington, 1900), 45–46, 55, 57, 62.

could to keep that memory alive. Hence, the familiar emphasis in the program of the DAR and other such organizations on the erection of statues to Revolutionary heroes, the marking of the graves of Revolutionary soldiers, the hanging of Washington's picture, together with framed copies of the Declaration of Independence and of the Constitution, on our schoolroom walls, and the establishment of prizes for school essays on the history or government of the United States.[67]

In view of the stand the DAR took on some of the issues of the period running down to the First World War, it can be said perhaps that the daughters made some compromises with their original statements of policy. They lent support to movements for the regulation of the hours and conditions of labor for women and children. They enlisted in the cause of conservation. A little later they were caught up by the ideal of arbitration and of a world court as a means for the settlement of international differences. They favored legislation for the establishment of a national university. When war came in Europe, they gave substantial help to Belgian relief and later to American preparedness, this last being a pointer perhaps to further divergences from the line of original policy.[68] But such departures as one finds before 1917 suggest chiefly that the DAR had been infected by the virus of Progressivism.

In thus selecting the DAR for examination, I may be guilty of giving too much emphasis for this period of time to the Revolutionary societies. It may well be that the primary emphasis belongs rather to those societies that stressed the importance

[67] Both Davies' *Patriotism on Parade* and John Higham's *Strangers in the Land* (New Brunswick, 1955) indicate that the attitude of the DAR toward immigration restriction was representative of the position taken by most such societies.

[68] Reports of D.A.R., Sen. Doc. 117, 61st Cong., 1st Sess. (Washington, 1909), 41; Sen. Doc. 517, 61st Cong., 2d Sess. (Washington, 1910), 41; Sen. Doc. 371, 62d Cong., 2d Sess. (Washington, 1912), 35, 47; Sen. Doc. 9, 63d Cong., 1st Sess. (Washington, 1913), 46; Sen. Doc. 392, v, 14, 64th Cong., 1st Sess. (Washington, 1916), 22, 43–44; Sen. Doc. 710, 64th Cong., 2d Sess. (Washington, 1917), 18, 27, 74.

of a colonial ancestry, if only because their activity is suggestive of a continuing resistance to a new tendency for the Revolutionary fathers to acquire the dominant position in the
national tradition. The aims of the colonial societies were basically the same as those of the Revolutionary societies, and the
programs they developed were in no essential way different.
But there was one difference. By the very conditions imposed
on membership, the members of the colonial societies were
identified by a special sense of belonging to the older stock of
settlers. I am not so interested in the extra degree of social
snobbery that may or may not have been involved as in the
evidence of a fear that the colonial forefathers, no less than the
Revolutionary fathers, might be forgotten.

This fear seems to have been especially acute in New England,
where in the words of James Phinney Baxter, for many years
president of the New England Historic-Genealogical Society,
"the American idea" had long been viewed as "essentially the
New England idea." [69] Disturbed by the thought that "the New
England type of civilization" might "give way here in Massachusetts to that of the Old World races who have been reared
in subjection, ignorance and poverty," Mr. Baxter came to advocate the building in Boston of a "New England Pantheon or
Temple of Honor" as a memorial to the men "who laid in New
England the foundations of popular government." For that
purpose he left $50,000 in his will at his death in 1921, but the
city of Boston refused the gift.[70]

However understandable may have been this fear for the
future of a long cherished tradition, it was clearly based upon
some misunderstanding of the attitude of the more recent immigrant. The immigrant in this country has rarely been an
enemy to its established tradition. He may have been puzzled
at times by some aspects of it. He may have suffered from a

[69] *New England Historical and Genealogical Register*, LVII (1903), xiv–
xvi.
[70] *New England Historical and Genealogical Register*, LXXI (1917), xi–
xiii; XCIX (1945), 185–87.

sense of rejection by his neighbors and chiefly by their suggestion that he had no part in the founding of the country. He
has often shown his shrewdness by recognizing that one interpretation of that tradition served his own interest better than
did another. But he has never really rebelled. Whatever the
difficulties experienced by the first and the second generations,
he has come in time to be no different from all his predecessors.
He has accepted the tradition in all its essentials, and he has
accepted it by making it his own. In so doing, he has not
quarreled with the rules of the game as established by those
who played it before him. He agrees that this country owes its
greatness to the ideals of those who first established it, and he
agrees that it was established some time before 1789. He argues
only that his own people were here before that date and that
they played the part they should have played. And in making
his argument, let me suggest, he shows a degree of filial piety
that would put a descendant of the Mayflower Pilgrims to
shame.

The Irish always provide a good example, if only because
they have a colorful way of expressing their sentiments. "A Call
for the Organization of an American Historical Society whose
Special Line of Research Shall Be the History of the Irish Element in the Composition of the American People" went out
from Boston, that old seat of Puritanism, in 1896.[71] The letter,
addressed to gentlemen of Irish ancestry in various parts of the
country, gave vigorous expression to a deep-seated resentment
toward all efforts by others to establish an exclusive claim on
the founding fathers in these words: "Certain elements in the
make-up of the American people have not hesitated on occasion
to masquerade, at the expense of the Irish, in borrowed plumes,
and to pose under plundered laurels." The time had come,
therefore, "for honest historians to look after the rights of the
lawful owners." In somewhat less bombastic terms, the constitution of the American-Irish Historical Society expressed the

[71] *The Journal of the American-Irish Historical Society,* I (Boston, 1898),
1–5.

hope that had inspired its organization in these words: "In the days to come, that lie in the womb of the future, when all the various elements that have gone and are going to make the republic great, are united in the American,—the man who in his person will represent the bravest elements of all the old races of earth,—we desire that the deeds and accomplishments of our element shall be written in the book of the new race, telling what we did and no more; giving us our rightful place by the side of the others." [72]

Charles A. DeCourcey of Lawrence, Massachusetts, probably came closer to explaining the basic reason for organizing such a society when he commented on the slurs "cast upon every school child of Irish parentage in the past, and to some extent today." Said he: "We were foreign. We did not feel at home. But we began to know. We began to feel at home. We learned of our race's participation in the up-building of the nation. We will prove our part in America's history; then the children as Americans can feel as Americans." [73]

This was the end to which the American-Irish Historical Society devoted its energies, as did others like it. There were no requirements for membership other than those of a good moral character and an interest in the purposes of the organization—tests, incidentally, that both Theodore Roosevelt and Woodrow Wilson readily agreed to meet, Roosevelt in 1897 and Wilson in 1911.[74] When members and guests of the society assembled for its second scheduled meeting on April 19, 1897, the anniversary of the Battle of Lexington, they listened after a good dinner to a reading of "Paul Revere's Ride," and then to papers on "The Irish Bacons who Settled at Dedham, Mass., in 1640," on Major John Sullivan's seizure of the gunpowder at Fort William and Mary, on the men of Irish name who stood on the green at Lexington in 1775, and on "The Irishman,

[72] *Ibid.*, I, 7–14.   [73] *Ibid.*, I, 18.

[74] Roosevelt signed the letter of invitation to the original meeting for organization. On Wilson, see Michael J. O'Brien, *An Alleged First Census of the American People* (New York, 1930), 4.

Ethnologically Considered." [75] And so went other very satis-factory programs. Especially noticeable is the continuing effort, depending upon the names of the first settlers, to prove that many of the supposedly English founders of the colonies had been actually Irish.

The subject, however, to which early speakers most often turned, to the obvious satisfaction of the audience, was the sub-ject of "The Scotch-Irish Myth." This term "Scotch-Irish" is one that has come to be well established in the national usage as a convenient designation for the Protestant Ulstermen who migrated to America in large numbers during the eighteenth century, but its establishment has come only over the vigorous protest of the American-Irish Historical Society. How early the subject was introduced into its deliberations is indicated by the opening remarks made from the chair by Thomas J. Gargan at the society's first meeting. His remarks began: "We claim that due credit has not been given to the Irish contributions. That through prejudice or through gross ignorance there has grown up a myth about the Scotch-Irish. Of all the myths that have crept into history this is the most mythical. Why any man should be ashamed of his honorable Irish ancestry surpasses my comprehension and subjects the man who attempts to deny it to the scorn and contempt of all honest and intelligent men." [76] Later in the evening, Mr. Flatley returned to the sub-ject in an impromptu speech but unhappily the minutes record only that he "handled the 'Scotch-Irish' myth without gloves." [77] It remained a favorite theme of Mr. Gargan, who at the third meeting of the society declared: "We respect the Germans, the French, the Italians, and the genuine Scotchman; but for that masquerading misnomer, the Scotch-Irishman, who claims no ancestry and no country as his own, we have only contempt; and he will go down to posterity as he deserves, 'unwept, un-honored, and unsung.' " [78]

This last statement was a prediction lacking in caution, for

---

[75] *Ibid.*, I, 31–54.   [76] *Ibid.*, I, 14–15.
[77] *Ibid.*, I, 18.   [78] *Ibid.*, I, 65.

the Scotch-Irish Historical Society had been organized at Columbia, Tennessee, in 1889, and a grand occasion it was for all the sons of Ulster who were privileged to be present. Laying claim at the very outset of the proceedings to Patrick Henry, Thomas Jefferson, John Witherspoon, John Paul Jones, James Madison, John Marshall, Andrew Jackson, James K. Polk, James Buchanan, Abraham Lincoln, Ulysses S. Grant, Robert Fulton, Horace Greeley, and the McCormick reaper, the Scotch-Irish Congress of some 6,000 to 10,000 representatives of many different parts of the country assembled in President Polk's home town of Columbia for a three-day session beginning on May 8, 1889.[79] There were parades and many speeches delivered in a tent that had been pitched for the purpose. "This race," declared Mr. McClelland of the German Theological Seminary of Dubuque, Iowa, "has the strong will, religiosity, and shrewdness of the Hebrew, the philosophic profundity of the German, the political sagacity and conservatism of the English, and withal, when needs be, the audacity of the French." [80] The most acceptable evidence of this audacity was perhaps that presented by Col. Joseph F. Johnston of Birmingham and late of the Confederate army, who as temporary chairman invited attention to certain statistics as to the bloodiest engagement of the recent Civil War. It had been at Gettysburg when the 26th North Carolina Regiment and the 151st from Pennsylvania had the great misfortune to meet on a battlefield as representatives of the two states most heavily populated by the Scotch-Irish. Needless to say, the statistics were appalling and most gratifying to the audience.[81]

The Scotch-Irish Historical Society, which resulted from these deliberations, was organized for social as well as historical purposes. It was observed, not altogether accurately, that every other people in America had banded together "for purposes of mutual pleasure and assistance." The society, in addition to

[79] *The Scotch-Irish in America; Proceedings of the Scotch-Irish Congress at Columbia, Tennessee, May 8–11, 1889* (Nashville, 1896).
[80] *Ibid.,* 20.   [81] *Ibid.,* 28–29.

promoting a desirable social intercourse, would collect historical data, of which the College of New Jersey at Princeton had agreed to become the custodian.[82]

The Scotch-Irishman to whose glorification this society was dedicated was no new figure in American history. He had emerged during the first half of the nineteenth century, through the efforts chiefly of the Presbyterian clergy, as a paragon of all the Calvinistic virtues, and he was now taken over by the Scotch-Irish Historical Society without having his stature reduced by even an inch. In our modern textbooks he continues to be depicted very much as his sponsors would wish.

The special offense the Scotch-Irishman gave to members of the American-Irish Historical Society was not attributable to his Protestantism, for there were many Protestants in that society, but to the fact that as an Irishman emigrating to America in the eighteenth century he might have eased the path for all Irishmen who emigrated in the nineteenth century. Instead, with a hyphenated name which placed the emphasis first upon a Scottish ancestry, this man seemed to deny that he was Irish —or rather his descendants did. The Scotch-Irish designation is as old as the eighteenth century, but it seems not to have become a fixed and unvarying usage until well into the nineteenth century.[83] It would appear to be definitely an Americanism, unknown in the usage of other parts of the English-speaking world and serving principally to distinguish between immigrants from Ireland.

In thus using the Irish as an example, I have no intention to suggest that they alone bestirred themselves at this time in the interest of justice to their ancestors. The Massachusetts Historical Society in May, 1887, was much disturbed because of a

---

[82] *Ibid.*, 9. Inquiry indicates that no such archives have been deposited with the Princeton University Library.

[83] On this question, see discussion in Wayland F. Dunaway, *The Scotch-Irish of Colonial Pennsylvania* (Chapel Hill, 1944), 4–8. My own observation is that the term "Scotch-Irish" remained until the middle of the nineteenth century merely one of the ways in which the Irish settlers of the eighteenth century might be designated.

bill recently passed by both houses of the state legislature for erection of a monument to the five men killed in the Boston Massacre of 1770. It was agreed by the members of the society that the victims in that celebrated incident had been rioters, not patriots, for the true patriot, it was agreed, had consistently followed a peaceful and orderly method of protest. The society, consequently, expressed its opposition to the measure in a resolution for presentation to the governor, but in so doing recorded its own lack of hope for success. Not only had one of the victims been Irish, but another was a Negro. The governor, it was assumed, would yield to pressure.[84]

The insistent demand for special recognition of the contributions a variety of ethnic groups had made to the founding of the country is most impressively recorded for us in an enormous bibliography that began now to be built of works devoted to the place in American history belonging to the Jew, the German, the Welshman, the Huguenot, the Scot, the Scotch-Irishman, and others. I do not need to go into detail. All of us who have studied American history are familiar in some degree with this bibliography and know the extent of our continuing dependence upon it in the effort to capture the full grandeur of a truly great migration. In using these works, we have known impatience with the antiquarian's care to include every available detail on the first settlers of a particular race, if I may use the term common to the time. We have been frequently repulsed by a filial piety exceeding that found in the earlier comments of Daniel Webster on the Pilgrim Fathers. In our search for useful material, we have skipped over the long lists of presidents of the United States, of justices of the Supreme Court, of members of the Senate, of state governors, or of military leaders who carried in their veins the blood of Scotland,

---

[84] Massachusetts Historical Society *Proceedings,* 2d ser., III, 313–18; Randolph G. Adams, "New Light on the Boston Massacre," American Antiquarian Society Proceedings, new ser., XLVII, 259–354. See the later protest of Samuel A. Green in American Antiquarian Society *Proceedings,* new ser., XIV, 40–53.

Ireland, Wales, Germany, Scandinavia, France, Italy, and so on. And in the skipping we have noticed not a little duplication.

The question I would like to raise in the time that remains is the question of why all this effort was expended. In the first place, it should be said that this was a natural development representing the normal pride of ancestry that already had stimulated so much of the attention given to questions of our national origins. The very circumstances of our national life, the many divisions and subdivisions into which we fell in our political or religious life, from the beginning had encouraged a somewhat competitive approach to the problem of our common origins, with each group looking out for its own ancestors. That certain groups who had not yet taken care of that responsibility—because they had been too few or too scattered to find the necessary encouragement, or because they had been too rapidly assimilated to sense the need, or because as more recent immigrants they had been too busy with the hard problem of getting established in a new world—should now have recognized the need to prove their contribution to the founding of America, was, I repeat, only natural.

But this is hardly a sufficient answer, and as one attempts to find the additional influence, he can not help but notice the very heavy emphasis upon ethnological distinctions. The very phrasing commonly used speaks now not just of a familiar pride of ancestry but of the pride of race. In a way already made familiar by the genealogist who brought his history of the family to a fitting conclusion with a summary of family traits, the historians of our varied ethnological groups showed a strong inclination to specify the particular qualities of character their own groups had contributed to America. I need not attempt to be specific, for it would be difficult to discover an original trait any one of them had contributed.

Had this historical effort been restricted only to such groups as had entered the country so recently as to feel victimized by the attitude of their predecessors, the explanation would be a simple one. But here were representatives of the Huguenot and Dutch settlers, who had given their names to some of the most securely established of our families, and of the Scotch-Irish and the Germans, who had settled in large numbers well before the Revolution. In short, this new demand for recognition came in no small part from those who had no great trouble in qualifying for membership in more than one of our patriotic societies. What was it that bothered them?

The answer, I suspect, is that the Anglo-Saxons seemed to be on the point of taking over the legend of the founding fathers. We had been very largely an English people in our first origins, and many of us had never lost a sense of pride in that fact. It had been as Englishmen that we fought the Spaniard and the Frenchman for the possession of North America, and the first steps we had taken toward overcoming a strong sense of provincial distinctions had been in the effort to guarantee that an English type of civilization would be dominant on this continent. Not even the Revolution had repudiated all our English heritage, and important elements in our population had been quick to identify themselves thereafter with a tradition basically English. This was especially true of New England, whose influence on the writing of our history was greater than that of any other section of the country. And now came still other encouragements to a special emphasis on our English origins.

One of these was the encouragement given by the new professional historian, whose growing influence is conveniently marked by the organization of the American Historical Association in 1884. By the professional historian I mean of course some one like myself, who has been professionally trained for the study of history in a graduate school devoted to the training of professional scholars, who has been accredited as a professional by award of the Ph.D. degree, and who teaches history for a living—a man to whom the study and writing of history is something more than the avocation pursued by a gentleman in his spare time. As our colleges and universities increasingly sought his services for instruction in the field of history, his influence was a growing one. In the development of university training, as is well known, we leaned most heavily upon the German universities, from which we borrowed the seminar method of instruction and the Ph.D. itself. Many of the most influential of our early university professors of American history were German-trained, and from their German professors they had taken over much of the Teutonic view of history. This was a view, if I may put it so briefly as perhaps to do violence to fact, that depended upon the concept of an Aryan race that had found its fullest development, especially in its services to the cause of civilization, in Northern Europe. In saying this, I do not mean to suggest that we were in the process of being Germanized, for as Edward N. Saveth has shown in his admirable study of *American Historians and European Immigrants,* American students with few exceptions translated the concept of Teutonic supremacy into the terms of Anglo-Saxon supremacy.[85] They thus tended to identify themselves with the views of E. A. Freeman, the English historian who saw the greatest development of Teutonic character in England, where men, despite the Norman conquest, had been less subject to the diffusion resulting from association with the Romantic peoples. Mr. Freeman, it should be noted, owed a part of his influence in America to his willingness to admit that the English emigrants to America in the seventeenth century had carried many of the virtues of their race with them and thus to find in the New England town meeting one more proof in support of his view of history.

This, of course, was a racist concept of history and it should be said that by no means all our historians accepted it. But many of them did, among them John Fiske, perhaps the most influential historian of the age insofar as popular opinion was concerned. Mr. Fiske put some qualification on his acceptance of Aryanism and even to a lesser extent of Anglo-Saxonism, but he was ready enough to accept the English view of our origins. As a man who had gained fame as the popularizer

[85] Edward N. Saveth, *American Historians and European Immigrants, 1875–1925* (New York, 1948), 15.

of Charles Darwin and Herbert Spencer before he turned his attention to his immensely successful books on American history, he easily became a spokesman for the view that the greatness of this nation was attributable largely to its English origins.[86]

How far this view might be carried could be suggested by many quotations. But it will be enough to cite only Philip Alexander Bruce, whose *Institutional History of Virginia in the Seventeenth Century* outranks all other works of the time on Virginia's early history, except for his own earlier *Economic History of Virginia in the Seventeenth Century*.[87] In a frequently eloquent conclusion to his two-volume study of Virginia's institutional origins, Mr. Bruce paid tribute to the English settlers of Virginia.[88] They had been men who knew the traditions and conventions of old England. He found their divergences from the patterns of social and institutional usage in old England to be few, only such as were required by the different circumstances of life in America. Not even the Revolution, said he, "could efface on our Continent the mighty work which England had done through the growth of Virginia, and the other American communities, however far, even in Colonial times, some of the latter may, in many respects, have drifted from the distinctive landmarks of the Mother Country." Bruce was too honest a historian not to recognize that non-English stocks had emigrated to America in large numbers, but he argued that these people were destined "to see their children grow up almost as deeply affected by the spirit of the fundamental institutions of England, . . . as if they were of the purest Anglo-Saxon stock." And so he saw in the settlement of Jamestown "the greatest of all events in the modern history of the Anglo-Saxon race, and one of the very greatest in the history of the world."

[86] *Ibid.*, 32–42.

[87] Bruce, *Economic History of Virginia in the Seventeenth Century* (2 vols., New York, 1895); *Institutional History of Virginia in the Seventeenth Century* (2 vols., 1910).

[88] *Institutional History,* II, 605–36, and for quotations, 634–36.

On his last page, Bruce speaks almost as if he were an Englishman. "If to-morrow," said he, "a vast wave from the Atlantic, set in motion by some appalling convulsion of nature, should sink England for ever below the level of the ocean, and thus destroy the last remnant of her population and the last vestige of her cities and her fields, yet in her spirit, which represents all that is highest in nations as in individual men, she would still survive in that great Power overseas, whose seed she planted, whose growth she nourished, and whose chief claim to the respect of mankind will always consist in upholding those general ideas of law, government, and morality, which its people inherited from that little island lying like an emerald in the stormy seas of the North." Whatever might be the future fate of England, said Bruce, Virginia and America offered the guarantee that the Anglo-Saxon "conception of social order, political freedom, individual liberty, and private morality" would "not perish from the face of the earth."

As the American people entered into the twentieth century, they showed many evidences of progress toward achieving a common view of their national origins. Particularly encouraging was the desire of the South to claim its full share in the political heritage of the nation, and the promise that exclusive claims based upon nothing better than provincial jealousy might soon become out of date. But with this promise came also a new tendency to draw distinctions based upon considerations of ethnological origin and priority of settlement that threatened to establish dangerous standards of exclusion. However limited may have been the professed objectives of the patriotic order, and however important it may be to draw some contrast between the earlier and later phases of its activity, the implications of the movement were unmistakably dangerous to national unity. Or should I say they could have been dangerous? When one looks at the activity of those societies that challenged the pretensions of the self-styled patriots, it would seem to be a very difficult thing to keep any American from proving to his own satisfaction that he is an American by right of inheritance.

CHAPTER VI

A Legend Debunked and Restored

IT may seem that my choice of title for this last lecture is entirely misleading as to the true story of popular attitudes toward our national origins in the twentieth century. For one thing, you will have noted in the printed program for these lectures that it was just at the close of the First World War that Mr. James Stokes left to New York University the generous bequest making possible the Anson G. Phelps Lectureship on Early American History, a lectureship intended especially to inculcate "a knowledge of the principles which animated the Puritan Fathers and early colonists; and of the influence they have exerted upon modern civilization." In this phrasing, surely, one finds no suggestion of an intent to encourage the debunking of any of the nation's founders, least of all the earliest of them.

There may be one or two persons present who were privileged to attend the celebration at Plymouth in 1920 of the three hundredth anniversary of the landing of the Pilgrim Fathers. If so, you no doubt recall the tribute to those fathers spoken by Governor Calvin Coolidge of Massachusetts, a tribute that certainly broke none of the established conventions governing such celebrations. You probably have an even more sharply defined recollection of Governor Coolidge's long-distance telephone message to the governor of California, staged as an interruption of the major address by Senator Henry Cabot Lodge. The Senator, you will recall, had just quoted from Webster's great oration of 1820 the passage in which Webster looked forward to the next centennial, and in which he predicted that by 1920 "the voice of acclamation and gratitude, commencing on the Rock of Plymouth, shall be transmitted through millions of the sons of the Pilgrims, till it lose itself in the murmurs of the Pacific seas." As Lodge paused at the end of this quotation, a telephone previously placed on the platform began to ring. A representative of the telephone company, on answering, turned to the governor of Massachusetts, who was seated in Governor Bradford's chair, to indicate that the governor of California was on the line, and Governor Coolidge then spoke a few words into the instrument "to be lost in the waves and roar of the Pacific." Actually, Governor Stephens of California was out hunting at the time and his secretary took the message, but that circumstance was unknown to the audience at Plymouth. Senator Lodge picked up his address with a transitional disclaimer of any responsibility for the interruption.[1]

These morning exercises, held under the auspices of a state tercentenary commission, were followed by the town's own celebration in the afternoon. Among other orators, Vittorio Orlandini of Boston spoke on "The Immigrant's Share in Our Heritage—What Part May He Fairly Expect?" Tercentennial observances at Plymouth continued on into the summer of 1921, reaching their high point on August 1 in a celebration of the town's tercentenary that drew an estimated 100,000 people and featured President Warren G. Harding as the chief speaker. Mr. Harding had reached Plymouth, appropriately enough, aboard the presidential yacht, the *Mayflower*. Meanwhile, some of the early settlers had been reburied at the expense of the Society of Mayflower Descendants, and Plymouth

[1] Frederick W. Bittinger, *The Story of the Pilgrim Tercentenary Celebration at Plymouth in the Year 1921* (Plymouth, 1923), 11–16.

Rock had been given a new portico. During the latter part of the summer, thousands of visitors were entertained by a historical pageant requiring a cast all told of 1,300 persons.[2]

It hardly needs saying that other centennial celebrations have followed—among them the sesquicentennial at Philadelphia in 1926 that is remembered chiefly for the first Dempsey-Tunney fight, the Washington bicentennial of 1932 remembered chiefly for Congressman Sol Bloom of New York, and Grover Whalen's great show that in 1939 featured New York's observance of the establishment of our federal government one hundred and fifty years before.[3] Once again, the decade of the '30's belonged especially to New England. In 1930 the tercentennial of the Massachusetts Bay Colony was marked by some 2,000 events sponsored by state, municipal, and other agencies throughout the commonwealth.[4] Maryland broke into the picture in 1934 with ceremonies at Baltimore and St. Mary's, but Connecticut and Harvard soon took the center of the stage. We are now approaching the three hundred and fiftieth anniversary of the settlement of Jamestown, for which occasion plans are being drafted for another celebration in Virginia. It would appear that we are not yet as tired of the centennial type of observance as perhaps we might be.

That popular interest in the earlier chapters of our history showed no real deviation from previously established patterns is also suggested in other ways. The study of family history continued to hold the attention of many of our citizens, enough of them at any rate to encourage the publishers of *Who's Who* to issue in 1925 an expensive *Abridged Compendium of American Genealogy* carrying as a subtitle *The First Families of America.*[5] The publisher's foreword began: "In the entire field of American bibliography there is, perhaps, at the present time, no single subject of more interest to so great a number

[2] *Ibid.*, 17, 43–87.

[3] Mention belongs also to the Yorktown sesquicentennial of 1931.

[4] *Celebrating a 300th Anniversary; A Report of the Massachusetts Bay Tercentenary of 1930* . . . (Boston, 1931).

[5] Edited by Frederick A. Virkus (Chicago, 1925).

of people . . . as genealogy." No doubt this statement should be discounted as an obvious promotional device, but the fact remains that the publisher already had underwritten the statement with hard cash. In confirmation of his judgment, it would be possible to compile a most impressive bibliography of modern genealogical publications. But there would seem to be little point in so doing. It will be enough perhaps simply to ask that you recall the evidence of a continuing interest in genealogy offered by the files of our state historical magazines until a relatively recent date.

As in years past, much of this interest can be attributed to a desire on the part of many individuals to find evidence of their qualification for membership in one or more of our patriotic societies. Most of these organizations had come into existence no earlier than the 1890's, and thus they represented a development in our national life that had not yet run its course. Indeed, as late as 1933 there remained a few unexploited opportunities for the organization of a new order, as is suggested by the establishment in that year of the Society of the Descendants of the Colonial Clergy.[6] The years of the First World War had provided new stimuli to the activity of such organizations, and after the war many of them enlisted wholeheartedly in the effort to protect the country against the radical. That effort took more than one form, but of particular interest to this discussion was the attempt to perpetuate in our school histories an ultranationalistic and patriotic view of the American experience.

The idea that the school should serve a civic purpose was as old as the first school law in Massachusetts, which in 1642 required that all children be instructed to a point that would permit them "to read and understand the principles of religion and the capital laws of the country." [7] Our public school system had developed in the nineteenth century with a strong sense of

[6] *Historical Societies in the United States and Canada* (American Association for State and Local History, Washington, 1944).

[7] Quoted in Bessie L. Pierce, *Public Opinion and the Teaching of History in the United States* (New York, 1926), 3.

its obligation for the perpetuation of the republican form of government, and the teaching of American history had been required as early as 1827 by laws enacted in Massachusetts and Vermont. Six other states followed suit before the Civil War. After the war, as our public school system was rounded out, such a requirement became commonplace.[8]

Well before the First World War, moreover, some concern had been shown for the interpretation of American history that would be taught, especially in legislation specifying the use of particular texts or requiring the adoption only of such as were "impartial." In this development, leadership seems to have belonged to the South, where in the middle of the nineteenth century there was some effort to escape dependence upon texts reflecting too much of the madness of the abolitionist. After the Civil War, the United Confederate Veterans, and even more noticeably their daughters, stood guard in behalf of "a true and reliable history" of the War between the States. Indeed, they stood guard so well that members of the Grand Army of the Republic, suspecting that they were being maligned, presented their own demands for a true history of the Rebellion.[9] The Catholic Church also showed an inclination, in the development of its parochial schools, to seek texts that would better illustrate the part played by Catholics in the history of America.[10] In the rapid development of the patriotic orders after 1890 one finds a heavy emphasis on the need for education in the history and government of the United States, but these societies seem at first to have interpreted their own responsibilities quite broadly. Only with the coming of the war did their efforts find a special focus on the question of textbooks used in the school.[11]

The difference between prewar and postwar attitudes is probably best explained in terms of different estimates as to the

[8] *Ibid.*, 6–23.   [9] *Ibid.*, 136–71.   [10] *Ibid.*, 171–84.

[11] Miss Pierce's discussion (*ibid.*, 244 ff.) indicates that the turning point came in 1917, with a focus first on charges of pro-German sentiment in texts on European history.

danger confronting the country. It is my impression that before the war the members of our patriotic societies were guided chiefly by fear of the ultimate consequences of a failure to educate the alien, but that after the war they saw themselves grappling with an immediate conspiracy for destruction of the American way of life. One should not overlook the estimate by the United States Flag Association in 1926 "that $1,000,000 a month is being spent in this country for communistic and other anti-American propaganda," an estimate pointing, among other things, to the overshadowing influence on American sentiment of the Russian Revolution.[12] When the president-general of the Daughters of the American Revolution addressed the national congress of that society in this same year 1926, she pictured the daughters as "sentries" on guard against "studied and unremitting assaults" upon the "sacred heritage bequeathed to us in the Declaration of Independence and the Federal Constitution." [13]

Lest I be misunderstood to suggest that these fears were only the fears of women, let me mention that the U. S. Flag Association, a body seeking to co-ordinate the activities of all patriotic groups in the interest of a proper reverence for the chief symbol of our national union, had as its honorary president none other than President Coolidge and as its active president the distinguished elder statesman, Elihu Root. In accepting the invitation to become the honorary president of the organization in 1926, Mr. Coolidge declared: "Unless there is an eternal readiness to respond with the same faith, the same courage, and the same devotion in the defense of our institutions which were exhibited in their establishment we shall be dispossessed, and others of sterner fiber will seize on our inheritance. It is, therefore, well that the fires of patriotism be kept burning and that our national ideals and traditions be emphasized and kept before the people." [14]

[12] Bessie L. Pierce, *Citizens' Organizations and the Civic Training of Youth* (New York, 1933), 5.
[13] *Ibid.*, 19–20.   [14] *Ibid.*, 5n.

As the existence of this association indicates, the older patriotic societies did not have to stand guard alone. A good
many of the organizations that at this time undertook to
function as self-appointed guardians of the national tradition
can be dismissed, for they existed "on paper alone" and had
no significant following.[15] But there were others that fall into
an entirely different category, and this is especially true of the
veterans' organizations. The American Legion became suffi-
ciently concerned about the problem of school histories to
commission the writing of a textbook in American history that
would conform to its own concept of the interpretation of that
history the child should receive. The specifications, written in
1923, have interest. It was declared that the text should "inspire the children with patriotism," and "preach on every page
a vivid love of America." The book should "emphasize that our
ancestors accomplished great deeds," and so encourage "the
children to attempt brave deeds themselves." The "old patriotic legends" should be preserved, though it would be permitted to point out wherein they were legendary. Sectarianism
or anything calculated to encourage religious or racial hatreds
was to be avoided, but spiritual values and a belief in God
were to be kept ever in mind. The history must "speak the
truth, so that no child learns afterward to distrust it," but "in
telling the truth it must be careful to tell truth optimistically."
The "blunders of the past" might be mentioned to make the
child "careful," but the history should "dwell on failure only
for its value as a moral lesson" and should "speak chiefly of
success." In short, a school history of the United States should
"encourage patriotism, strengthen character, stimulate thought
and impress the worth of truth." [16]

Two years later, in the preface to a report on existing texts,
the Legion restated its convictions in somewhat more sober
language. The report itself—covering texts written by Pro-

[15] *Ibid.*, 3.

[16] Pierce, *Public Opinion and the Teaching of History*, 329–30. The text
was Charles F. Horne's *The Story of Our American People* (2 vols., New
York, 1925).

fessors Muzzey of Columbia, Hart of Harvard, McLaughlin of Chicago, and Van Tyne of Michigan, among others—rejected the charge of unpatriotic intent that had been leveled against these authors by less responsible critics. More specifically, the Legion rejected any suggestion that our textbook writers had sold out to the British. It was maintained, instead, that the professors had merely confused the function of teacher and "investigator." Consequently, they had included in their texts interpretations that might be properly brought to the attention of advanced students but that were unsuitable for instruction of "the public school pupil." The Legion considered it dangerous to place "before immature pupils the blunders, foibles and frailties of prominent heroes and patriots," for a pupil "led to believe that a great National hero was guilty of weakness and crime" was the more likely "to excuse such failings in himself and others." The purpose of a school text was "to influence good citizenship," not to record the "critical results of recent historical research." [17]

The charge that our history was being consciously slanted in favor of the British usually came from some Irish-American or German-American source. It is my impression that most of our ethnic groups by the 1920's were passing out of the period of their greatest excitement over the honors that were due their own particular ancestors. Certainly, the major works identified with this development in American historiography had been published before the war—such works as those of C. W. Baird on the Huguenot immigration, of C. A. Hanna on the Scotch-Irish, or of A. B. Faust on the German element in our population.[18] There are indications also of declining zeal in some of

[17] *Ibid.*, 331–33.

[18] C. W. Baird, *History of the Huguenot Emigration to America* (2 vols., New York, 1885); C. A. Hanna, *The Scotch-Irish; or, the Scot in North Britain, North Ireland and North America* (2 vols., New York, 1902); A. B. Faust, *The German Element in the United States with Special Reference to Its Political, Moral, Social, and Educational Influence* (2 vols., Boston and New York, 1909). Studies like those of T. C. Blegen on the Scandinavians fall into a quite different class, both as to their inspiration and their execution.

the organizations identified with this movement.[19] But other groups were still motivated by a sense that due recognition had not yet been accorded them.[20]

Had it not been for the war, the German-American might now have been as relaxed as the descendants of the Scotch-Irish settlers seem to have been. But there had been a war, and the war effort in the United States had depended in no small degree upon an indictment of Germany and the German people that was often attributed in postwar years to the influence of British propagandists. It was only natural that a newly organized Steuben Society should have been particularly sensitive to suggestions that our history was being distorted in the interest of Anglo-American union.[21] When the American Legion dismissed the charge that our texts were deliberately colored by British propaganda, it identified the complaint as one rooted basically in pro-German sentiment.

The Legion might have been on better ground had it laid the responsibility at the door of the Irish-American. As an Irishman, he was influenced by the still agitated question of Ireland's own political future. As an American who for several years past had been making a vigorous bid for acceptance, he was still bothered by the tendency of the "Scotch-Irish Myth" to obscure the case for the Irishman's contribution to the founding of the nation. A good example is that provided by Michael J. O'Brien, historiographer of the American-Irish Historical Society, who published in 1919 a volume entitled *A Hidden Phase of American History, Ireland's Part in America's Struggle for Liberty*.[22] In this the author claimed that Ireland

[19] Thus, the tenth and last volume of the *Proceedings* of the Scotch-Irish Historical Society was published in 1902.

[20] Among the demands made at public hearings in 1922 on texts used in New York City schools were those for fuller recognition of Jewish and Negro heroes. Pierce, *Public Opinion and the Teaching of History,* 281–82.

[21] *Ibid.,* 239–44.

[22] Michael J. O'Brien, *A Hidden Phase of American History, Ireland's Part in America's Struggle for Liberty* (New York, 1919).

had contributed more importantly to the success of the American Revolution than did any other European country, challenged the Scotch-Irish once more by laying claim in the name of Ireland to some of the more important of the heroes and virtues of the "Scotch-Irish" settlers, and argued that the time had come for America to repay its debt to Ireland. In this connection, mention may also be made of the Knights of Columbus, who in 1921 established a historical commission under the leadership of Edward F. McSweeney for the purpose of encouraging historical studies and distributing historical materials "free from propaganda of any kind as to the origin and development of this country." [23]

It would not be difficult to find documentation for the proposition that the superpatriot and the filio-pietist were more representative of prevailing attitudes during this postwar era than was the debunker. But any such attempt could end in nothing conclusive, and would draw attention away from the many indications, including the very shrillness of the "patriot's" protests, that the debunker spoke, however extremely, for the dominant mood of his time. It can not be said even that the "patriot" was in full control of the effort to dictate the interpretation of our history to be taught in the schools, for there were other groups no less insistent because of their fear that an excessive patriotism might endanger the hope of a new international order.[24] I do not mean to discount the danger to our schools of the effort to censor the textbooks, or the need for the warning of this danger that was issued by the American Historical Association as early as 1923.[25] I mean only to suggest that we should turn our attention now to the debunkers.

[23] Pierce, *Public Opinion and the Teaching of History,* 225–38, and for quotation, 233.

[24] For a discussion of the efforts to influence the curriculum by peace societies of one sort or another, see Pierce, *Citizens' Organizations and the Civic Training of Youth,* 71–94.

[25] Pierce, *Public Opinion and the Teaching of History,* 296–97.

It may be helpful to remember that it was not just the founding fathers who were being debunked in the 1920's—that the towering figure of the industrial magnate and the methods of modern advertising were also objects of the debunker's attention. Some of you will recall, or will have had your memory recently prompted by William E. Woodward's autobiography to recall, that the word "debunk" itself came originally into our language without any reference at all to problems of historical interpretation. It was first used by Mr. Woodward in a novel he published in 1923 under the simple title *Bunk*.[26] On the second page of this book one of the two central characters is introduced as a debunking expert, a professional no less, whose immediate assignment was to take the lead in revealing the far from admirable qualities of the other chief character, who was a financial magnate. For the benefit of a young Englishwoman who found the term unfamiliar, it was explained: "Why, de-bunking means simply taking the bunk out of things. . . . You've heard of deflation—of prices, wages, and so on—taking the fictitious values out of merchandise. Well, debunking is simply an intellectual deflation. It's the science of reality." The term "bunk" itself not being familiar to the young lady, it had to be explained as "the diminutive of buncombe." And when she began to catch the idea that the debunker struck at hypocrisy and pretense, she received the additional answer: "Not altogether. . . . It is a kind of illusion. Hypocrisy's a mean word. Illusion, that's it. It's a big thing in life. Millions of people make their living with no other asset." In his later autobiography, Mr. Woodward added for the benefit of readers who did not know the meaning of bunk that it meant "buncombe, trickery, false pretenses." [27]

In the same place, Mr. Woodward records for us the origin of the word "debunk." He had written some six chapters of the novel before going to Europe in the spring of 1922 for a vacation. It was a pleasant vacation extending through the summer,

[26] W. E. Woodward, *Bunk* (New York, 1923).
[27] W. E. Woodward, *The Gift of Life; an Autobiography* (New York, 1947), 243–44.

but as the Woodwards boarded their ship at Southampton for the return trip in September, he was beginning to ponder an unresolved problem in his unfinished manuscript. He had discovered no shorter way of describing this character he had created than as a specialist in "taking the bunk out of ideas and opinions." Something better than that was obviously needed, and to Mr. Woodward's delight he found the inspiration on the editorial page of that day's London *Times*, which he had picked up as he approached the gangplank. The editors of the *Times* were concerned at the moment, for some reason, with the all too familiar "delousing" operations of the First World War. Mr. Woodward had his word. If you could delouse a man, you also could debunk him.[28]

In his novel of the next year, Woodward did a thorough job of debunking the financial and industrial magnate. It was a first novel, but he had the advantage of previous experience as a banking executive, an advertising man, a newspaper reporter, and as the dispenser of literary news and criticism through syndicated columns. He was no youth, having been born in South Carolina in 1874, but he was encouraged now to devote his energies entirely to writing. A second novel, demonstrating that it did not take brains to make money, was followed by a third, and then he turned to biography.[29] In 1926 he published his *George Washington, the Image and the Man,* a venture so successful as to encourage him to write his *Meet General Grant,* which appeared in 1928.[30] Other historical works followed, including a *New American History,* of which several hundred thousand copies have been sold. His last work before the autobiography was *Tom Paine: America's Godfather,* published in 1947.[31]

Mr. Woodward became tired of the word "debunk," a term

[28] *Ibid.,* 244–45.

[29] The titles were *Lottery* (1924) and *Bread and Circuses* (1925).

[30] W. E. Woodward, *George Washington, the Image and the Man* (New York, 1926); *Meet General Grant* (New York, 1928).

[31] *A New American History* (New York, 1936); *Tom Paine: America's Godfather, 1737–1809* (New York, 1945).

that naturally continued to be especially identified with him and his works. "I don't like the word and I never use it," he complained in his autobiography.[32] He protested that his *Washington* had contained not a single "debunking paragraph." He admitted that he had included some criticism of Grant as president, but he expressed the hope that his *Tom Paine* at least might pass free of the charge of debunking. Woodward explained: "I think he has been cruelly maligned, that his influence for good has been powerful, and that he should be respected, even revered." But Woodward overlooked the obvious fact that in becoming an advocate of Tom Paine, a Revolutionary father repeatedly rejected by the American people, he was still engaged in the old business of debunking the national legend. The New York *Herald Tribune* gave the front page of its book review section to the Paine biography with the caption: "Woodward Debunks the Debunkers of Tom Paine." The author closes his discussion of his chief contribution to the English language—and may I say, I think he was really rather proud of it—with the plaintive observation that he supposed the autobiography would be greeted with "Woodward Debunks Woodward." [33]

For all his protest that the Washington biography was not a debunking book, it is actually a good example of the debunker's approach to American history. It may not be the best example, for it is not a good book and it is an extreme example. Others who shared with him the debunking spirit were more moderate, and thus perhaps more effective. Mr. Woodward wrote as a professional writer, and as a former businessman and publicist who had gauged the market well. He wrote, I think, with the deliberate purpose of writing a shocker, and he knew the satisfaction of receiving some very nasty correspondence from patriots around the country about what he had written. The most satisfying of all, I suspect, was the letter from an irate lady who promised to leave money in her will to

[32] Woodward, *The Gift of Life,* 245.
[33] *Ibid.,* 245–46.

buy up as much as possible of the publisher's stock for the purpose of keeping the book out of the hands of the public. At any rate, Woodward reprints the letter in his autobiography and records that he made some calculations as to what he might get out of the will at sixty cents a copy.[34] The opening sentence of the biography gave its own announcement of what would follow: "George Washington came of a family that must be called undistinguished, unless a persistent mediocrity, enduring many generations, is in itself a distinction." The conclusion was even more shocking, for after Mr. Woodward had stripped away what he considered to be the misleading accumulations of tradition, George Washington emerged clearly delineated in all essential details as the American businessman—an appalling picture indeed, especially in view of Mr. Woodward's well-publicized opinion of the American businessman.

And yet, I fear I may have done an injustice to the author in this brief summary. I think it should also be said that an honest purpose underlay the whole effort, and that Mr. Woodward did not have too much of a quarrel with George Washington, whatever may have been his quarrel with the modern business magnate, of whom Washington now became the prototype, or with the genealogists who had so industriously explored an ancestry to which Washington himself had been apparently indifferent. Woodward did not dispute the evidence these genealogists had discovered of a royalist background in England. He accepted it and then argued that "none of this has any value. . . . If it proved anything at all it would prove that the Washingtons were habitually opposed to democracy and progress, but it does not prove even that. The study of heredity is of small worth in appraising human values, because its conclusions are so often contradicted by facts." [35] Perhaps the author spoke here as the son of old stock in South Carolina who had been reared on a tenant's farm and in a cotton mill town where the company owned everything, including the store in which his father had worked after giving

[34] *Ibid.*, 320–21. [35] Woodward, *George Washington*, 11.

up farming. The son had gotten an education by winning in
competition a scholarship to The Citadel at Charleston. After
graduation, he had learned the newspaper game with the
Atlanta *Constitution,* and then he came north, where he prospered and found a happy marriage with a brilliant girl of
Jewish birth. In his *George Washington,* Woodward struck
violently at what he considered to be a false image supporting
some of the false values in his own society. Washington was
portrayed as a man who often lacked control of his own emotions, a man imperfectly educated and with no inclination
toward intellectual growth, a man who may have married for
money and who certainly was strongly motivated by the acquisitive instinct, a man who was indifferent to religion, as he
was to the suffering of an Indian, a man who should be remembered as a slaveholder, and a man whose career owed much
simply to good luck. In his effort to destroy the image, Woodward undoubtedly distorted the portrait of the man, but that
is a technique frequently employed by the artist who paints
for a purpose.

It is the attempt to humanize Washington—to destroy the
myth and find the man—that explains the extraordinary concern of the debunkers with the less important detail of his life.
In this same year, 1926, Rupert Hughes published the first
volume of his *George Washington,* subtitled *The Human
Being and The Hero.*[36] It was a much more careful work than
was Woodward's, and one much less marked by a straining for
the sensational effect. Even so, the mystery of Sally Fairfax
receives attention all out of proportion to the true significance
of the subject, simply because of its bearing on the question of
whether Washington did in fact marry Martha Custis while
loving another woman.[37] But perhaps that is not quite it. The
question really was whether George Washington had been

[36] Rupert Hughes, *George Washington* (3 vols., New York, 1926–30). The
remaining volumes carried as subtitles: *The Rebel and the Patriot, 1762–
1777* and *The Savior of the States, 1777–1781.*

[37] *Ibid.,* I, especially 176–204, 398–419.

subject to the normal passions of man. After quoting in full his famous letter to Sally of September 12, 1758, and after nearly four pages of comment on the letter, Mr. Hughes rejected the popular notion of Washington as "a man under almost perfect self-control" with the exultant cry: "But he could love. He did love. His letter, however, confusing to his idolaters, redeems him to humanity and, however pitiful as a confession, is magnificent as passion." [38]

The debunkers felt a strong obligation to correct the false impressions conveyed by certain pictures that had enjoyed great popularity. Listen for a moment to Hughes in the chapter entitled "He Wins a Rich Widow"—"One of those painters who have done so much to fasten picturesque falsehoods on the public mind, has shown the wooing, with the widow's pretty children playing on the floor while George and Martha stand by the mantelpiece as still as the statuary they have since become; though the tradition-builders have had the kindness to make Martha of bisque instead of the marble they selected for George. And she is the more lovable of the two; they allow her humanity at least. Even in legend she is such a woman as everybody knows, while nobody ever knew such a man as the George Washington of myth. If such a man ever lived, he himself was not that man, but the opposite." [39] Another picture that bothered Mr. Hughes was the one depicting Washington praying in the woods at Valley Forge. It took all of a twenty-eight page chapter in the third volume, not to mention an appendix in Volume I on a related subject, to dispose of the very uncertain evidence on which this part of the tradition rested and to establish the proposition that Washington had been indifferent to all but the formalities of religious life.[40] Little wonder that a study started as a one-volume biography had by 1930 reached three volumes without getting the subject beyond the victory at Yorktown. Little wonder, too, that Mr. Hughes met many citizens who, in his own words, "take a pa-

[38] *Ibid.*, I, 410.   [39] *Ibid.*, I, 351.
[40] *Ibid.*, I, 552–59; III, 270–98.

triotic pride in denouncing this biography while boasting their
innocence of having read it." [41]

In an "Afterword" appended to the third and last volume,
Hughes answers his critics with this protest: "The more I study
Washington the greater and better I think him, yet I am not
trying to prove him great or good. I am trying solely to describe him as he was and let him speak for himself. He was a
man of such tremendous undeniable achievement that he does
not need to be bolstered with propaganda, protected by a
priestcraft of suppression, or celebrated by any more Fourth
of July oratory." [42] This was written in defense of a study that
had been vigorously attacked, and it came at the end of the
third volume and not at the beginning of the first. Nevertheless, it merits respectful attention, for it is true enough that the
debunkers did not deny Washington's achievement. If anything, they made that achievement all the greater by focusing
attention on the immense difficulties he faced as a result of the
shortcomings of other Revolutionary fathers. "The graft and
profiteering of the times was stupendous," wrote Hughes, "and
it is unjust to Washington as well as to truth, to conceal any
longer the fact that the generation of Americans which coin-
cided with the Revolution, was far from being the supremely
virtuous race its descendants have been pleased to pretend." [43]
For the traditional view of the Revolution Hughes sought to
substitute this: "A few soldiers, a few statesmen, a few devoted
men did all the work, suffered all the hardships, and saved the
country in spite of itself, while the majority ran away or kept
aloof, grew fat and looked on." [44]

In this conclusion one finds little, if anything, that should
have bothered a daughter of the Revolution who had unimpeachable evidence that her own ancestors belonged to the few
who had been willing to make a sacrifice for our independence.
Indeed, there was no real reason why any of us should have
been seriously disturbed, except perhaps for those tied by filial

[41] *Ibid.*, III, 688.   [42] *Ibid.*, III, 689–90.
[43] *Ibid.*, III, 691.   [44] *Ibid.*, III, 694

piety to the proposition that the very presence of an ancestor in America at the time of the Revolution argued in behalf of his patriotism. The debunker gave both implicit and explicit endorsement to the Revolution itself, which is to say that he raised no really fundamental issue regarding its interpretation. We did for a time show some favor for a literature dwelling on the virtues of those who had been Tories at the time of the Revolution, partly because of the satisfaction we found in repudiating the legendary view of a united America in 1776, but this was hardly more than a luxury we could well afford because of our continuing agreement that the decision in favor of independence had been the right one. Certainly, those of us who are old enough to have read the debunkers in the 1920's will find, if we go back to reread them, that their works are neither so shocking nor so gratifying as we first found them to be. And certainly the explanation for this difference of reaction is a simple one. We are today a people much more inclined to accept the central proposition of the debunker—that the founders of this country were human beings—and for that more sophisticated attitude we undoubtedly owe something to the debunker.

I do not mean, however, to give too much of the credit to the debunker, who capitalized on a mood he had done little to create, as much of the literature of his day will serve to demonstrate. The effort to debunk our history actually had been under way for some time. In a paper delivered before the American Philosophical Society in 1912 on "The Legendary and Myth-Making Process in Histories of the American Revolution," Sydney G. Fisher demanded a substitution of "truth and actuality for the mawkish sentimentality and nonsense with which we have been so long nauseated." [45] As one of the more prolific writers in the field of American history, Fisher already had contributed to the attainment of that goal by publishing his *True Benjamin Franklin,* his *True William Penn,* and a *True History of the American Revolution,* works whose very

[45] Read April 18, 1912, reprinted from *Proceedings,* LI (April–June, 1912).

titles bore testimony to a hope that the misleading impressions of tradition might be corrected.[46] The pattern for these studies had been set by Paul Leicester Ford in *The True George Washington,* a biography published in 1897 for the purpose of "humanizing Washington, and making him a man rather than a historical figure." [47] Like Rupert Hughes a generation later, Ford insisted that this approach served to make Washington all the greater.[48]

Other and more important works could be cited, among them Charles A. Beard's *Economic Interpretation of the Constitution* which, in 1913, successfully demonstrated that the authors of our federal constitution had been guided by something less than divine inspiration.[49] If another example of earlier date is desired, mention can be made of John Bach McMaster's essay on "The Political Depravity of the Fathers," which in the 1890's undertook to show that "in all the frauds and tricks that go to make up the worst form of practical politics, the men who founded our State and national governments were always our equals, and often our masters." [50]

As the mention of McMaster and Beard suggests, a major share of the responsibility for correcting the popular tradition had been assumed by the professional historian. In days past the clergyman, or some other gentleman who in his spare time pursued the avocation of history, had exerted the dominant influence on the writing of our history. But that influence was now passing into the hands of the professional—a scholar who usually had received special training for his work as a historian, who usually made his living by teaching school, and who looked for leadership to the rapidly developing graduate

[46] All published at Philadelphia, the first two mentioned in 1900, the last in 1902. The single volume of 1902 was expanded into *The Struggle for American Independence* (2 vols., Philadelphia, 1908).

[47] *The True George Washington* (Philadelphia, 1897), 6.

[48] *Ibid.*   [49] At New York, 1913.

[50] First published in the *Atlantic Monthly,* this essay was reprinted in McMaster's *With the Fathers, Studies in the History of the United States* (New York, 1896), 71–86.

schools of our major universities. In saying this, I am well
aware that the professional historian has been subjected to
much criticism for failure to appreciate the full extent of his
public responsibility, as in his tendency to write primarily for
the attention of other professional historians. But there can
be no question as to his growing influence. Not only did the
so-called popular historian—a twentieth-century designation
for the historian who sought immediately to win the public
ear—depend heavily upon the monographic studies of the professional, but the professional himself has been less guilty of
neglecting the larger audience than has been assumed. For one
thing, in an age marked by the most extraordinary expansion
of formal education at all levels, it was the professional historian who wrote most of the textbooks used for the study of
history in our schools, as the members of the American Legion
and the Daughters of the American Revolution well understood in their campaigns of the 1920's. When the president-
general of the DAR in 1923 condemned the schoolteacher who
thought there were two sides to every question, there could be
no doubt as to the real target of her remarks.[51]

From time immemorial, I suppose, all historians have
claimed the virtue of writing honest history, but certainly no
group of historians has placed heavier emphasis on the need
for an objective interpretation of the full record than did these
new professionals. Their standards reflected the rigorous training of the modern seminar, a training founded on the hope that
a scholarly ideal might make possible an objective analysis of
human experience. That hope was in no way peculiar to
America, but it undoubtedly gained additional importance for
American historians from the fact that the traditional view of
their own history, which had found its classic expression in
Bancroft's volumes, fell so markedly short of the new ideal.

Bancroft had built his great themes upon the sacrifice of
those who settled the country and who fought for its independence, and upon the evidences of a common goal uniting

[51] Pierce, *Citizens' Organizations and the Civic Training of Youth*, 21.

peoples of diverse origins and interests. One can hardly dispute the utility of such a view of our history in the nineteenth century, or perhaps in any century. Nor can any one deny that it has in it important elements of truth. But the need to promote national union no longer had its old urgency, and themes that had once been fresh and stimulating had lost through monotonous repetition much of their former appeal. There was in Bancroft's writings too much patriotism, and too much that smacked of special pleading, for them to be regarded any longer as good history.

Worse still was the filial piety that continued to inspire so much of the writing of our earlier history, and the continuing competition for special recognition among different groups in which everybody seemed intent on talking about subjects of no conceivable interest to anybody else. From our newer ethnic groups, struggling against the tendency for Anglo-Saxonism to dominate the national legend, some of our historians caught a new insight into the American adventure that would lead in time to systematic study of immigration as a major factor in our history. And yet, in the efforts of these groups one found also the worst sort of antiquarianism. Having accepted the proposition that priority of settlement counted most, they insisted on pushing their inquiries back to the point of least return, and so helped to demonstrate for us all how arid could be a scholarship dedicated primarily to the honoring of one's fathers.[52] It was this example, I suggest, that helped some of us to understand that there were a few details about the *Mayflower* and the Pilgrim Fathers that we really did not need to be bothered about.

The new approach to the study of American history may be seen at its best in the works of George Louis Beer, one of the ablest historians this country has produced. In many ways Mr. Beer was representative of the gentleman scholar, who fortu-

[52] Notice Edward Channing's comment in 1910 at the end of his chapter on "The Coming of the Foreigners" (*History of the United States,* II, 421–22).

nately did not disappear from the scene with the coming of the professional historian. Although Beer taught for a few years, he found that he disliked the task and, after a few more years devoted to the family business, he was able to give his full attention to the study of British colonial policy from the time of Elizabeth to 1765. Four distinguished volumes, published in the years extending from 1907 through 1912, elaborated and documented more fully a thesis he had earlier submitted at Columbia for the master's degree on *The Commercial Policy of England toward the American Colonies,* a study of such merit as to have received publication in 1893.[53] In these works Beer presented an interpretation of the development of Britain's colonial policy that was both sympathetic and comprehensive in its coverage.

I have no desire to oversimplify the historiographical problem. Any full discussion of Beer as a historian would require attention to general considerations leading scholars in the later years of the nineteenth century to view with new sympathy the mercantilist assumptions that had shaped the old imperial policy. But in the context of our present discussion there may be some advantage in considering Beer's efforts as an attempt to escape the limitations heretofore imposed by patriotic loyalties. The duty of the historian, as he saw it, was neither to condemn nor to justify, but to understand and interpret faithfully the forces that have shaped history. He sought, therefore, to see the problems of the old empire as Britain's merchants and statesmen had seen them, and for that purpose he spent many long hours in the British archives.[54] There he followed the development of a policy that was shaped only in part with

[53] In the Columbia *Studies in History, Economics, and Public Law.* His later works were *British Colonial Policy, 1754–1765* (New York, 1907); *The Origins of the British Colonial System, 1578–1660* (New York, 1908); *The Old Colonial System, 1660–1754* (2 vols., New York, 1912), this last being incomplete in that the two volumes did not get beyond 1689.

[54] See especially the appreciation by C. M. Andrews in *George Louis Beer, A Tribute to His Life and Work in the Making of History and the Moulding of Public Opinion* (New York, 1924), 9–43.

a view to the thirteen North American colonies. To put the point briefly, Beer's work argued that a significant chapter in the history of the United States could be understood only by taking it out of the narrow confines of United States history.

This was a view that was also espoused by Charles M. Andrews, who shared with Beer the dominant influence on the writing of early American history in the first half of the twentieth century. "The years from 1607 to 1783 were colonial before they were American or national," said Andrews in 1924, "and our Revolution is a colonial and not an American problem." [55] In his later magnum opus, entitled *The Colonial Period of American History*,[56] Andrews devoted one volume to imperial policy and administration, the area of Beer's chief interest. The other three volumes dig deep into the English background of settlement, with attention to the development of English projects of settlement in Bermuda and the West Indies as well as on the North American continent, and with not a little evidence of a flagging interest in the subject once the colonists had crossed the Atlantic. The work would have been better described had its author labeled it an introduction to the history of the colonial period, for Andrews gave little attention to the history of the colonies after the initial period of settlement, except as that history had a bearing on the problem of imperial policy. Although Andrews was an amazingly productive scholar, he found time to deal directly with the problem of the Revolution in only one work, *The Colonial Background of the American Revolution*, published in 1924. Nevertheless, his immensely valuable studies emphasize the continuing tendency for the twin problems of original settlement and the Revolution to dominate the interest of those who concern themselves with the question of our national origins. He differed from his predecessors chiefly in his insistence that these problems could be interpreted aright only in the broader context of Britain's imperial history.

[55] C. M. Andrews, *The Colonial Background of the American Revolution* (New Haven, 1924), ix.
[56] In four volumes (New Haven, 1934–38).

Between them Beer and Andrews exerted a more profound influence on the interpretation of American history than did any of their contemporaries, except for Frederick Jackson Turner and possibly Charles A. Beard. It is to the special emphasis of the so-called imperial school they founded that we must attribute in part the complaint of the 1920's that our school texts carried British propaganda. The charge itself was transparently superficial, but there can be no question that American historians, in their desire to rise above the limitations of nationalism, responded enthusiastically to this new point of view.[57] Nor can there be any doubt that the new point of view encouraged a new appreciation for the ties binding us to England, with results that led some of our citizens to suspect that the new point of view represented nothing better than an old emphasis on the virtues of the Anglo-Saxon race. Even those who subscribed fully to the superiority of the Anglo-Saxon might find in the new history a dangerous loss of national emphasis. I doubt that many daughters of the Revolution bothered to read Beer's *British Colonial Policy, 1754–1765*, but among the few who may have done so there must have been some who were disturbed by the author's concluding sentence. "It is easily conceivable," said he, "and not at all improbable that the political evolution of the next centuries may take such a course that the American Revolution will lose the great significance that is now attached to it, and will appear merely as the temporary separation of two kindred peoples whose inherent similarity was obscured by superficial differences, resulting from dissimilar economic and social conditions." [58] But perhaps I had better leave the point, at this point, to those among my colleagues who call themselves diplomatic historians.

[57] See Miss Pierce's discussion in *Public Opinion and the Teaching of History*, 206–8.

[58] Beer, *British Colonial Policy, 1754–1765*, 316. Beer himself later became a leading advocate of our entrance into the war on Britain's side, and in his *English-Speaking Peoples* (New York, 1917) argued "the advisability and necessity of a co-operative democratic alliance of all the English-speaking peoples."

Of greater interest for this discussion is the long-term influence of the imperial school of historians on the periodization of American history, and so on its interpretation. Whatever may have been the shortcomings of the older national school, it had encouraged us to view American history as being all of one piece, as a story having both unity and continuity from the beginning to the end, and as a story that quite definitely had its beginning in the seventeenth century. In contrast, the newer view tended to break that story into two parts—the one British, the other American. For so long as we shared the debunker's inclination to challenge the filio-pietist, or the pretentious claims of the genealogist, we continued to have an active interest in the question of our colonial origins. But in time our interest began to flag, and the history of the United States came to have its beginning, as almost any textbook will demonstrate, with the Revolution.[59]

Again, I would like to avoid seeming to oversimplify the problem. From the first, our Revolution had cast its shadow over the whole of the earlier period of our history. The interpretation placed upon that Revolution had been of the most critical importance to the great constitutional debates of the nineteenth century, and in our own century, when the hopes and fears of men have turned so much on the use that was made of national authority, it has been only natural that our attention should be drawn forward to the period in which the nation first took shape. And there were other, if less important, influences, among them the simple fact that so many more of us in the twentieth century could find a closer personal or group identification with the Revolution than with the more remote period of settlement. People, after all, have a way of showing more interest in their own history than in the history of other people, which brings us back to Beer and Andrews. Were they perhaps too successful in their effort to establish the proposi-

[59] For discussion, see Carl Bridenbaugh, "The Neglected First Half of American History," *American Historical Review*, LIII (April, 1948), 506–17.

tion that our colonial history should not be viewed primarily as American history?

In raising the question, I have no inclination to place blame on Beer and Andrews, whose works will probably stand longer than will the work of any of their contemporaries, and for the simple reason that they brought great skill to the task of giving us a new appreciation for the place our history has in the history of the modern world. Were I inclined to assign blame, I probably would pick on Frederick Jackson Turner, who demanded attention to influences peculiar to America while Beer and Andrews argued for the study of our history in a broader context. But there are enough people picking on Turner, as it is. I have no other purpose than to suggest that Turner's theories helped to add very greatly to our interest in the national period just when Beer and Andrews seemed to suggest that the history of the colonial period was nothing more than a chapter in the history of the British Empire.

The growing tendency to consider the Revolution as the true beginning of our national history is strongly suggested by the work of the debunkers. Indeed, the debunkers concentrated their fire so largely on the Revolutionary fathers as almost to suggest that we had no other fathers worthy of attention. Almost but not quite, for there still remained the bothersome problem of our Puritan fathers. The debunking of the Puritan was an old national pastime, one that had been enjoyed on occasion even by his own descendants. As we saw in the last lecture, John G. Palfrey had hardly completed the most elaborate of the defenses of Puritanism before the Adams brothers began to strike at its very foundations. That it should have been felt necessary now to go beyond what they had accomplished is partly explained by their disposition, while damning the Puritan's intolerance, to leave him great credit for the establishment of political liberty in America. Another reason stemmed from our tendency to confuse Puritanism and Victorianism at a time when we felt the strongest impulse to repudiate the latter.

One of the more influential of the histories published in the 1920's was James Truslow Adams' *Founding of New England.*[60] In fact, the book gave such substance to its author's reputation as to set him on the way to becoming as influential a historian as had been John Fiske in an earlier day.[61] Adams, who incidentally had no connection with the family of John Adams, dismissed the "old conception of New England history, according to which that section was considered to have been settled by persecuted religious refugees, devoted to liberty of conscience, who, in the disputes with the mother country, formed a united mass of liberty-loving patriots unanimously opposed to an unmitigated tyranny" as a legend that for some time had been passing out of view. He argued the need for fuller clarification of the part played by economic factors in the settlement of New England and substituted, for the long favored story of New England's defense of its rights of self-government against the encroachments of English authority in the seventeenth century, a narrative of "the domestic struggle against the tyranny exercised by the more bigoted members of the theocratic party" in Massachusetts.[62] In the final overthrow of the theocratic control established by the first fathers, Adams saw one of the major victories for liberty in American history.

As this brief statement suggests, Mr. Adams' chief quarrel was with the leaders of the Bay Colony, but he did not ignore the Plymouth Pilgrims. The Pilgrims were presented as a community of relative insignificance in their own day, which was true enough, and as a people who were so far from having been "harried out of the land" that the authorities in England were actually to be credited with leniency toward them in their efforts to flee the country illegally. In discussing the question of their second flight from Holland to America, Mr. Adams

[60] *The Founding of New England* (Boston, 1921).

[61] Nowhere is Adams' influence more apparent than in the attention that has been given to correcting him.

[62] See the preface.

stressed the similarity of their purpose to that of the latest arrival at Ellis Island. He was too good a historian to dismiss the religious factor, but he considered that to be more pertinent to an explanation for the first flight to Holland than to the question of why the Pilgrims came to America. In Holland they had found tolerance, and Mr. Adams' tribute to the principles that guided Dutch policy in the seventeenth century was warm enough to satisfy any member of the Holland Society. Yet, as if to prove that he would play no favorites, he denied that the Pilgrim's character owed anything to his sojourn in Holland. The Pilgrim had remained an Englishman and had migrated to America partly because of the hope that his children might remain English, which was also true enough.[63]

It would be unfair and misleading to suggest that Adams was nothing more than a debunker. Despite the uneven quality of his work over the years, I have respect for him as a historian, and I think his widely read books served on the whole a useful purpose. For example, we were a people badly in need of someone who would stress the similarity between the Pilgrim Father and the latest arrival at Ellis Island. And when Mr. Adams, in his later and immensely influential *Epic of America,* suggested that all of us were descended from immigrants who were so far from being the strongest of their race as actually to have shown their weakness by seeking escape in the New World from the difficulties of the Old, he at least gave us some common bond.[64] But this may be merely to say that the themes of the debunker were socially useful, and that all of us shared in some degree the impulse to debunk the national legend.

In the heavy emphasis he placed on the economic motivation of the first settlers, Adams denied the transcendent importance of a religious ideal in the settlement of New England.

[63] See pp. 87–90.
[64] James Truslow Adams, *The Epic of America* (Boston, 1931), 241–42.

Like Vernon Parrington a few years later,[65] he took time to demonstrate how undemocratic and illiberal were the ideas that guided the ruling fathers of early New England. But like some of the others who sought to debunk legendary views of the nation's origins, he offered an agreeable substitute for the old legend. The heroes of Adams' history were the people, for the most part anonymous and by his estimate a clear majority, who through the years had opposed the leadership of a narrow-minded oligarchy and finally had overthrown it. In "the leaders and citizens of Rhode Island, the martyred Quakers, and the men and women of Massachusetts and the other colonies, who so lived and wrought and died that the glory of an heritage of intellectual freedom might be ours," he found men and women whom "it should be our duty to honor." [66]

Can it be argued that the act of debunking was also an act of restoration? Did the debunker's violence express chiefly his resentment at what had been done to something he cherished? Is it true that we are a people so committed to the idea that our rights have been inherited that we dare not tolerate anything that cheapens the inheritance? In short, should the debunking of our history be viewed as a step toward returning the legend of the founding fathers to its traditional place in our national life? Certainly, in the years since the 1920's we have done much to restore the good repute of our founders.

Especially notable has been the effort made in behalf of the Puritan. Many of us can say today what S. E. Morison said in 1930: "My attitude toward seventeenth-century puritanism has passed through scorn and boredom to a warm interest and respect." And for this change in our view, Mr. Morison himself is in no small part responsible. In his *Builders of the Bay Colony,* which helped to mark the tercentenary of Massachusetts, he felicitously brought to life men and women who represented, in his own words, "a courageous, humane, brave,

[65] Vernon L. Parrington, *Main Currents in American Thought,* Vol. I: *The Colonial Mind* (New York, 1927).

[66] Adams, *The Founding of New England,* 277.

and significant people." [67] In the Phelps Lectures of 1934, as some of you will recall, he devoted not a little of his time to correcting some of the mistakes J. T. Adams had made.[68] But *The Puritan Pronaos,* which remains perhaps the most widely read of the Phelps series, provided more than an expert's example of knuckle-rapping. In these lectures, Morison helped us to judge the Puritan for his constructive contributions to the American way of life, and more especially for his work in the founding of schools and colleges and in the transmission of a cultural heritage that has greatly enriched our lives. That Professor Morison should have had to emphasize these points is the measure of our recent rejection of the Puritan, for the points were new only in the sense that some of us had recently forgotten them. The lectures were a by-product of Morison's tercentennial history of Harvard, a major work in the field of our intellectual history that may well include the most distinguished of its author's books.[69] The *Pronaos* thus reflected the spirit in which New England was then celebrating the third centennial of its founding—a spirit speaking often in protest of the common tendency to defame the Puritan.[70] Since the Second World War, Mr. Morison has devoted his attention chiefly to his history of naval operations, but fortunately he has also found the time to edit and publish for the general reader a new edition of Bradford's history.[71]

[67] Samuel Eliot Morison, *Builders of the Bay Colony* (Boston and New York, 1930), vi, for both quotations.

[68] Samuel Eliot Morison, *The Puritan Pronaos; Studies in the Intellectual Life of New England in the Seventeenth Century* (New York, 1936).

[69] In my judgment, that distinction belongs to *The Founding of Harvard College* (Cambridge, 1935). In the next year he published two volumes on Harvard in the seventeenth century.

[70] For example, see Clifford K. Shipton's sharp attack on Adams, Parrington, and others in "The New England Clergy of the 'Glacial Age,'" in Colonial Society of Massachusetts *Publications,* XXXII (1933), 24–54.

[71] *Of Plymouth Plantation, 1620–1647, by William Bradford, Sometime Governor Thereof,* a new edition, by Samuel Eliot Morison (New York, 1952).

Perry Miller's complex studies of *The New England Mind* have had appeal for only a few readers outside academic circles.[72] Nevertheless, they have been one of the more significant influences affecting more popular studies of the Puritan —such a study, for example, as Ola Elizabeth Winslow's artistic attempt to re-create the life that once centered about *Meetinghouse Hill.* Her story, as she described it, was "a village story in a day of small things," but in its course from 1630 to 1783, it repeatedly gave hint "that some things in contemporary life and what we are pleased to call the 'American character' may still be measured, as colonial records tell us distances from town to town were once measured; namely, 'in a straight line from the meetinghouse door.' " [73]

Several years before this was written, and at a time when our energies were concentrated on preparations for the invasion of Hitler's Europe, Ralph Barton Perry had undertaken to explain the essential elements of the American character in a stimulating work entitled *Puritanism and Democracy.*[74] There is no time for discussion. I must be content merely to establish the existence of a new sense that the national character had deep roots in the colonial period, and that our history can be properly interpreted only with due regard for its essential continuity.

This was the inspiration of Thomas J. Wertenbaker's very readable three volumes on *The Founding of American Civilization,* and of his *Torchbearer of the Revolution,* a study of Nathaniel Bacon and the rebellion he led in the seventeenth century.[75] In Max Savelle's *Seeds of Liberty,* and Clinton

[72] Especially his *Orthodoxy in Massachusetts* (Cambridge, 1933); *The New England Mind: The Seventeenth Century* (New York, 1939); *The New England Mind: From Colony to Province* (Cambridge, 1953).

[73] Ola Elizabeth Winslow, *Meetinghouse Hill, 1630–1783* (New York, 1952), 2–3.

[74] Ralph Barton Perry, *Puritanism and Democracy* (New York, 1944).

[75] Thomas Jefferson Wertenbaker, *The Founding of American Civilization: The Middle Colonies* (New York, 1938); *The Puritan Oligarchy* (New York, 1947); *The Old South* (New York, 1949); *Torchbearer of the Revolution; The Story of Bacon's Rebellion and Its Leader* (Princeton, 1940).

Rossiter's *Seedtime of the Republic,* one finds a vigorously argued thesis that the Revolutionary fathers can be understood only by understanding their fathers, a view we may be certain John Adams would have endorsed.[76] Certainly, too, it would have won the endorsement of George Bancroft, whose *History of the United States* receives today much more favorable comment than it did at the beginning of the century.[77]

To mention but one other example, we find in Louis Hartz's very recently published study of *The Liberal Tradition in America* an argument that draws the old and familiar contrast between the American and the French revolutions. The author would have us believe that the key to an understanding of our own Revolution is to understand what it did not need to accomplish.[78] In other words, the Revolution becomes, as it does in other recent studies, not so much a revolution as simply a war for independence fought by those who would not surrender the liberties their fathers had given them. Perhaps those among my colleagues who in recent years have been bothered about the neglect of colonial history need not have been bothered at all.

In saying this, I do not mean to suggest that the Revolutionary fathers suffer now from neglect. Since Carl Van Doren published his *Benjamin Franklin* in 1938,[79] the year of Munich, we have been much inclined to view our Revolutionary fathers with sympathy. They have remained human beings, very human indeed at times, but they have been men who in an hour

[76] Max Savelle, *Seeds of Liberty; The Genesis of the American Mind* (New York, 1948); Clinton Rossiter, *Seedtime of the Republic: The Origin of the American Tradition of Political Liberty* (New York, 1953).

[77] For example, see N. H. Dawes and F. T. Nichols, "Revaluing Bancroft," *New England Quarterly,* VI (1933), 278–93; Michael Kraus, "George Bancroft, 1834–1934," *ibid.,* VII (1934), 662–86.

[78] Louis Hartz, *The Liberal Tradition in America, An Interpretation of American Political Thought since the Revolution* (New York, 1955). See also his earlier discussion in "American Political Thought and the American Revolution," *American Political Science Review,* XLVI (June, 1952), 321–42.

[79] Carl Van Doren, *Benjamin Franklin* (New York, 1938).

of uncertainty and challenge took a stand for principle. We have yet to produce a distinguished multivolumed history of the Revolution, unless that distinction belongs to Bancroft. But we have produced in recent years, or are in the process of producing, multivolumed biographies by Irving Brant of Madison, by Dumas Malone of Jefferson, and by the late Douglas Freeman of Washington.[80] And this emphasis on the individual leaders of the Revolution has been reinforced by an extraordinary effort to collect and publish the full writings of the more important of our Revolutionary fathers. Princeton University, with help from *The New York Times,* has undertaken the publication of Jefferson's papers on a scale more ambitious than anything tried before. Yale and the American Philosophical Society, with the aid of the Luce publications, plan to issue Franklin's writings on a comparable scale. Harvard, the Massachusetts Historical Society, and the Luce publications have launched still another project for making known the long-hidden resources of the Adams family papers in Boston. In New York, Columbia University has undertaken to publish more fully than heretofore has been done the works of Alexander Hamilton. Meantime, the so-called popular writer has rarely been more popular than when directing our attention to the Revolutionary fathers, as in Catherine Drinker Bowen's artistic *John Adams and the American Revolution* or Esther Forbes's engaging tour through the Boston of Sam Adams in her *Paul Revere and the World He Lived In.*[81]

Meantime, also, the fathers have become a leading tourist attraction. One thinks first, of course, of John D. Rockefeller's restoration of Williamsburg, but the first thought belongs really to Henry Ford, who was more responsible than any

[80] Irving Brant, *James Madison* (4 vols., Indianapolis, 1941–); Dumas Malone, *Jefferson and His Times* (2 vols., Boston, 1948–); Douglas S. Freeman, *George Washington, A Biography* (6 vols., 1948–54).

[81] Catherine Drinker Bowen, *John Adams and the American Revolution* (Boston, 1950); Esther Forbes, *Paul Revere and the World He Lived In* (Boston, 1942).

other man for giving us the automobile that has become well-nigh the one indispensable thing in our life. As early as 1920, the traffic problem in Plymouth, on the occasion of the tercentennial, seems to have caused as much comment as did any feature of the celebration.[82] During the next summer the success of the historical pageant, which featured the year's program, owed much to those who found the pageant a convenient excuse for a nice drive. And today the number of historical pageants that invite the tourist's attention, including Paul Green's show at Roanoke Island, is almost unbelievable.

We had been somewhat slow to recognize the need for preserving our historical monuments, and slow to raise monuments where none had existed. Plymouth, by the care of local residents, had its monuments to the Pilgrim Fathers, but Jamestown had remained an abandoned site given over to nature, and the river itself was threatening to wash it away by the later years of the nineteenth century. The Association for the Preservation of Virginia Antiquities, chartered in 1889, took the lead in efforts to save the site of our first settlement during the years preceding the Jamestown tercentennial.[83] Three years later, a Society for the Preservation of New England Antiquities was organized.[84] Meanwhile, the federal government had become active in behalf of the preservation of archaeological treasures under the authority of a bill "for the preservation of American antiquities." The National Park Service followed in 1916, with attention first to the preservation of the natural and archaeological treasures of the continent, but by 1930 the Park Service was becoming interested in historical monuments. The Washington bicentennial was approaching, and a newly organized Wakefield Monument Association was interested in

[82] See Bittinger's comment on the traffic jam of August 10, 1921, *The Story of the Pilgrim Tercentenary,* 89–91.

[83] The APVA acquired some twenty acres on Jamestown Island in 1893, a small part of which was subsequently deeded to the federal government for the location of the tercentenary monument. *Jamestown National Historic Site* (National Park Service, 1947).

[84] The society issued its first *Bulletin* in May, 1910.

"restoring" the birthplace of Washington as nearly as it could be done by the erection of a new building. Though the site belonged to the United States Army, the Park Service secured the necessary legislation for a transfer and in so doing added a new type of activity to its responsibilities.[85]

State governments have helped in various ways, among others by erecting the roadside markers that by 1930 were becoming familiar to many a tourist. Local governments have not been indifferent, any more than have local chambers of commerce or the oil industry, which hands us a road map so attractively illustrated as to invite us to prolong the trip, simply because of the area's historical interest.

I have no complaint to make. It does seem to me that at times we may have been carrying this business of historical restoration a bit far, that we may need to ask on some occasions at least if the funds could be put to better use. I am willing, for example, to ask our patriotic societies, which have been active in the effort to preserve and mark the relics of our past, if they might not instead give to our universities fellowships for the aid of young men who are seeking graduate training in American history. We are going to need many more men with that training in the years ahead of us, not only because of greatly swollen enrollments in our colleges but because this taste of ours for historical restorations creates its own demands for the guidance of trained scholars. As an officer of Colonial Williamsburg has recently commented, many of us "accustomed to exercising skepticism toward the printed word . . . are not so ready to disbelieve in brick and mortar or furniture and furnishings." [86] We tend to preserve or restore only that which by some artistic or other standard seems worth preserving, and so the picture can be distorted. Who among us can wander

[85] Jenks Cameron, *The National Park Service: Its History, Activities and Organization* (New York, 1922), 1–44; Robert Shankland, *Steve Mather of the National Parks* (New York, 1951), 297–305.

[86] E. P. Alexander, quoted in *Colonial Williamsburg News*, February, 1955.

down the streets of Williamsburg, with promptings on every side to remember Washington and Jefferson, and still remember that it all rested originally on the back of a Negro?

But I am not here to exhort. What I have been trying to do in these lectures is to suggest some of the influences that have shaped, in successive periods of our history, the American's interest in the origins of his country. In general, I have avoided attempts to correct his conclusions, and I have passed up many opportunities to analyze the content of his assumptions. This has been because I have felt the story of this interest might be worth reviewing in broad outline.

Index

DATE DUE

Demco, Inc. 38-293